BUDDHIST EXTREMISTS AND MUSLIM MINORITIES

BUDDHIST EXTREMISTS AND MUSLIM MINORITIES

RELIGIOUS CONFLICT IN CONTEMPORARY SRI LANKA

EDITED BY

JOHN CLIFFORD HOLT

OXFORD
UNIVERSITY PRESS

Oxford University Press is a department of the University of Oxford. It furthers the University's objective of excellence in research, scholarship, and education by publishing worldwide. Oxford is a registered trade mark of Oxford University Press in the UK and certain other countries.

Published in the United States of America by Oxford University Press
198 Madison Avenue, New York, NY 10016, United States of America.

Library of Congress Cataloging-in-Publication Data
Names: Holt, John, 1948– editor.
Title: Buddhist extremists and Muslim minorities : religious conflict in contemporary Sri Lanka / edited by John Clifford Holt.
Description: New York City : Oxford University Press, 2016. |
Includes bibliographical references and index.
Identifiers: LCCN 2016009998 (print) | LCCN 2016035303 (ebook) |
ISBN 9780190624378 (cloth : alk. paper) | ISBN 9780190624385 (pbk. : alk. paper) |
ISBN 9780190624392 (updf) | ISBN 9780190624408 (epub)
Subjects: LCSH: Islam—Relations—Buddhism. | Buddhism—Relations—Islam. |
Islam—Sri Lanka. | Buddhism—Sri Lanka.
Classification: LCC BP173.B9 B83 2016 (print) | LCC BP173.B9 (ebook) | DDC 297.2/843095493—dc23
LC record available at https://lccn.loc.gov/2016009998

1 3 5 7 9 8 6 4 2
Paperback printed by Webcom, Inc., Canada
Hardback printed by Bridgeport National Bindery, Inc., United States of America

CONTENTS

ACKNOWLEDGMENTS

Books of this nature are collaborative ventures. I thank the other seven contributors to this volume for their time and efforts needed to formulate their essays on relatively quick notice.

I have benefited from the support and resources of four institutions while working on this project. First, the inspiration for this work derives from a 2014 conference organized by the International Centre for Ethnic Studies (ICES, Kandy) that focused on relations between Buddhism and other religions in South and Southeast Asia. Papers presented and discussions engaged within that context motivated me to focus more particularly and in greater depth on the nature of recent relations between Buddhists and Muslims in Sri Lanka. Second, the library and faculty resources of the Intercollegiate Sri Lanka Education (ISLE) Program in Kandy proved critical in supporting the project at various moments. Third, the Bowdoin College Faculty Development Committee provided a generous grant for the preparation of a detailed index for the volume. And fourth, the lion's share of my time needed to solicit contributions, to edit them, to write an introduction to the volume, and to write my own contribution was made possible by a fellowship awarded to me by the John Simon Guggenheim Foundation in New York. My great indebtedness to ICES, ISLE, Bowdoin, and Guggenheim is gratefully acknowledged.

BUDDHIST EXTREMISTS AND MUSLIM MINORITIES

INTRODUCTION

John Clifford Holt

I have followed, as best as I could through the media and through short visits to the island, the tensions and intermittent violence that occurred between Sinhala Buddhists and Sri Lankan Muslims from 2012 through 2015. I was living in Kandy during the time violence had broken out between Buddhist and Muslims in the upcountry town of Mawanella in 2001. At that time, every one I had talked to in Kandy had hoped that the imbroglio had been a "one-off" moment of a purely local origin and that a return to the kinds of tensions that had occurred between Buddhists and Muslims earlier in the first part of 20th century was genuinely unthinkable. But that "unthinkable" hope evaporated with the emergence of militant Buddhist groups following the conclusion of Sri Lanka's long civil war between 1983 and 2009. Between 2012 and 2015, hundreds of incidents were documented in which Muslims, their homes, and their places of worship and business were attacked by Sinhala Buddhists who had mounted a public campaign envisaged as a defense of their country and religious culture. Although Christians and their interests were also frequent targets, Muslims bore the brunt of most of the violence.

The rise of a Buddhist militancy victimizing Muslim communities strikes most Euro-American observers as surprising. Popular stereotypes often articulated in the West profile Buddhists as peace-loving, meditative, if not otherworldly oriented agents of a religion that consummately represents the interests of pacifism and gentility. Muslims, on the other hand—often branded through Islamophobic renderings engendered by centuries of confrontation with Christianity and recent geopolitical developments emanating out of the Middle East, Africa, and Afghanistan—are imagined in almost the polar opposite manner: as aggressive radical militants intent on establishing an international Islamic civilization in juxtaposition to the norms of civilized Western society. Such monolithic depictions, of course, are illusory. Unfortunately, that Buddhists are aggressive perpetrators of violence and intolerance who are victimizing relatively innocent Muslims has been a staple of political culture in Sri Lanka and Myanmar in recent years, although the local situations in both countries are far more complex than I can indicate here in this introductory essay or by what is written by the authors of the chapters that follow. This book is a nascent attempt at understanding how and why the tensions between Buddhists and Muslims have become so aggravated recently in Sri Lanka.

Before addressing the situation specifically in Sri Lanka, I need to point out that Sri Lanka is not the only Theravada Buddhist dominated society where tensions and violence between Buddhists and Muslims have flared in recent years. There has been, and continues to be, a violent insurgency mounted by ethnic Malay Muslims that has been severely repressed by the Thai government in southern Thailand, a confrontation in which at least 6,500 people have been killed since the early 2000s. Although the situation in Thailand has cooled a bit at the time of this writing, at least in terms of the number of violent deaths during recent years, the root problems of the conflict have yet to be addressed practically. At base is this question: how does a community that defines itself primarily in terms of language, religion, and history (Malay, Muslim, and a distant historical memory of autonomy) accommodate itself or not to a country that identifies itself essentially with the Thai language, Buddhist religion, and almost a thousand years political independence marked profoundly by lineages of Buddhist kingship? This fundamental structural problem, the issue of how a minority people can fully belong within a state that has insisted, for more than a century, on religious, cultural, and linguistic homogenization, is the fundamental issue at hand. On the Thai Buddhist side of the problem, there is a question about whether Thais can summon the political will to embrace a pluralistic conception of their society or political culture so that regional and ethnic tensions might abate. There is little sign that such a conception will be translated into public policy in the near future. The link between religion and the state, embodied by the symbolism of Buddhist kingship and the state's formal administration of the Buddhist *sangha,* is thoroughly entrenched and embraced, enthusiastically so, by a vast overwhelming majority of the Thai Buddhist demographic. Thailand remains "the most Buddhist" of all Theravada-dominated countries, with 95% of its citizens regarding themselves as nominally Buddhist in identity. A formula for peaceful coexistence with Malay Muslims seems elusive at the moment. What is common between the Thai context, and the Sri Lankan and Burmese contexts as well, is that many people in the majoritarian Buddhist communities of each identify their countries as essentially Buddhist. This identification has been institutionalized in different ways within each state, but the problem of belonging remains basically the same for minority peoples, respectively.

Meanwhile, relations between Buddhists and Muslims in Myanmar[1] have taken a dramatic and tragic turn, especially since 2012 when a fiery riot broke out in the Rakhine state (Arakan, also called Rakhine) in western Myanmar leaving hundreds dead, more than a hundred thousand Muslim Rohingyas (a now contested self-identification) in squalid refugee camps, and many more thousands attempting to flee the country by boat for Malaysia only to find themselves intercepted and funneled into human-trafficking rackets based in Thailand, rackets that have sometimes enjoyed the collusion of members of the Thai military or police. The plight of these refugees has now come to the notice of the international community, including the United States and Myanmar's ASEAN (Association of Southeast Asian Nations) neighbors (chiefly Thailand, Malaysia, and Indonesia). The situation for these Muslims has become so dire that the Rohingyas are often referred to in journalistic accounts as "one of the world's most vulnerable peoples." Why the trouble broke out in such a spectacular fashion in western Myanmar is a complex question to ponder and is still being debated at length. But the crux of the current problem in Myanmar involves a triangle of historically troubled relations between the Muslim Rohingyas and

Arakanese Buddhists, Rohingyas and the Burmese-dominated government, and Arakanese Buddhists and the Burmese-dominated government. Perceptions in each community about the cause of conflict vary spectacularly, abetted by differing anachronistic renderings of history (e.g., are the Rohingyas only recent Bengali Muslim border-jumpers or interlopers, or have these Muslims been in place within this region for centuries, in the process becoming part of the emergent mosaic of society within the Arakan region?). Each of these three constituencies articulates a narrative of siege. The riotous violence in Arakan—sparked by the purported rape of a Buddhist woman by Muslim men, followed by the murder of 10 Muslim men by Arakanese Buddhists—subsequently spread to other regions of Myanmar, stoked in no little way by radical Buddhist monks, including the now infamous U Wirathu, who has been a driving force of the Ma Ba Tha ("preservation of Buddhism society") and 969 movements aimed at repelling what is perceived as a Muslim threat to the future of Buddhist Myanmar. Many observers, both within and outside of Myanmar, know that Wirathu enjoyed the support of influential leaders within the military-dominated government who believed that Wirathu could articulate a powerful voice of Buddhist nationalism advantageous to their continued aspirations for power and disadvantageous to the aspirations of the National League for Democracy (NLD) led by Aung San Suu Kyii—who, as well, also remained very circumspect in her comments about the deteriorating Rohingya plight. The exclusionary and nationalist substance of Wirathu's movement bears an uncanny resemblance to the ideology espoused in Sri Lanka by the hardline Bodu Bala Sena (BBS) movement, a radical and debatably fringe movement that has claimed responsibility for wreaking havoc on Muslims in Sri Lanka since 2012. Indeed, Wirathu was brought to Sri Lanka by the BBS for a high profile visit in September 2014, during which the leaders of both movements pledged international cooperation in defending Buddhism from what they perceive as the rising tide of Muslim encroachment in the region. The recent November 2015 election in Myanmar may bring changes in the desperate situation confronting the Rohingyas and the concerns of other Muslims in other regions of Myanmar. Although no Muslim candidates were allowed to compete for seats in parliament, and the Ma Ba Tha actively campaigned for the surrogate and military-dominated United Solidarity and Development Party (USDP), Aung San Suu Kyii's NLD won a spectacular landslide election victory by claiming more than 80% of the contested seats in parliament. How and if this change in power will translate into a new era of greater inclusion is the question of the hour. The antipathy recently expressed for Muslims by both Arakanese and Burmese Buddhists runs deep, but apparently not as deep as their hatred for the military that had ruled the country in dictatorial fashion since 1962. As this book goes to press, it is too early to know if the Rohingya Muslims in Myanmar will continue to be disenfranchised, or whether the new NLD government will gradually begin to take steps to address the Rohingya situation in Arakan in a manner that provides a place for them in a newly democratized Myanmar.

In Sri Lanka, many observers, both international and domestic, had held out hope that the end of Sri Lanka's protracted 26-year civil war between Sri Lankan government armed forces and the Liberation Tigers of Tamil Eelam (LTTE) in 2009 would occasion the re-establishment of relatively harmonious relations among the various religious and ethnic communities in the country. Unfortunately, immediately following the war's conclusion, an aura of militant triumphalism pervaded public discourse,[2] catalyzed by various members and supporters of President Mahinda Rajapaksa's Sinhala-dominated nationalist government, a government preponderantly controlled by members of Rajapaksa's own family who commanded as much as 80% of all budgetary expenditures. In the aftermath of its electoral defeat in January 2015, Rajapaksa's regime was tarnished with charges of nepotism, corruption, and human rights abuses (especially in relation to the harassment and disappearances of scores of journalists). It's heavy-handed tactics became very apparent during the first year following the government's military victory in 2009 when almost three hundred thousand Tamil people in the Northern Province were detained within hurriedly constructed make-shift camps where they were closely scrutinized by squads of military investigators to determine whether they might pose a future threat to the security of the country. Although almost all of these people had been released and resettled by 2011, the Rajapaksa government did not introduce, nor did it apparently ever seriously entertain, any significant measures of power devolution that could be discussed in concert with newly elected Tamil political officials, measures that might have created meaningful degrees of autonomy in the northern regions of the country that remain dominated demographically by Tamil peoples. Following the war, these regions remained monitored very closely by the Sri Lankan military. Private lands that had been confiscated by the military were not returned, and ritual actions in civil society were closely monitored such that any public demonstrations, such as honoring those who had died during the war, were patently disallowed. Following the election of the government headed by President Maitripala Sirisena in January 2015, restrictions in the north were eased somewhat.

Meanwhile, beginning in 2012, the US government three times annually successfully petitioned the United Nations Human Rights Council (UNHRC) in an effort to promote accountability for war crimes that were committed during the final phase of Sri Lanka's civil war. In 2014, after the third petition and continued Sri Lankan recalcitrance, the UNHCR agreed to begin formally an international investigation into war crimes. The Rajapaksa government fiercely resisted UN efforts by refusing to cooperate with the UN commission and surreptitiously organized periodic public demonstrations against such an inquiry in the vicinity of the American embassy and UN offices in Colombo. It insisted that the UN inquiry was an intrusion on its sovereignty.

During the postwar years, the Sri Lankan government under Rajapaksa grew increasingly autocratic, in the process attempting to assert its control over the local media and nongovernmental organizations while at the same time reorienting its foreign policy away from the United States, the United Kingdom, the European Union, and Japan, which previously had been its primary group of economic supporters, to an orbit that included China, Myanmar, Russia, and Iran. High profile diplomatic exchanges between Rajapaksa and the political leaders of these countries were orchestrated, and China agreed to loan vast amounts of money while supplying its own cadres of manpower to construct a new seaport and an international airport in Rajapaksa's rural native place, a small regional town located in a remote area on the southern coast of the island. Under the leadership of his brother, the Secretary to the Defense Ministry Gotabhaya Rajapaksa, a major scheme with Chinese financing was also launched to create a new seaport in Colombo, a massive harbor reclamation project that would include a golf course, hotels, and casinos. Another major project in Colombo for urban renewal, especially in the Slave Island area of the city, displaced hundreds, if not thousands of longtime, low-income residents.

During this time, hardline right-wing groups of Sinhala Buddhists emerged (some with the government's not so tacit approval) to propagate an interpretive vision asserting the presence of an international conspiracy designed to destabilize Sri Lanka. The local targets of these extremist groups, the so-called fronts of this alleged conspiracy (or those regarded as having close relations to the "machinations" of the "international community") were identified as Christians and Muslims. But the conspiracy theory was only the international side of the attack. On the specifically domestic side, the Muslim community was singled out as engaged in economic practices that unfairly placed burdens on the Sinhala consumer and disadvantaged the competitiveness of Sinhala businessmen. Although many Christian churches, especially those of the Protestant evangelical variety, suffered numerous attacks at the hands of these Buddhist extremists, the Muslim community bore the brunt of harassment. Rauf Hakeem, a Muslim politician and leader of the Sri Lanka Muslim Congress (SLMC), who was actually the Sri Lankan government's Minister of Justice during the Rajapaksa regime, submitted a list of 240 documented attacks on Muslims and mosques during the calendar year of 2013 to the UN. Many more, with increasing intensity, were mounted thereafter. In June 2014, a very serious riot instigated by hardline Sinhala Buddhists followed a mass rally organized by the BBS, a rally filled with hate speeches delivered by Buddhist monks, including the BBS's outspoken monastic leader, Gnanasara Aththe Thero. The chaos that ensued resulted in the deaths of three Muslims; the serious injury of more than sixty; and the destruction of more than eighty shops, mosques, and private residences in the towns of Aluthgama, Beruwala, and Dharga Town, all located about fifty kilometers south of Colombo. Most of the damage occurred with police and military personnel passively observing. (The details of the Aluthgama riot will be provided with more precision in Farzana Haniffa's chapter later in the book.) It is safe to say that relations between Buddhists and Muslims in Sri Lanka had not become so embittered at any time during the past 100 years.

This, then, is the general setting for the more detailed assessments that follow in the chapters comprising this book. The first four chapters of the book are each dedicated to providing various background explanations for aspects of the Buddhist/Muslim conflict in Sri Lanka. The last four chapters are aimed more at ascertaining the dynamics of the conflict that remained in play until at least January 2015. But before briefly introducing the substance of those chapters, there are three introductory issues that I will address.

First, the reader will look in vain for a discussion of a specifically Buddhist *religious* rationale for the aggression against minority groups perpetrated by the BBS and other Buddhists who have joined in their cause. Whereas I discuss in the eighth chapter what I call a "religious syntax" to violence mounted by Buddhists or between Buddhists and Muslims, all of the reasons actually articulated by Buddhists for their actions have been economic, political, or social in nature. There has been no specifically Buddhist religious rationale appealed to, or formulated, that is consonant with ethical or doctrinal understandings. For instance, at an academic conference in Sri Lanka in 2014 where members and sympathizers of the BBS were present, I specifically raised the issue of whether or not the BBS protest against *halal* food was related to concerns about cattle slaughter and thereby rooted in the Buddhist sensitivity for nonviolence, or the taking of life. In response, I was informed by the leading lay advocate for the BBS that the issue at hand had only to do with how the manner in which *halal* food is certified in Sri Lanka puts Sinhala Buddhist business competition and the Sinhala Buddhist consumer at an economic disadvantage. Indeed, if one looks at the statements and assertions that derive from BBS sources in Sri

Lanka, or from the Ma Ba Tha or 969 in Myanmar, there are virtually no appeals to Buddhist philosophical or moral traditions at all to legitimize their anti-Muslim stances. These movements may be led or orchestrated by Buddhist monks, but their aims are almost purely economic and political in nature. Moreover, what seems to be at stake is how these movements define the political culture of these countries. That is, the assumption in play, one that I have noted previously, is that Myanmar and Sri Lanka are essentially Buddhist countries. Indeed, in Sri Lanka, there is a well-worn adage that "the country exists for the sake of the religion." Tessa Bartholomeusz explored this adage in depth when ferreting out the dimensions of "just war theory" in her book, *In Defense of Dharma*.[3] But there is nothing explicitly Buddhist (in the philosophical sense) about this articulation, no religious assertion that can be traced to the teachings of the Buddha preserved in Pali canonical literature. In the Sri Lankan political context, one can definitely find assumptions in play that may have their bases within episodes of the monastic chronicles (*Mahavamsa, Culavamsa, Dipavamsa*, etc.) but not appeals to *buddhavacana* ("words of the Buddha") in the *Abhidhamma, Sutta*, or *Vinaya pitaka*s.

Second, militant groups like the BBS arose in a specific political context. There seems to be little doubt that they were allowed to operate with impunity or given cover by the state's security forces. Early on, police often accompanied the BBS "moral police" on their raids of Muslim or Christian premises, and state television generously covered many of their activities. Secretary to the Ministry of Defense Gotabhaya Rajapaksa was the chief guest and keynote speaker at the formal inauguration of the BBS "academy." In fact, in the months following the Rajapaksa regime's electoral defeat in January 2015, the BBS announced that it would form its own political party and publicly invited Gotabhaya Rajapaksa to assume a leadership role. It would be stretching the point, at least in terms of the available evidence, to say that actions of the BBS, Ravana Balaya, and others were simply arms of a repressive state. However, it is not a stretch to say that their political interests seem to align with the interests of the Rajapaksa regime and that the state gave them a relatively free rein. In point of fact, no one from the BBS has yet to be charged with any criminal wrongdoing, even in the post-Rajapaksa era. Maitripala Sirisena's government is holding various hearings about corruption issues, but there has been no effort to bring the perpetrators of violence against Muslims or Christians to book. That said, the social and political climate in Sri Lanka has improved significantly, and many in the Muslim community seem more assured of their safety these days.

Third, it follows from this that in considering the issue of criminal actions being undertaken with impunity that not only was there a considerable amount of collusion in play between Sinhala Buddhist monastic interests and the Sinhala Buddhists business community that has helped to fund the activities of the BBS, but that the absence of other Sinhala Buddhists speaking out against the abuses of the BBS was rather striking. As Tudor Silva observes in his chapter in this book, perhaps the reason for this is that the BBS was building on deeply entrenched prejudices held by many Sinhala Buddhists against Muslims. Although that may be the case, other Sinhala Buddhists were certainly aghast at what they observed occurring in their midst. Privately, they would confide their dismay. And yet very few of these progressively oriented people spoke out. Ostensibly, the reason for this silence was the repressive political climate that had devolved under the Rajapaksa regime. Most morally conscious people simply stayed off the radar screen and kept their silence. But did this progressive section of the Sinhala Buddhist community turn out in force by voting against Rajapaksa on the January 2015 national election day? Did the antics of the BBS and other hardline, strident, "patriotic" groups and their public endorsements of the Rajapaksa regime cost the Rajapaksas the election, owing to their outrageous, embarrassing, and simply irreligious public behavior? There is no doubt that the Muslim population voted as a bloc against the Rajapaksa regime. And given the fact that Muslims comprise roughly 9% of the Sri Lankan population, and that Rajapaksa lost by a 3 or 4% margin, one could argue that the BBS became a serious political liability. On the other hand, to what extent did the actions of the BBS actually strengthen the hand of Rajapaksa's appeal among rural Sinhala Buddhists (as Dennis McGilvray suggests as a possibility in his chapter in this book), particularly in the far southern regions of the country? If the BBS strengthened Rajapaksa's hand among some sections of the Sinhala Buddhist community, and alienated the more progressive others as well, thus producing a "wash effect," there were also a myriad of reasons why many other Sinhala Buddhists voted against Rajapaksa in the end: for the educated (upper middle class) people, there were governance issues (scant regard for law and order by Rajapaksa's family, cabinet ministers, and ruling party Members of Parliament)—that is, corruption; for lawyers, it was the impeachment of the Chief Justice that Rajapaksa had orchestrated; for the military, it was the court-martial and imprisonment of General Sarath Fonseka after he unsuccessfully ran against Rajapaksa for the presidency; for the urban poor, it was issues like "Samurdhi" (the microcredit style savings and loan scheme) that was not functioning well, in addition to the rising cost of living; among the Free Trade Zone garment workers, it was serious problems with their pension scheme, including an embarrassing scam; for fishermen, it was the sudden increase in kerosene and oil prices; and many of the slum-dwelling poor turned against the Rajapaksas because of Gotabhaya's urban beautification programs, which meant their displacement. There were also many people, particularly non-Sinhalas, who were adamant about the abolition of the all-powerful executive presidency.[4] In the final analysis, it would be difficult to argue that although the public antics of the BBS surely aggravated some Sinhala voters, their active presence and endorsement was a crucial factor that cost Rajapaksa the election. Whatever the past political significance of the BBS, it is likely that this reactionary force, one that aspires to create a profile similar to Hindutva in India, is somewhat diminishing at the moment but will undoubtedly surface again in the future. It is unclear, at this juncture, how far their antics would be tolerated by the new Sirisena regime. It is now a foregone conclusion that they would not be encouraged.

With these preliminary issues addressed, readers will find pertinent discussions of each in what follows, I will succinctly introduce the substance and parameters of the eight chapters that comprise this volume.

M. A. Nuhman's wide-ranging chapter addressing Sinhala/Muslim relations over the past hundred years opens the volume by providing an extensive background consideration of the manner in which colonialism and modernization impacted both Sinhala and Muslim communities. Prof. Nuhman's fundamental thesis is that the current problem between Buddhists and Muslims is one that is not essentially religious in nature, but that "the religious element is a surface manifestation of socioeconomic and political competition." How and why this is especially so becomes the crux of his chapter. His chapter is specifically illuminating insofar as it outlines an understanding of how the Muslim community, especially following the 19th century modernization reform efforts of Siddi Lebbe, evolved into its current makeup, and how ethnic Muslim identity became institutionalized in terms of education, the mosque, business establishments, and politics. On the Sinhala side of the equation, Nuhman asserts that the *jatika cintanya* ("indigenous people's thought") movement, an attempt to critique and resist Western modes of thinking and practice, a movement that has its origins in the early 20th century in figures like the Anagarika Dharmpala and one that gained a new fruition in the 1990s, is the root and common ideology of today's Sinhala nationalists, including the BBS.

Dennis McGilvray's chapter, "Rethinking Muslim Identity in Sri Lanka," also provides a historical overview of the Muslim community in Sri Lanka and then proceeds to catalogue the rather outlandish claims made by the BBS movement about Sri Lanka's Muslims. The heart of his chapter is given over to an analysis of four different ways in which Muslim identity has been constructed over the past 100 years: (1) as "caste-like," an understanding that never gained too much traction in Sri Lanka but has an affinity for the manner in which Muslims in south India are sometimes categorized and understood there; (2) as "Islamic Tamils," an identity that some non-Muslim Tamil politicians sought to impose to further bolster Tamil political claims on the island; (3) racial and ancestral Moors, an identity derived from the claim that Sri Lanka's Muslims descend from Arab sea traders of the 8th century on; this view remains a common or popular migration myth among many Sri Lankan Muslims today; and (4) Sri Lanka's Muslims as simply

"Muslims," the alternative to the other three preceding formulations and an umbrella designation based on religion that has now defined the Muslim community as a distinctive ethnic identity; yet "Muslim" identity does not preclude serious differences that remain within the community with regard to what is actually meant by "Muslim." In the final section of his chapter, McGilvray takes stock of Muslim reactions to BBS onslaughts and how they "have ranged from civil indignation and alarm, to international conspiracy theories, to collective community introspection." With regard to the last issue, and in his concluding remarks, McGilvray suggests that "[i]n the current xenophobic situation, the priority would presumably be to assert a more distinctively Sri Lankan cultural identity with deeper ancestral roots in the island and in the South Asian region, rather than emphasizing itinerant Arab seafarers or a connection with global Islam."

Jonathan Young in his chapter squares up directly to the question about why Buddhist monks in Sri Lanka are so involved in the political arena in the first place. This is a question often raised in the West by surprised observers. His answer is that monks have been involved politically for a very long time in Sri Lanka and that the political involvement seen so evidently during the early years of the 21st century is by no means a historical anomaly. Specifically, he examines the manner in which monks served as teachers to royalty in the 18th century Kandyan Nayakkar dynasty in efforts to cultivate virtuous "governmentality," borrowing a term from Michel Foucault. He asserts that fielding the nature of political assertions of Buddhist monks historically is a first step in trying to ascertain the reasons and rationales for monastic interventions now in play within the contemporary Sri Lankan context.

Benjamin Schonthal's chapter "Configurations of Buddhist Nationalism in Sri Lanka" sees the BBS as a third type of militant Buddhist nationalism that has arisen since the country's political independence in 1948, a movement that follows predecessors that, like the BBS, were produced by a "siege mentality." That is, insofar as Buddhism was thought to be under siege by an advancing Christianity up to the 1940s and early 1950s, and then under siege by a Tamil insurgency from the 1970s through the conclusion of the civil war in 2009, the

Muslim community now is also seen as an invasive force threatening Sinhala Buddhist civilization. What differentiates the BBS from its predecessors, Schonthal points out, is that its aims are clearly business or capitalist in orientation, and its self-professed goal is to inhibit what it believes is a market manipulation being perpetrated by Muslim economic forces.

Whereas these first four chapters contribute to a historical understanding of the conflict between Muslims and Buddhist militancy, Kalinga Tudor Silva's chapter entitled "Gossip, Rumor, and Propaganda in Anti-Muslim Campaigns of the Bodu Bala Sena" examines in detail the manner in which the BBS was started, is structured, and how it articulates its messages of hatred for Muslims. After theorizing how rumor is an instrument used to mobilize political ill will and violent public actions toward an "ethnic other" to incite "moral panic," Silva reviews BBS literature that allegedly exposes the manner in which Muslims seek to gain a population advantage in Sri Lanka; how Muslims have deployed political strategies to gain power far beyond their proportional representation in the country; and how elected Muslim members of parliament, especially those with cabinet portfolios, have maximized the effectiveness of the patronage system to benefit Muslim businesses in conducting trade. He concludes by suggesting that the rise and relative persistence of the BBS may reflect entrenched prejudices among the Sinhala Buddhist population in an era of postwar political triumphalism.

Philip Friedrich's "Adjudicating Antiquity: The Politics of Historical Confrontation at Devanagala, Sri Lanka" chapter is a close examination of the manner in which local history has been appropriated by Buddhist nationalists, including Buddhist nationalist BBS sympathizers, to locate the "intrinsic religiosity of Devanagala," a hillock of some cultural antiquity in the vicinity of modern Mawanella, some 15 miles west by southwest of Kandy in the central highlands. In this effort, Devanagala comes to be identified with either the 8 or 16 traditional places of Buddhist pilgrimage on the island. Here, Friedrich notes the role of a government archeology department under pressure from Buddhist interests to establish a buffer zone around the hillock that would result in the exclusion of many Muslim families, families who have held legal title to their lands for generations. According to the BBS and its local sympathizers, the presence of Muslims is an infringement on Devanagala's *intrinsic* Buddhist religiosity. Friedrich's analysis, like Silva's preceding it, provides keen insight into the aims and machinations of the BBS within the context of specific local campaigns.

Farzana Haniffa's "Stories in the Aftermath of Aluthgama" chapter analyzes how narratives of the violence that occurred in Aluthgama reflect the manner in which that violence has been framed, rationalized, understood, or condemned by both Muslims and Sinhalese in the affected areas. After theorizing storytelling as a manner in which political power can be narrated, she compares the ethnic violence that occurred in Aluthgama with the 1983 Sinhala pogrom against Tamil people living in the Sinhala regions of the island. Indeed, many people on the island feared that Aluthgama was a harbinger of a return to the watershed widespread violence of 1983. Although noting similarity between Aluthgama and 1983 regarding the fact that security forces were complicit in both contexts, insofar as they were passive bystanders who allowed the violence to occur, she notes that the Aluthgama violence in 2014 was more "economically oriented." Consequently, in many of the narratives she collected among Aluthgama's Muslims in the aftermath, a persistent complaint was the state's failure to protect property, an outright abrogation of governmental responsibility. As Haniffa remarks rather succinctly, yet profoundly, ". . . the rationality and integrity of the market was eclipsed by the ethnicity of the state." Now that the Rajapaksa regime has been removed from power, Muslim sentiment is such that there is hope that vilifications by the BBS in the future will not gain as much legitimacy among Sinhala Buddhist people.

My own chapter, "A Religious Syntax to Communal Violence in Sri Lanka," chronicles the transformation of my own perspective regarding the complicity of religion in Sri Lanka's communal violence. Although previously arguing in sympathy with the view articulated in M. A. Nuhman's lead chapter that economic issues lie at the base of Sri Lanka's communal conflicts, I now argue that elements of religious culture, particularly the performance of ritual and the evocation of symbol, are either venues or flashpoints for the incitement of violence, or are purposively targeted by enemies of ethnic communities to wound, insult, or injure. I note not only the recent history of attacks on sacred places in South Asia in general and in Sri Lanka specifically, but how the collision of ritual cultures at specific times and specific places, and how the targeting of sacred spaces at sacred times (e.g., mosques during the time of Ramadan), are elements of strategy deployed by militants. Moreover, the so-called infringement of Muslims on Buddhist sacred places such as Dighavapi, Dambulla, and as Friedrich notes, Devanagala, notes how elements of religious culture are carefully considered or deployed for the martial assertion of political ends.

There is no doubt that the nature of Buddhist/Muslim tensions in Sri Lanka will devolve further in the future. Although there is hope that the newly elected government signals a change of fortune, the fact of the matter is that many politicos who served in Rajapaksa's government are also occupying key positions within the new government as well. And one has to pause at how nationalistic President Maitripala Sirisena posed during the waning days of his campaign, as if he was worried about not being Sinhala Buddhist nationalist enough for the Sinhala constituency. Moreover, one also has to worry about the dark thought offered by Tudor Silva in this volume that there remains a deep-seated prejudice among Sinhalas for Muslims in their midst. Stereotypes of Muslims as predominantly rich businessmen will be difficult to deconstruct. Moreover, the increasing propensity to underscore the uniqueness of Muslim identity within the Muslim community, as M. A. Nuhman has described, unique differences articulated through the apparel that Muslim men and women wear, through the certification of the food that Muslims eat, through the conservative ideological emphases now prominent within Muslim educational institutions, through the imitations or appropriations of other cultural fashions deriving from the Middle East, and so forth, all highlight a sense of separateness from other Sri Lankans and beg the conclusion provided by McGilvray in his chapter, that perhaps a helpful strategy for Muslims would be to emphasize their Sri Lankan historical roots and cultural affinities in the foreseeable future.

NOTES

1. Myanmar was formerly known as Burma. How to refer to Myanmar or Burma has become an interesting, contested issue for the past 20 years. "Burma" was the English rendering that the British determined for "Bamar," an indigenous term that signifies the language and people now commonly referred to as Burmese. Like so many other terms (e.g., "Calcutta" for Kolkata; "Bombay" for Mumbai; or "Vizag" for Visakhapatnam; etc.) invented by the British during their extended colonial experience in South Asia, it is a linguistic corruption. "Myanmar" is the term within the Bamar language for the country. However, since the name of the country was formally changed from Burma to Myanmar by a repressive military junta in the 1990s, there has been considerable resistance to its adoption by politically progressive forces within the country and by some in the international community who have not wanted to sanction any definitive political actions of consequence by the long-standing, antidemocratic forces that have ruled the country since 1962.
2. For a description of the scene in the days following the defeat of the LTTE, see Doug Saunders, "Kingship-in-the-Making," in my *The Sri Lanka Reader: History, Politics, Culture* (Durham, NC: Duke University Press, 2011), 731–733.
3. Tessa Bartholomeusz, *In Defense of Dharma: Just War Ideology in Sri Lanka* (New York: Routledge, 2002).
4. I am grateful to Carmen Wickramagamage for an exchange that brought these issues of Sinhala discontent to light. Some of the wording in this protracted sentence is hers.

CHAPTER ONE

SINHALA BUDDHIST NATIONALISM AND MUSLIM IDENTITY IN SRI LANKA

One Hundred Years of Conflict and Coexistence

M. A. Nuhman

INTRODUCTION

As a religious and ethnic community in Sri Lanka, Muslims have at least a thousand years of history on the island. The relationship between them and the Sinhalese, the majority community, has been, in general, very cordial until the end of 19th century (Dewaraja 1994). We do not find any record of conflict between them during the long history of their coexistence until then. However, the situation began to change from the late 19th century due to the new phenomenon of sectarian ethnic identity among different communities, a phenomenon that was induced by economic and political competition created during the British colonial rule. The new sociopolitical changes caused ethnic tension and communal violence between Sinhalese and Muslims from time to time in the early 20th century in colonial and in postcolonial Sri Lanka.

The first major ethnic violence between Sinhalese and Muslims in modern Sri Lanka took place in May 1915. A number of anti-Muslim violent episodes after independence have also occurred from the mid-1970s (Anes et al. 2008). The most recent and brutal violence against Muslims by Sinhala Buddhist extremist forces took place in June 2014 in Aluthgama, Dharga Town, and Beruwala in the Kalutara District of the Western Province (Farook 2014a).

In this opening chapter, an attempt is made to trace the sociohistorical and political roots of the conflict between the Sinhalese and Muslims that has continued intermittently for the last hundred years. It would be an oversimplification to assert that this conflict is only religious in nature. I will argue instead that religion is a surface manifestation of socioeconomic and political competition.

This chapter is divided into two parts. The first part deals with the formation of ethnic identity and the emergence of Sinhala Buddhist nationalism and Muslim identity in the late 19th century and the early phase of the conflict culminating in the 1915 anti-Muslim riots that were brutally suppressed by the British. The second part deals with the new phase of Sinhala Buddhist nationalism and Muslim identity in postindependent Sri Lanka and the re-emergence of anti-Muslim sentiment and violence.

THE EMERGENCE OF SINHALA BUDDHIST NATIONALISM AND MUSLIM IDENTITY

The Early Phase

The history of modern Sri Lanka, beginning with the latter half of the 19th century, is also the history of the development of ethnic consciousness and conflicts among the major ethnic communities, namely, the Sinhalese, Tamils, and Muslims who were largely living in harmony throughout the premodern period except for some dynastic or royal conflicts between Sinhalese and Tamils. The social transformation from the feudal system to the mercantile capitalism that gradually took place during the 19th and early 20th centuries, the introduction of the British educational and political systems, and the consequent competition for economic and political power between the different social groups heavily contributed to the polarization of Sri Lankan society along ethnic lines during British colonial rule. In the postindependence period, we witness a virtual ethnic segregation propelled by the consolidation of ethnonationalisms and 30 years of ethnic war (Wilson 1988, 2000; Tambiah 1986, 1992).

Language and religion played a major role in ethnicity formation during the colonial and postcolonial period in Sri Lanka. Sinhalese and Tamil ethnicities are marked mainly by languages (Sinhala and Tamil, respectively). Each of these ethnic groups includes minority religious groups, for example, Protestant Christians, Catholics, and Buddhists. Sinhala Buddhists and Sinhala Christians are primarily identified as Sinhalese by their language. In the same way, Tamil Hindus and Tamil Christians are primarily identified as Tamils because they choose the Tamil language as their primary ethnic marker. However, religion was also used by the elites of the majority religious groups of the Sinhala- and Tamil-speaking communities during the late 19th and early 20th centuries to consolidate their ethnic identity and to differentiate themselves from the Christians, the economically and politically privileged groups dominating the British administrative sector, because of their English education and Christian identity.

The emerging Buddhist elite promoted a Sinhala–Buddhist identity to secure their domination in the sociopolitical arena (Obeysekere 1979; De Votta 2007). Anagarika Dharmapala (1864–1933) was the strongest proponent of Sinhala–Buddhist identity during the period. Parallel to this development, the Tamil-speaking upper class elite appealed to Hindu Saivaism to promote Tamil Hindu identity against Christian domination especially in the North. Arumuga Navalar was the leading figure in the Hindu revivalist movement in Jaffna in the late 19th century. However, during the postindependence period, the Tamil language became the primary marker of Tamil identity in Sri Lanka mainly because of the domination of Sinhala in the public administration and the marginalization of Tamil (Kearney 1967). This political change brought Tamil Hindus and Tamil Christians together to fight for their linguistic and civil rights, submerging their religious identities. Thus, religion and language played a major role in the formation of Sinhala–Buddhist and Tamil–Hindu identities in Sri Lanka. The Sinhalese and Tamil elites chose either language or religion, or both, as their ethnic markers depending on the sociopolitical and historical situation (Brass 1991).

However, the Sri Lankan Muslims behaved differently. They used only their religion—Islam—as their primary ethnic marker. Although they are also linguistically Tamils like the Tamil Christians and speak Tamil as their mother tongue, not only in the North and East but also in the interior Sinhala-dominated villages in the South, they don't want to be identified as Tamils. Ethnicity and religion are inseparable, two sides of the same coin, as far as Sri Lankan Muslims are concerned. Sri Lankan Muslims constructed their identity on religious lines only, rejecting the Tamil language as their ethnic marker and to safeguard their sociopolitical and economic interests. The Sri Lankan Muslim elite rejected Ponnambalam Ramanathan's claim in the late 19th century that Sri Lankan Muslims were ethnologically Tamils (Azeez 1907).

Sinhala Buddhist nationalism emerged as a sociopolitical mobilizing force in Sri Lanka from the mid-19th century to consolidate the sociopolitical interests of the Buddhist elites. The revivalist activities of Sinhala Buddhist and the Tamil Hindu elites were in full swing at the time against Christian domination. By the late 19th century, Christianity had been well rooted through English education and proselytization activities of the Christian missionaries with the patronage of the British Government. Although it started from the Dutch period, as Jayawardena (2000: 250) points out, "aggressive proselytization, combined with the prospect of economic and political advantage from the foreign occupiers, led sections of the inhabitants of coastal areas of the island to adopt various brands of Christianity." Sinhala Buddhists and Tamil Hindus converted to Christianity in large numbers during this period. According to the 1881 census, 162,270 Sinhala Christians and 82,200 Tamil Christians were in Sri Lanka. These converts also included landowners and local capitalists. Their conversion ensured them "a greater involvement and entrenchment in the whole colonial establishment" (Jayawardena 2000: 250). Understandably, Buddhist and Hindu nationalists feared that Christianity would swallow their religion and culture. Ananda Guruge expressed this fear with a degree of exaggeration as follows: "By the middle of the nineteenth century, the

British efforts at denationalizing the Sinhalas and weaning them away from their religion, culture and tradition had reached the zenith and the disappearance of Buddhism from Ceylon was imminent" (Guruge 1967: 9).

In this sociocultural context, Buddhist resistance to Christianity arose as a revivalist movement during the late 19th century. The Buddhist revivalist activities against the domination of Christianity became stronger during and after the 1860s, after which the Sinhala merchant capitalist class started to financially support the Buddhist revivalist movement (Jayawardena 2000). A Society for the Propagation of Buddhism was established in 1862. "With the arrival of Colonel Olcott in 1880 the Buddhists found an efficient leader who was capable of translating their religious and national aspirations to action through a well conceived plan and programme" (Guruge 1967: 13). Henry Olcott formed the Buddhist Theosophical Society in the same year, and he started an island-wide movement to establish a Buddhist school system that marked the beginning of Sinhala Buddhist nationalism.

Anagarika Dharmapala gave a strong leadership to Buddhist revivalism in Sri Lanka. He left government service in 1886 to serve the Buddhist Theosophical Society. He was also the manager of newly founded Buddhist schools and the Assistant Secretary of the Buddhist Defense Committee. He started the Maha Bodhi Society in 1891 and the nationalist journal *Sinhala Bauddhaya* in 1906 (Guruge 1967). His conviction was that the Sinhala Buddhists were "the sons of the soil," and all the other minorities were "alien" people. This ideology, which was rooted deeply in the minds of Sinhala Buddhist nationalists, has been an important factor that alienated the minorities from mainstream politics in the later years.

Islamic Revivalism and Muslim Identity

Islamic revivalism and Muslim identity in Sri Lanka arose in the late 19th century not directly against Christianity or Christian missionary activities, as was the case of Buddhist and Hindu revivalisms, because Christianity was not a direct threat to Islam in that period, and Christian missionaries could not convert any significant number of

Muslims to Christianity. Muslim revivalism arose basically to consolidate elitist desires to create wider community awareness in response to Sinhala and Tamil revivalist programs. Islamic nationalist and revivalist movements in the larger Islamic world, such as those in Turkey, Egypt, and India from the late 19th century, also had an impact on Sri Lankan Muslims in this respect.

Mohamed Casim Siddi Lebbe (1838–1898) was the initiator and the leading figure in the Islamic revivalist movement in Sri Lanka in the late 19th century. He set out the ideological framework for Islamic revival and Muslim ethnicity in Sri Lanka. Siddi Lebbe was seriously concerned about the backwardness of his community and thought that modern education was the only way to bring Muslims into the main stream of social and political life in the country. He realized that without English education, his community would not get its share in the public life and would not advance further. However, the Muslim community at that time was reluctant to accept modern English education because of the fear that their children might be converted to Christianity.

Siddi Lebbe tried to make a breakthrough in the education of Sri Lankan Muslims by opening separate schools for them, following the model of Syed Ahmad Khan in India and the Buddhist and Hindu revivalists in Sri Lanka. Giving modern education in a religious environment was the common feature, a kind of mixture of tradition and modernity.

1891 was an important year in the history of Muslim education in Sri Lanka. An individual effort was transformed into a collective effort, and the Muslim Educational Society was established in that year. The Society worked hard to establish a new school for Muslims in Colombo and they succeeded in establishing *Al Madrasathul Zahira* in 1892 near the Maradana Mosque in Colombo. It is presently known as Colombo Zahira College. Siddi Lebbe also took the initiative to open more schools for Muslim boys and girls in Kandy, Kurunegala, Galle, and Matara. Although the Muslim-educated elites campaigned for modern English education from the late 19th century, the Muslims were more reluctant in comparison to the other communities.

As the religion, Islam, is the primary marker of the ethnic identity of the Sri Lankan Muslims, one can see increasing religious awareness among them from the late 19th century as they had to face challenges from the other ethnic groups. Re-emerging Islamism in the Muslim world also had an impact on Sri Lankan Muslims at this time.

The educated Muslim elite who were in the forefront of the revivalist movement in the late 19th century strongly felt that promoting religious awareness was essential for the social mobility and ethnic consolidation of the Muslims. It was with this motivation that the *Jamiyatul Islamiya*, the first specifically Islamic organization in Sri Lanka, was formed by Siddi Lebbe and his companions in 1886. The objective of this organization was to promote Islamic awareness among the Muslims to consolidate Muslim identity and to work toward the social and political progress of the Muslims. Thus, Islamization of the Muslim community was the underlying ideology of the formation of *Jamiyatul Islamiya*. This organization wanted to eliminate sociocultural and religious practices that were considered un-Islamic and superstitious. For example, shrine worship, belief in devils and spirits and related folk customs, and rituals of healing were their targets.

Islamization in the late 19th century was an effort to unite the Muslims spiritually and culturally based on Islamic principles that were interpreted by the modern educated elite and the traditional *ulama*, and which often lead to controversy and conflicts between them because of their different interpretations of Islam. Siddi Lebbe propagated a modern rationalist version of Islam, which he thought was true Islam that could lead Muslims into the modern world. He, as most of the Muslim revivalist leaders of the Islamic world of his time, was on a double track of modernization and Islamization. He thought that Islam should be the foundation for any modernization process.

In an effort to keep the Muslim community within a traditional Islamic frame, attempts to sustain or establish traditional Islamic teachings in Sri Lanka, as against modern education and modernization, were also started in the late 19th century. The *Madrasatul Bari*, the first Arabic college in Sri Lanka to train Sri Lankan Muslims in traditional Islamic scholarship, was established in 1884 at Weligama in the Southern Province. Following this several Arabic colleges were established in Galle (1892), Kinniya (1899), Maharagama (1931), and

Matara (1915). Hundreds of *ulamas* were educated at these colleges. They were responsible for preaching Islam and to develop religious consciousness among the Muslims.

The British colonial policy of governance was one of the important factors that contributed to the rise of ethnic consciousness in Sri Lankan society from 1830s. The British introduced communal representation to the Legislative Council in 1833 following the recommendations of the commission of Colebrooke and Cameron. Six unofficial members were appointed by the Governor to the council from Europeans, Sinhalese, Tamils, and Burghers. A low country, upper class Sinhala Christian was appointed to represent the whole Sinhalese; and a Colombo based, upper class Tamil was appointed to represent the Tamils, including the Tamil-speaking Muslims. This was the first time that Sri Lankan communities were politically divided into ethnic groups, and those who did not get representation started to agitate for separate representation. In 1889, the government made some changes and appointed two additional members to the Legislative Council, one from among the Kandyan Sinhalese and one from the Muslims. The communal representation in the Legislative Council was increased from time to time. There were 37 unofficial members in the council by 1924, including 3 Muslims.

Ethnic consciousness developed among Muslims also in response to hostility from Sinhala Buddhist nationalists that reached its peak between the late 19th and early 20th centuries. This hostility developed mainly because of colonial politics and competition in trade and commerce in the urban areas.

As we have noted earlier, until the arrival of the British, the Sinhala–Muslim relationship was one of mutual trust and cooperation. The Muslims were also recruited to the high civil posts and "structurally assimilated" into society. However, after the arrival of the British, the situation changed. As Dewaraja (1994: 140) points out "the good relationship that had prevailed over a thousand years deteriorated into one of competition, suspicion and ill will. This was the result of the policy of divide and rule and communal politics which the British initiated from 1796 onwards."

After the British captured the Kandyan Kingdom, some influential Muslims cooperated with them. One of them was appointed to one of the highest administrative posts, which in turn was considered as an affront to Sinhala aristocratic families. This person was Hajji, an influential Muslim who was appointed as the *tavalam madige muhandiram* of the Vellassa area. There was widespread resentment against this appointment, and the British received several petitions against Hajji Muhandiram. However, the British authorities defended his appointment. But the Sinhala aristocrats did not accept Hajji Muhandiram, and that was one of the causes for the Kandyan rebellion that took place in 1817 against the British, mainly in the areas of Uva and Vellassa. Hajji Muhandiram was abducted and killed during the upheaval (Najimudeen 2002: 9–39). Because the Muslims were loyal to the British and collaborated with them during the upheaval, the British wanted to safeguard their interest; and a proclamation, favorable to Muslims, was issued on the 2nd of March, 1818, by the Secretary of the Kandyan Provinces. According to this proclamation, within the Districts of the Kandyan Provinces

> it shall not be lawful for any Kandyan Chief to exercise any jurisdiction whatever over the Moor men of this country; and the civil and the criminal justice shall in future, in all cases where a Moor man is a party, be impartially administered to them by a British official. . . . any Moor men who may suffer in his person, or, property by his adherence to the British Government, shall receive the fullest compensation as the nature of the injury will admit of.

This proclamation clearly shows the divide and rule policy of the British. They wanted to keep Muslims loyal while also alienating them from the Sinhalese to manage the rebellious Sinhala chieftains. As Dewaraja points out, "the proclamation had a disruptive effect on Sinhala-Muslim relations. . . . The British Government ensured that the Muslims would henceforth look up to the new rulers as their saviors and at the same time disturbed the traditional interdependence that prevailed between the two communities" (Dewaraja, 1994:141–142).

Unlike the Portuguese and the Dutch who had suppressed the Muslims, the British granted them some concessions to win their loyalty. They abolished the poll tax imposed by the Dutch, and the Muslims began to accumulate capital by buying land and property in Colombo and other urban areas.

Owing to the development of the plantation industry and mercantile capitalism from the early 19th century, some Muslims also were able to accumulate wealth and formed an elitist upper class within the community. They mainly accumulated capital through trade and urban property. They were involved in the export trade of various goods such as cinnamon, pearls, tobacco, areca nuts, coffee, tea, rubber, coconut, and gems. Southern Muslims dominated the gem trade. Some of the Colombo-based Muslims became wealthy through building contracts. Other Muslims became rich through wholesale and retail trade in the local market. As I. L. M. Abdul Azeez (1907) proudly pointed out in replying to Ponnambalam Ramanathan, in the late 19th century, the newly emerged Muslim elites included "wholesale merchants, large shop keepers, planters, and wealthy landed proprietors and in point of wealth, they were only next to the Sinhalese among the native races of the Island." It was this elitist group that was ethnically sensitive and politically motivated and led the Muslim community into the modern era through their revivalist activities.

During the 19th century, new economic channels were opened up for all indigenous ethnic groups as well as foreign trading communities. Ameer Ali's (1989: 247–248) concluding remarks, after giving a detailed account of the Muslim participation in the export sector, are relevant here. He says

> Between 1800 and 1915, the export sector of Sri Lanka underwent a radical change marked by the advent of the plantation economy in the 1840s. The Muslim community participated actively in the export sector both before and after the transition. The extent of their participation and the manner in which they did varied, depending partly on the political and the administrative rules governing the various export items,

partly on the economic profitability promised by the different articles, and partly on the religious values that generally governed the Muslim life. Overall theirs was an enterprising contribution to the 19th century economic development of Sri Lanka. Nevertheless, there were problems confronting the community which arose partly from competition from foreigners and partly from the local reaction to the Muslim economic dominance. These problems kept on adding to undermine the image of the Muslims which eventually culminated in the Sinhalese-Muslims racial riots of 1915.

Kumari Jayawardena (1984, 1990) also gives some details about the situation in trade in the late 19th century. According to her, by 1880, the Pettah trade was dominated by 86 Chetty and 64 Muslim firms; and at the beginning of the 20th century, the external trade (export and import) was dominated by seven leading Borah firms (Chetty and Borah are business communities of Indian origin who live in Sri Lanka.) Retail trade was also dominated largely by Muslims, especially the Coast Moors in the urban as well as in the rural areas.

Understandably the emerging Sinhala mercantile class faced severe competition from the minority communities, especially from the Muslims. Dewaraja (1994: 147) points out that "the animosity of the Sinhala small retail traders against this foreign domination of the Island's trade was directed mainly against the Coast Moors who had established their little shops, or boutiques, not only in the suburbs but also in the remote villages where they came in contact with the poor section of the Sinhala society."

Sinhala Buddhist nationalists, who had the strong support of the Sinhala mercantile capitalists, started to agitate against the Muslims from the late 19th century. K. M. De Silva (1981: 382) points out that "the Sinhala traders (mainly low-country Sinhalese) had no compunctions about exploiting religious and racial sentiments to the detriment of their well established rivals, since (they) were an influential group within the Buddhist movement, religious sentiment often given sharp ideological focus and a cloak of respectability to sordid commercial rivalry." But very often this commercial rivalry was expressed removing the "cloak of respectability" and with an overt racial tone. For example, in 1915, just before the communal riots against Muslims began, Anagarika Dharmapala, the veteran Buddhist revivalist leader, wrote this:

> The Mohammaden, an alien people by Shylockian method, became prosperous like the Jews. The Sinhalese sons of soil, whose ancestors for 2358 years had shed rivers of blood to keep the country free from alien invaders ... are in the eyes of the British only vagabonds. ... The alien South Indian Mohammaden comes to Ceylon sees the neglected villager without any experience in trade ... and the result is that the Mohammedan thrives and the son of the soil goes to the wall. (Guruge 1965)

Anagarika Dharmapala had developed a hostile ideology toward Islam and Muslims. If we go through his speeches and essays, we find numerous negative references on Muslims. He was unreasonably convinced that the Muslims were responsible for the elimination of Buddhism in India, its birthplace, even though Buddhism was almost eradicated from India before the arrival of the Muslims due to internal religious conflicts. I give one quotation from Dharmapala as an example:

> Superstition again took hold of the thought, and in an evil hour the Mohammedan conquerors entered India. The vestiges of Buddhism were destroyed by this inhuman, barbarous race. Thousands of Bhikkhus were killed, temples were destroyed, libraries were burned and Buddhism died in India. (Guruge 1965: 207)

This kind of animosity, with its real roots due to the competition in the economy, was the main reason for the anti-Muslim riots in 1915.

The immediate cause of the riots was a religious controversy between the Coast Moors and the Buddhists over an *Esala Perahera*, an annual religious practice of the Buddhists in Gampola, an ancient town in the Central Province, where the Sinhalese and the Muslims have coexisted for centuries. The controversy started in 1907 when the

Coast Moors for the first time objected to the *perahera* passing their recently built Mosque. The police and the Government Agent had to be involved in that issue each year after 1907, but both parties were not agreeable to a compromise. In 1912, the Basnayake Nilame of the Wallahagoda Devala, one of the parties of the controversy, filed a case against the Attorney General of Ceylon with regard to this issue at the District Court, Kandy and the Court gave the verdict on July 4, 1914, in favor of the Devala. The Attorney General appealed to the Supreme Court, and the Supreme Court reversed the District Court's judgment on February 2, 1915. The judgment was considered a defeat to the Buddhists and aroused island wide anti-Muslim sentiment among the Sinhalese. It was also considered a breach of the Kandyan Convention signed between the British and the Kandyan chieftains exactly a century before in March 1815. The Sinhala newspapers—*Sinhala Bauddhaya*, edited by Anagarika Dharmapala, and *Sinhala Jathiya*, edited by Piyadasa Sirisena—mouthpieces for the Sinhala nationalists, propagated a strong anti-Muslim sentiment, arousing Sinhala nationalist feelings (Blackton 1967).

The riots erupted first not in Gampola but in Kandy at midnight on May 28, 1915, when the police blocked the Vesak *perahera* near the Hanafi Mosque on Castle Street. Kandy was in turmoil for 3 days. A few died, seven mosques were damaged, and Muslims' shops were looted. Subsequently, the riots spread to the entire Central Province and Colombo, Kurunagala, Badulla, and all over Sri Lanka except the Northern, Eastern, and North Central Province. This was the first major communal riot in the history of modern Sri Lanka. It lasted for more than two weeks, and the government had to proclaim martial law to suppress the riots. The Muslims were severely affected by the riots. According to a government report, 25 Muslims were killed, 189 were wounded and 4 women were raped. 4,075 shops were looted, 350 were burnt to the ground and 103 mosques were destroyed or damaged (Najimudeen 2002: 143). The statistics vary in different literatures on the subject. The Inspector General of Police, at that time, reported 52 murders and 14 rapes during the riots (*Ceylon Administrative Report for 1915*). The estimated damages to the properties of the Muslims during the riots was Indian Rupee (Rs.) 5,527,745, of which 58%, that is, Rs. 3,195,271, was in the Western Province, revealing that Colombo was severely affected (Blackton 1967: 61).

Much of the writing on the riots blames the Coast Moors as the main cause of the riots and the main target of the rioters (De Silva 1981; Wimalaratna 1989; Shukri 1989; and Ali 2001). The Coast Moor trader was painted as an extreme exploiter and plunderer of the poor village Sinhalese. According to Dewaraja (1994: 147) "the Coast Moors have been accused of exploiting the poor by readily extending credit and selling at higher prices ... the Coast Moor was again accused of profiteering." This negative image of the Coast Moors is derived from the construction of the late 19th century Sinhala Buddhist nationalists such as Anagarika Dharmapala and Piyadasa Sirisena, which excludes the other traders—especially the Sinhala traders—and implicitly vindicates them from such allegations of exploitation and profit making. This is the image of the Muslim trader that prevails in the Sinhalese mind to now. The category of Coast Moor no longer exists in Sri Lanka.

In fact, poor Sinhala villagers were exploited equally by many traders in the late 19th and early 20th centuries, and the Moor trader was only one among them. If we look at this issue impartially without ethnic prejudices, we see that more Sinhalese (the Sinhala trader, the village headman, and the like) were involved in this exploitation. This was the reality. It was realistically depicted by Leonard Woolf, who was a civil servant in Ceylon from 1904 to 1911, in his celebrated novel *The Village in the Jungle*, a modern classic on Sri Lankan rural life, which was published 2 years before the 1915 riots against the Muslims. In the following, I give a relevant passage of his description:

> Nanchohami had touched the mainspring upon which the life of the village worked—debt. The villagers lived upon debt and their debt were the main topic of their conversation. A good kurakkan crop, from two to four acres of chena, would be sufficient to support a family for a year. But no one, not even the headman, ever enjoyed the full crop which he

> had reaped. At the time of reaping a band of strangers from the little town of Kamburupitiya, thirty miles away, would come in to the village. Mohamadu Lebbe Ahamadu Cassim, the Moorman boutique keeper, had supplied clothes to be paid for in grain, with the hundred per cent interest, at the time of reaping; the fat Sinhalese Mudalali, Kodikarage Allis Appu, had supplied grain and curry stuffs *on the same terms*; and among a crowd of smaller men the sly-faced low-caste man, who called himself Achchige Don Andris (his real name Andrissa would have revealed his caste), who, dressed in dirty white European trousers and coat, was the agent of the tavern-keeper in Kamburupitiya, from whom the villagers had taken on credit the native sprit, made from the juice of the coconut flowers, to be drunk at the time of marriages. *The villagers neither obtained nor expected any pity from this horde.* With the reaping of the chenas came the settlement of debts. With their little greasy notebooks, full of unintelligible letters and figures, they descended upon the chenas; and after calculations, wrangling, and abuse, which lasted for hour after hour, the accounts were settled, and the strangers left the village, their carts loaded with pumpkins, sacks of grains, and not infrequently the stalks of Indian hemp, which by Government order no man may grow or possess, for the man that smokes it becomes mad. And when the strangers were gone the settlement with the headman began; for the headman, on a small scale, lent, grain *in the same terms* in times of scarcity, or when seed was wanted to sow the chenas.
>
> In the end the villager carried but little grain from his chena to his hut. Very soon after the reaping of the crop he was again at the headman's door, begging for a little kurakkan to be repaid at the next harvest, or tramping the thirty miles to Kamburupitiya to hang about the bazaar, until the Mudalali agreed once more, to enter his name in the greasy notebook. (Woolf, 2000)

Here, Mohamadu Lebbe Ahamadu Cassim, the Moor trader (his identity as a Coast or Ceylon Moor is not known), is only one among the exploiters. Kodikarage Allis Appu, the Sinhalese trader, is another exploiter on equal terms. The tavern keeper and his agent Don Andris and the headman all are Sinhalese and all exploit on the same terms.

"The villagers neither obtained nor expected any pity from this horde." Although there was no difference in exploitation between them, if Allis Appu, "the son of the soil" in Dharmapala's term, wants to monopolize the exploitation and make more money without competition, he can easily exclude Ahamadu Cassim ethnically, accusing him of being an "alien who uses Shylockian method[s] and became prosperous like Jews." This was the situation in the late 19th and early 20th centuries, and the final result was rioting against the "Moors" in 1915. It was a culmination of continuous rivalry of the trading groups of two different ethnic communities. However, the writers on the riots easily found a scapegoat in Coast Moors who were the major victims of the riots. I think it is equally ridiculous to blame the Tamils for the 1983 violence against them.

The harsh methods deployed by the government to suppress the riots were severely criticized by the Buddhist nationalists. During the riots, the police and the military killed 63 rioters, mostly Sinhalese, under martial law. The total accused of being involved in the riots was 8,736. Among them, 4,497 were convicted; 412 "serious cases had been remitted to the field general court martial which found 358 guilty"; 83 were sentenced to death; and finally, 34 of them were executed, and most of them (26) were convicted of murder (Blackton 1967: 61). The government also arrested several important nationalist leaders including D. S. Senanayake and F. R. Senanayake. "Some of the leading Buddhist activists, who were from the most successful Sinhala business families, were killed or died in jail; one among [them] was Edmund Hewavitarana, the brother of Anagarika Dharmapala, who died in the jail owing to the illness" (Jayawardena 2000: 271).

The government's attempt to suppress the riots further flared up anti-Muslim sentiments among the Sinhalese elite. Dharmapala "leveled a surprising burst of hate against Muslims: 'What the German is to the British, that the Muhammedan is to the Sinhalese . . . shoot, hang, quarter, imprison or do anything to the Sinhalese but there will always be bad blood between the Moors and the Sinhalese' . . . [A] few months later the London *Daily Chronicle* received from Dharmapala an anti-Muslim diatribe and clippings listing death-sentences meted out to Buddhists in Ceylon" (Blackton 1967: 55–56). This anti-Muslim sentiment of the Sinhala Buddhist elite and the 1915 riot had a lasting impact in consolidating Muslim identity in the late 19th and early 20th centuries.

The New Phase of Sinhala Buddhist Nationalism

Sinhala Buddhist nationalism and social hegemony were firmly rooted in Sri Lankan polity at the time; and so Tamil and Muslim nationalisms emerged as reactive political ideologies with the introduction of universal franchise, electoral and parliamentary politics under the Donoughmore and Soulbury constitutions in the 1930s and 40s, respectively, as well as consequent political developments after independence. These political reforms paved the way for ethnic and religious majority rule in the country, marginalizing ethnic and religious minorities who had enjoyed equal rights and even some privileges under British rule.

However, the Muslim political elites collaborated with the Sinhala majority political parties—the United National Party (UNP) and the Sri Lanka Freedom Party (SLFP)—without moving toward any political confrontation until the mid-1980s when they finally succeeded in politically institutionalizing Muslim identity. The Tamil minorities, especially the Sri Lankan Tamils, who were the majority in the North and East, had chosen confrontational politics immediately after independence because of the discriminatory policies of the mainly Sinhala Buddhist political parties. Although the main political parties, the UNP and the SLFP, were considered as inclusive national parties, in practice they were and remain dominated by Sinhala Buddhist ideology and mainly catered to the interests of the Sinhalese.

The Ceylon Citizenship Bill, which proved overtly discriminatory, was passed by the Sinhala majority party in the first parliament in 1948 to disfranchise a million plantation workers of Indian origin who were the backbone of the Sri Lankan economy and who became stateless overnight to eliminate a leftist threat to the power of the Sinhala Buddhists in the parliament. The bill also affected the Coast Moors who were the commercial rivals of the mercantile class of Sinhala Buddhists as well as the Ceylon Moors.

Sinhala Buddhist nationalism became a major political force in the country in the 1950s and thereafter. It took an anti-imperialist stance and loudly voiced promotion of indigenous culture, religion, and the language of the people under the leadership of S. W. R. D. Bandaranaike. He was an Oxford-educated Sinhala Buddhist nationalist who converted from the Anglican Christian faith for the sake of his political career while he formed the Sinhala Maha Sabha in 1936. He left the ruling UNP in 1951 and formed a new nationalist party, the SLFP, and gave a strong and articulate political leadership to the Sinhala Buddhist nationalists. He mobilized the *panca bala vegaya* (the five great forces), namely, Buddhist monks, vernacular teachers, indigenous physicians, peasants, and workers. He used Sinhala only official language policy (founded the Official Language Act) as a shortcut to power and announced that he would make Sinhala as the only official language of the country within 24 hours if he won the 1956 general election. That promise proved very attractive to the Sinhala masses. He also readily accepted the recommendations of the report on *The Betrayal of Buddhism* released by the All Ceylon Buddhist Congress in February 1956. The Eksath Bhikkhu Peramuna (United Front of Buddhist Monks) led by Mapitigama Buddharakitha Thero campaigned for him; and his coalition, the Mahajana Eksath Peramuna (MEP), swept to victory at the election. That was a crucial turning point in the political history of Sri Lanka.

The Official Language Act No. 33 of 1956, popularly known an Sinhala Only Official Language Act that was passed in Parliament in June 1956 had a long-lasting negative impact on Sri Lankan politics, as it gave rise to the cradle of Tamil nationalism and separatism, which in turn contributed to the further strengthening of Sinhala Buddhist nationalism (Kearney 1967). Bandaranaike also appointed a Buddha Sasana Commission in March 1957 to make recommendations based on the report submitted by the All Ceylon Buddhist Congress to the government in June 1959. Some of the recommendations of the commission were implemented later by his widow, Sirimavo Bandaranaike's, government.

But Bandaranaike had to compromise with the Tamil nationalists to subside their political agitation and signed an agreement known as the Bandaranaike–Chelvanayakam Pact to grant some concessions to the Tamil minority in 1957, a pact that was vehemently opposed by UNP and the Sinhala Buddhist nationalists, especially by the Eksath Bhikkhu Peramuna. Their vitriolic opposition caused him to eventually abandon it. The first ever major anti-Tamil violence occurred in 1958, a direct consequence of the Sinhala Only Act and the political developments immediately after that. The Tamil Language (Special Provision) Act was passed by the government in the Parliament in August 1958 to appease the Tamil sentiment, but it seems that Bandaranaike could not satisfy either the Tamils or the Buddhist extremists. He was too late and was unable to tame the Sinhala Buddhist extremists, whom he politically patronized, and unfortunately he became the victim of his own politics. He was assassinated at his residence by a young Buddhist monk, Talduwe Somarama Thero, in 1959 to safeguard "the country, race and religion." Another prominent Bhikkhu, none other than the head monk of the Kelaniya Vihara, Mapitigama Buddharakita Thero, was also convicted by the court for his involvement in the plot. It is ironic that Buddhist monks assassinated the political leader who had created political space for Sinhala Buddhist nationalism to flourish.

The Tamil national question became the major issue in Sri Lankan politics after the 1950s, and each of the major Sinhala political parties, the UNP and the SLFP, started to play with the issue to win over the Sinhalese votes. Parliamentary opportunism became the undeclared permanent policy of both of these parties. Both parties were competing to satisfy the Sinhala masses, the Buddhist clergy, and extremists with their discriminatory policies against the minorities. Like the Bandaranaike—Selvanayakam pact of 1957, the Dudley Senanayake–Chelvanayakam pact of 1965 was also abandoned due to extremist pressure. The new constitution of the Democratic Socialist Republic of Sri Lanka, enacted in 1972 by the newly elected SLFP government with a coalition of the leftist parties, elevated Buddhism to be virtually a state religion by giving Buddhism "the foremost place" and by specifying the duty of the state to protect and foster the Buddha Sasana. This provision ultimately transformed the hitherto secular nature of the constitution into a religious one. Tamil Language was not even given the status of national language in the constitution. The government also introduced a discriminatory policy for university entrance that severely affected Jaffna Tamil youths who had enjoyed greater opportunities in university admission, especially in the fields of medicine and engineering. There was also a hidden agenda of "Sinhalizing" the public sector and the administration. It was recently revealed in an Official Languages Commission Report of 2005 that only 8% of minorities are employed in the public sector. This also includes the teachers in government schools. Thus, the minorities, especially the Sri Lankan Tamils, were further alienated.

As the Sinhala Buddhist nationalists were not ready to come to any meaningful compromise with the Tamil nationalists, Tamil militancy started to emerge in the mid-1970s. The Tamil nationalist parties joined together to form a coalition, the Tamil United Liberation Front (TULF) and adopted the Vaddukkoddai Resolution in May 1976—declaring their desire to create a separate state, Tamil Eelam, in the North and East. The TULF swept to victory in the North and East in the 1977 elections and became the main opposition party in the parliament, thereby creating high ethnic tension within the parliament and outside. The UNP, which had promised in their election manifesto to amicably solve the ethnic question, came to power with a comfortable majority; but they were determined to suppress the Tamil political demand and militancy due to the mounting pressure of Sinhala Buddhist hard-liners within the party and outside. Unprecedented organized anti-Tamil violence in 1977, 1981, and especially 1983 was unleashed; and the Prevention of Terrorism Act (PTA) was brutally implemented in the North and East. These events created space for the emergence of a number of Tamil militant groups, including the Liberation Tigers of Tamil Eelam (LTTE), one of the strongest liberation cum terrorist organizations in the world. They dragged the country into a protracted ethnic war that lasted for nearly three decades and that came to an end in 2009 with heavy casualties and destruction.

Emergence of Jathika Chintanaya: An Extreme Form of Sinhala Buddhist Ideology

The mounting ethnic tension and war from the late 1970s also created space for the emergence of a number of extremist Buddhist groups and organizations, all of which shared a new ideology called *Jathika Chintanaya* as an indigenous ideology and alternative to Marxism and capitalism, which was propagated by two leading Sinhala Buddhist intellectuals, Gunadasa Amarasekara and Nalin de Silva, from the late 1970s (Seneviratne 2004). *Jathika Chintanaya* (literally, "national thought") is a sophisticated version of Sinhala Buddhist nationalist ideology. According to Amarasekara, "our national ideology is Sinhala Buddhist ideology that has evolved through a period of about two thousand years." Although they trace the origin of their ideology from early Buddhism, it is clearly an exclusive ideology of modern nationalist and religious chauvinism parallel to Hindutva in India and Talibanist Islamism in the Muslim world. They are ideologically anti-West, culturally conservative, and intolerant of the ethnic and religious "other." *Jathika Chintanaya* justifies war and militarism within Buddhism, which is generally believed to be a religion of nonviolence and compassion. Sri Lanka is regarded as the land of Sinhala Buddhists and not as a multiethnic and multireligious country; minorities are aliens, latecomers, troublemakers, and the enemies of Sinhala Buddhist civilization. This is the essence of this ideology, the genealogy of which can be traced to Anagarika Dharmapala and Walpola Rahula (1907–1997), a powerful Buddhist monk who was a strong proponent of Sinhala Buddhist nationalism from the 1940s until his death. Although there are severe critiques of *Jathika Chintanaya* within the Sinhala community, it had general appeal among a wider section of the Sinhala people.

Jathika Chintanaya paved the way for the formation of exclusive Sinhala Buddhist hard-line organizations and political parties. The *Sinhala Veera Vidhana* (SVV) and the National Movement against Terrorism (NMAT) have been active from the mid-1990s. The first exclusive Sinhala Buddhist political party, the *Sihala Urumaya* (the Sinhala Heritage Party) was launched in 2000. They stated in their manifesto that the Sinhala people form 75% of the population, but they have been reduced to the state of a minority. They also stated that Buddhism should be made officially the state religion, that the national anthem should be sung in Sinhala only, and they sought the eradication of LTTE terrorism by military means. The *Sihala Urumaya* got only one seat from their national list in Parliament at the 2000 general election, but their appearance was a harbinger of what was to follow.

Jathika Hela Urumaya (JHU; National Sinhala Heritage party), an offshoot of *Sihala Urumaya*, is a more vibrant Sinhala Buddhist nationalist organization that was launched in February 2004, mostly by prominent Buddhist monks such as Rev. Omalpe Sobhitha Thero and Rev. Athuraliya Ratana Thero, in wake of the death of Ven. Gangodawila Soma, an extremely popular charismatic nationalist monk who had raised the issue of Muslim encroachment on ancient lands purportedly given by Sinhala kings to the Buddhist *sangha*. According to their 12-point manifesto, Sri Lanka is a Sinhala Buddhist unitary state that should be ruled according to Buddhist principles. The Sinhala people made the country into a habitable civilization, and the national heritage belongs to them. Their hereditary rights should be granted while protecting the rights of the other communities who inhabit the island (Deegalle 2004). The JHU contested in the April 2004 general election by fielding 200 Buddhist monks island wide as candidates. They secured 9 seats in the parliament, getting a little more than 550,000 votes. This is the first time in the history of modern Sri Lanka that a Sinhala Buddhist nationalist party, led exclusively by monks, engaged directly in parliamentary politics and demonstrated their influence in public life. Immediately after they entered the parliament, the JHU demanded that the government enact and implement a Prohibition of Forcible Conversion of Religion Act. They also campaigned against cattle slaughtering in the country.

Sinhala Ravaya (SR), *Ravana Balaya* (RB), and *Bodu Bala Sena* (BBS) are also extremist Sinhala Buddhist organizations of recent origin that are led by Buddhist monks and actively engage in propagating hostility against minority religious communities in the country. The BBS recently announced that they are forming a political party and have invited the former secretary of the defense ministry and brother of the former president to join.

The emergence of militant Sinhala Buddhist nationalism during the last few decades has had a tremendous influence on the Buddhist community at large. This is evident in the increased number of temple goers among them, not only on *poya* days, but on most other days as well. The student numbers in the Sunday *Daham Pasal* (Buddhist religious schools) has also increased. Buddha's statues seem to have been erected everywhere in public. As Gananath Obeyesekere has observed

> By the 1980s the Buddha in the market place was an ubiquitous presence: he is found everywhere, outside public buildings, in every major road junction, at the entrance to towns, in almost every school, at the entrance to the university campuses, at hospitals, and disconcerting, to me at least, even in parts of the tea country where the population is almost exclusively Tamil and Hindu ... the Buddhist[s] have imitated the catholic example in their expression of projected nationhood but in recent times they have even invaded the catholic market place with Buddha statuary. There is a kind of warfare between religions through their statue construction. (Obeyesekere 2010: 70)

Muslim Identity after Independence

Muslim identity was strengthened and consolidated after independence due to various sociopolitical and economic factors. As I mentioned earlier, the introduction of universal franchise and electoral politics in the 1930s created a political awareness among the Muslims in the same manner as it did among the other communities and led them to compete to secure enough political representation in the State Council before independence and in the Parliament after independence. The political representation of the Muslims in the parliaments has been gradually increasing for the last five decades. Muslims had 8 members in the 1956 parliament, and it gradually increased to 16 in the 1977 parliament. Under the proportional representation system, it further increased to 23 in 1989 and reached its highest of 27 in the 2004 election before decreasing to 18 in 2010 (Jameel 2013).

Progress in education and employment also played an important role in consolidating Muslim identity in Sri Lanka. Muslims were backward in education until 1940. The compulsory education and free education introduced in 1931 and 1945, respectively, made a tremendous impact on the progress on Muslim education. The introduction of vernacular languages as the medium of education up to the university level in the late 1950s and the introduction of standardization and a special quota for backward districts to the university admission in early 1970s provided more opportunities for Muslims to obtain higher education qualifications and created a middle and a new professional class with an educated elite among them. They became ethnically a more sensitive and opinion making social group due to the competition they had to face with the other ethnic groups.

Muslims are traditionally known as a trading community, although only a small portion of them are actually traders. However, they visibly engage in commercial activities mostly in Sinhala dominated urban areas. Muslims' shops, big or small, are found in most cities and towns island wide. The open economic policy introduced in the late 1970s provided greater opportunities for some Muslim businessmen to become more prominent and to engage in larger commercial ventures. The gem industry was virtually monopolized by Muslim gem merchants for a long time until the 1970s. These trading communities are increasingly under pressure and in competition with the Sinhala trading groups. Those Muslims who are engaged in paddy cultivation and fishing in the East and some other parts of the country have also faced stiff competition from the majority ethnic group in the recent past. This competition in trade and commerce is one of the factors that has consolidated the collective Muslim identity.

Because of the collaborative politics of the Muslim political elites, they were able to institutionalize Muslim identity after independence. Two eminent political leaders, Sir Razik Fareed in the 1940s and 1950s and Badiuddin Mahmud in the 1960s and 1970s, made a significant contribution to institutionalizing Muslim identity. By institutionalization, I mean organizing separate social institutions in the public sector exclusively for Muslims, attempting to thereby legitimize Muslim interests (Nuhman 2007). The first such institutions were set up in the field of education. A separate category for government Muslim schools, separate training colleges, and colleges for the education of Muslim teachers was established. The Muslim schools are allowed to follow a separate calendar to accommodate a special Ramzan vacation. A separate university for Muslims, the Southeastern University of Sri Lanka, was established in 1995 as a university college and elevated to a full-fledged university in 1996 with predominantly Muslim students and staff; but subsequently, it has become a national university accommodating Tamil and Sinhala students and staff as well.

Another area of institutionalization of Muslim identity is the integration of Muslim Personal Law into the Sri Lankan Legal system with the establishment of special Quazi Courts in 1930 to deal exclusively with matrimonial disputes in the Muslim community. According to Savitri Goonesekere (2000: 9), "the introduction of special Quazi Courts was a unique development in the Sri Lankan legal system, since all other indigenous or customary laws were applied in the ordinary civil courts." The Muslim elite also succeeded in setting up government institutions to look after the maintenance of mosques and charitable trusts from the 1930s. The Muslim Interstate Succession and Wakfs Ordinance of 1931 was in operation until the mid-1950s. It was replaced by the Muslim Mosques and Charitable Trusts or Wakfs Act of 1956. Under this act a separate government department with an executive Wakfs Board was established (Ameen 2003).

Muslim identity was institutionally recognized also in government owned electronic media. A Muslim unit was set up in the Sri Lanka Broadcasting Corporation (SLBC) nearly 40 years ago. SLBC broadcasts a separate Muslim service catering exclusively to Muslim interests. There is also a small Muslim Unit at the Sri Lanka Rupavahini Corporation (SLRC), which telecasts weekly Muslim programs. These electronic media promote ethnic and religious awareness among Sri Lankan Muslims. But there is no strong print media owned by Sri Lankan Muslims as in the late 19th and early 20th centuries. A few tabloids and little magazines are published with a limited circulation, and they are ethnically and religiously very sensitive. Apart from these institutions, numerous social and cultural organizations and nongovernmental organizations (NGOs) are molding and activating Muslim identity in Sri Lanka for the last several decades.

Muslim Political Party

The emergence of Tamil militancy, the continuous separatist war and its effects on the Muslim community, combined with the unleashed atrocities by the LTTE against the Muslims of the North and East, intensified ethnic sentiment among the Muslims and paved the way for the emergence of a separate political party, the Sri Lanka Muslim Congress (SLMC) in the 1980s. With the emergence of the SLMC, Muslim politics in Sri Lanka became challenging, confrontational, and competing with Tamil and Sinhala nationalisms. The SLMC, under the charismatic leadership of M. H. M. Ashraf, gave rise to much inspirational sentiment with its verbal militancy laced with religious overtones and became almost a monopolizing political force in the East after the first Provincial Council elections held in 1988 (Nuhman 2007: 38–44). The SLMC became a very prominent and influential political party in the country after the 1989 and 1994 general elections held under the proportionate representative system, and they secured 6 and 9 seats in the parliament, respectively. In the 2000 general election, the SLMC contested under the United People's Freedom Alliance (UPFA) and the National United Alliance (NUA), a party created by Mr. Ashraff himself, and they secured 11 seats altogether. Although the SLMC divided into smaller parties after the untimely death of Mr. Ashraff in 2000, the Muslim parties had bargaining power in forming successive governments whether by the UPFA or UNP and managed to get some important portfolios in the cabinet that caused deepening anti-Muslim sentiments among Sinhala Buddhists. It has been said that "many Buddhist monks complained that the Muslim politicians from the East were using their disproportionate political power in the government to divert resources, including land and development funds, to support their Muslim constituencies, while Sinhala politician[s] merely looked after their own personal interests without helping their constituencies as such" (Spencer et al. 2015: 80). The

Eastern Muslims may have a converse opinion because they have faced many hardships due to Sinhala domination in the region.

Religious Awareness and Islamization

Religious awareness among Muslims intensely increased after independence for various reasons. Upward social mobility due to the educational and employment opportunities, increasing ethnic conflict, challenges to their identity, and the impact of a re-emergence of Islamism in the Muslim world are some of the important factors in this development.

Several Islamic *da'wah* (preaching) movements also emerged in Sri Lanka in the 1950s and after. *Jamaat e Islami, Tabligh Jamaat,* and *Tawhid Jamaat* are the most influential among them. The impact of these organizations on the process of Islamization of the Sri Lankan Muslim community, apart from the sociopolitical developments I discussed earlier, had been very significant. They played an important role in the development of religious awareness, in the deepening of ethnic consciousness, and in almost creating a cultural homogeneity among Sri Lankan Muslims during the past two or three decades, although there are serious ideological differences between them (Nuhman 2007:174–182).

After independence, Arabic colleges also mushroomed in Sri Lanka owing to Islamic resurgence. From 1884 to 1950, only 15 Arabic colleges were established in Sri Lanka. However, from 1950 to 2000, a little more than 100 colleges were established. That trajectory shows the dramatic trend of resurgence in traditional Islamic orientation during the period. Now more than 150 Arabic colleges are functioning in most parts of the country. In the year 2000, there were 101 Arabic colleges registered at the Department of Muslim Cultural Affairs. Others were not registered. Among the registered colleges, 88 were for men and 13 for women.

In all of these Arabic colleges, the main component of teaching—the Arabic and Islamic component—is accomplished mostly on a noted conservative traditional line. More emphasis is given to *sharia* as a sacred and static doctrine of Islamic law without a proper understanding of its evolutionary nature. The ever-changing nature of society is not taken into account, and therefore it remains a difficult task to interpret

Islam as a religion suitable for the contemporary modern world. Most of the *ulamas* who pass out from these Arabic colleges have developed an antipathy toward cultural change. No Arabic college has included the study of other religions or comparative religion in its syllabi.

The development of religious awareness among Sri Lankan Muslims is discernible in the extensively increased number of mosque goers during the past few decades and also in the increased number of mosques in rural as well as in urban areas. It is also discernible in the renovation and expansion of mosques in almost all cities and in many villages to accommodate more people who come to pray, especially for *Jumma* prayers on Fridays. The development of religious and ethnic consciousness has led the Muslims to seek a separate cultural identity based on the fundamentals of their religion, Islam, to differentiate themselves from the other Sri Lankan ethnic groups.

The question of whether specific cultural or religious practices are Islamic or un-Islamic has become very important, sometimes provoking violence among various religious groups and individuals throughout this period. Various sects and groups have developed their own interpretation of Islam, and they sincerely believe and try to prove that only their interpretation is truly Islamic and try to impose it in practice. Religious violence at Kathankudi, the largest Muslim village in Sri Lanka in the Batticaloa District in 2006, is a case in point (Spencer et al. 2015: 91–98). Muslim identity at the macro level seems to be superficially unifying the Sri Lankan Muslim community; but at the same time, Muslim religious and political groups are seriously polarized at the micro level. This is the contradictory reality of the Sri Lankan Muslim community today.

Muslim cultural identity is most prominently visible in male and female attire. There is a growing tendency among religiously conscious males to wear the white lace cap and to grow a beard with a trimmed mustache. Many of them, especially those who belong to *Tabligh Jamaat,* also prefer a long loose white upper garment and a lower garment worn at least 2 inches above their ankles. Although there is no prescribed dress for Muslim women, the *hijab* has become the acceptable Muslim female attire in Sri Lanka since the 1980s, as in the other countries, due to the emergence of Islamism globally. It has become the school uniform for Muslim girls in all the Muslim schools. The Muslim girls who attend non-Muslim schools also observe *hijab*. Various types of *hijabs* are in use. Most of them wear a black *habaya*. Some wear only a headscarf with their normal dress. Some extreme Islamist groups like *Tabligh Jamaat* promote a complete veil with gloves and socks (Nuhman 2007: 199–208).

Buddhist Extremism and Anti-Muslim Campaigns

Unfortunately, it is common to see in many underdeveloped plural societies increasing ethnic and religious consciousness creating sharp distinctions between "we" and the "other," thereby generating ethnic and religious segregation and polarization. If one group (majority or minority) gets political power, it tries to monopolize state resources and in the process marginalizes the other groups. Sri Lanka is a classic example of this. Sinhala Buddhists, who are the majority and who firmly believe that they are the rightful custodians of the country, having been earlier deprived of their rights by alien invaders—South Indian Tamils in the remote past and the Europeans in the recent past—have wanted to regain what they believe is their right to determine the destiny of the country.

After independence, the Sinhala Buddhist majority who came to power started to implement their agenda of "Sinhalizing" the country. Inevitably, this created serious conflicts between them and minority communities. The police, army, and the bureaucracy were all gradually "Sinhalized." The first major economic step in "Sinhalizing" was a state sponsored colonization project implemented from 1950 in the dry zone, especially in the East where Tamils and Muslims had been predominant settlers for a long time. A large number of Sinhalese from the southwest wet zone were brought and settled in these new colonies, disturbing the ethnic balance and creating ethnic tensions. The Gal Oya scheme in the southeast is a good specific example. It was first initiated and proposed by Mr. M. S. Kariyapper, a Muslim government servant who later became a politician in Kalmunai in 1937 with the hope that it would be beneficial to the Muslim farmers of that area (Nuhman 2009.) But when it became a reality in the 1950s, the major beneficiaries were the large number of Sinhala settlers who were brought from outside. A new district, the Ampara District, was created in the 1960s, carving out some parts from the Batticaloa District. Ampara, a new town that emerged after colonization, became the capital city; and the district administration that was located in Ampara was headed by a Sinhalese administrator. According to the 2007 enumeration, Muslims constitute 44%, Tamils 18.3%, and Sinhalese 37.5% of the district population. Although the Tamil-speaking minorities, Muslims, and Tamils constitute more than 60% of the population, they occupy only 26.5% of the land in the narrow coastal area of the district. Hundreds of acres of paddy land cultivated by Muslims were transferred to Sinhalese, and more land was distributed to the Sinhala settlers by the government for sugar cane cultivation. When the ruins of an ancient Buddhist temple, known as Digavapi, were rediscovered in the 1950s, it became a sacred site and a point of dispute between Buddhists and Muslims who had been cultivating adjacent lands for a long time. This land issue was an acute public problem that lasted for nearly four decades. It gained a national fame in the late 1990s. Mr. M. H. M. Ashraff, a Muslim minister from Ampara District, was accused by Buddhist nationalists, including Ven. Gangodawila Soma, of destroying Digavapi ruins. The TNL TV channel telecast a lengthy debate on the issue between Soma and Ashraff that had the effect of clearing Ashraff's name. A number of Buddhist organizations, politicians, and monks, including the JHU, became further involved in the dispute and filed a case in the Supreme Court in 2008. The verdict was given in 2009 in favor of the Buddhists, depriving the farming rights of Muslims (Spencer et al. 2015: 79). The courts clearly abetted the process of "Sinhalization."

When the tsunami hit Sri Lanka in 2004, the Ampara District was severely affected. More than 9,000 people, Muslims and Tamils, died and several thousand were displaced. The Sinhalese, who mostly settled in the interior, were marginally affected. According to the Department of Census and Statistics and its Basic Population Information on Ampara District in 2007, there were 18,213 displaced tsunami victims in the district who had not been resettled. A Saudi Arabia sponsored resettlement scheme with 500 housing units was completed by the National Housing Development Authority to address the problem among the

Muslim tsunami victims, but the distribution was blocked by Buddhist extremist groups accusing "Muslim politicians of using the tsunami as an excuse for encroaching on sacred Buddhist land," although the scheme is located 13 km away from the Digavapi temple (Spencer et al. 2015: 79). First the colonization scheme and then the land issue virtually marginalized the Muslims and Tamils of the Ampara District. Fortunately, however, there was no incident of violent clashes between Muslims and Sinhalese in Ampara.

A land issue, Sinhala colonization, and business competition were causes of ethnic violence that erupted between Muslims and Sinhalese in Putalam in 1976. It was the first major incident between Muslims and Sinhalese after independence (Anes et al. 2008: 39–57. Due to the Land Reform Law of 1972, some wealthy Muslims of Putalam lost thousands of acres of coconut estates. Their land and some crown land were redistributed to Sinhalese from outside to settle there. Deserving local Muslims, Tamils, or even Sinhalese were not given any of this land. Some Sinhalese also forcefully occupied some crown land close to Putalam on which some Putalam Muslims were negotiating with government officials to settle. These developments caused a bitter dispute and hatred between the two groups. Violent incidents occurred from time to time, but the police took stern actions only against Muslim youths.

There was also a demand to shift the Putalam bus stand close to the Sinhalese settlement. The demand was submitted to the Putalam government officials by the chief Buddhist monk of the Putalam Buddhist Centre. Putalam Transport Board officials and some of the local Sinhala leaders were also behind this. The bus stand had earlier been located close to the bazaar, so it had been mostly beneficial to Muslim businessmen and boutique keepers. It seems that the Sinhalese wanted to disrupt this arrangement to get benefits by relocating it close to their settlements. The bus stand was shifted in January 1976 following a violent incident between a Muslim youth and a Sinhalese bus conductor.

It was a longtime practice for Putalam town Muslims to block the road that goes in front of the mosque for about one hour by placing a "No Entry" sign during the Friday prayer. However, the board was removed by police on January 30, 1976, creating further tension among Muslims. Because of the protests by the Muslims and the involvement of a Muslim politician, the police officer who was responsible for the incident was transferred. The Sinhalese took it as a defeat and started anti-Muslim agitation and violence. Muslims were beaten, shops were looted and burned, and vehicles were stoned and burned. The riot spread to surrounding villages and lasted for 3 days. The riot came to an end when police fired shots into the Muslim mosque, killing 7 Muslims and seriously wounding 11. One innocent young Muslim boy was also killed in the violence. A total of 271 Muslim families were homeless and 44 shops were looted or burned, whereas losses on the Sinhalese side were minimal. Without any impartial inquiry, Prime Minister Sirimavo Bandaranaike issued a statement in parliament putting the blame on the Muslims for the riots. This clearly was an instance of victimizing the victims.

The Mawanella riot of 2001 was another example indicating how business competition is an important factor behind anti-Muslim campaigns by Sinhalese Buddhists. Mawanella is located in the Kegalle District of Central Province about 20 miles west of Kandy. It is a densely populated area mixed with Sinhala and Muslim communities. Muslims have lived in Mawanella and its suburbs for centuries' back into the times of Kandyan kings, without any problems with the Sinhalese. It is a semi-urban town with increasingly developing commercial activities by Muslims and Sinhalese. It is the only big shopping center in-between Kegalle and Pilimathalawa that caters to a large number of villages and small towns.

The riot took place in May 2001 (Anes et al. 2008: 150–169). There had been some minor incidents that had continued for 2 or 3 months before the outbreak. It was sparked by the refusal of a Muslim cashier in a hotel in the town to provide a ransom or bribe to a few Sinhalese thugs. A nonviolent protest by Muslims was met with violence by the Sinhalese, and that violence spiraled out of control. As usual, the police were passive in response. Nearly 150 shops, 2 mosques, 6 houses, several vehicles, one garment factory, and a filling station were completely destroyed; and 20 shops, 70 houses, and a mosque were seriously damaged within 2 days of the mayhem. The riot, as with many other instances, was not an accidental or spontaneous incident. It was a culmination of anti-Muslim campaigns carried out for a long time by the extreme Sinhala Buddhist organizations in the South. Between the Putalam and Mawanella incidents, a number of anti-Muslim violent events took place in many parts of the country. A total of 20 such incidents, small or big, were recorded (Anes et al. 2008) during this 25-year time frame. Another major attack occurred in Nochchiyagama in which 40 shops were burned in 1999 (Cheran 1999).

Some Mawanella residents blamed the Sihala Urumaya for the riot and also a politician from the ruling SLFP. The Sihala Urumaya, SVV, and JHU are inseparably linked with each other; and they successfully carried out Sinhala Buddhist supremacy and antiminority campaigns since the 1990s in the country with media support. SVV is an organization that carried out a campaign to boycott Muslim shops. The United Sinhala Traders Association (USTA), which constitutes more than 600 branches in predominantly Sinhala areas, works under the umbrella of SVV to promote the interest of Sinhala traders. It is reasonable to assume that the anti-Muslim hatred and most of the anti-Muslim violence stemmed from the economic interests of this group.

Although these incidents were disturbing to the Muslim community, the postwar emergence of BBS constitutes an important turn in Sinhala/Muslim relations in Sri Lanka. The BBS is an overtly extreme anti-Muslim organization with high level political patronage that began to carry out their anti-Muslim campaigns in 2012. This is the Buddhist organization that first asserted that cultural practices of the Muslims have an inverse effect on the Sinhala public. *Halal* was such an issue. After a lot of commotion and heated arguments, finally the All Ceylon Jammiyatul Ulama (ACJU) had to stop issuing *halal* certificates to various food-producing companies. We can assume that the BBS opposed a *halal* certificate not merely because it is a cultural practice of the Muslims but because it is also a commercial practice that affects Sinhalese producers. *Halal* had become a universal practice of the food producers to attract Muslim consumers.

The wearing of the *hijab* as a popular aspect of Muslim female dress was another issue that the BBS brought to the public's attention. They ridiculed the Muslim women wearing full head covers as "*goni billa*" (literally "sack devil"). Some thugs began to harass Muslim women wearing the *hijab* in public places. Due to anti-*hijab* propaganda and harassment, many Muslim women were afraid to go out for some time. Although the BBS could not succeed in banning *hijab*, as it is a fundamental right issue, it marked a serious damage in Muslim–Sinhala relations.

Cattle slaughtering is another issue that the BBS targeted. It had already been taken up by other extremist Buddhist groups including JHU, but the BBS tried to take direct field action by creating tension among Muslims, especially during the *Haj* festival time. Muslims had to find alternative arrangements to perform their *Haj* ritual.

The BBS, along with other extremist groups, began attacking Muslim places of worship in the last half of 2012. Mosques in Anuradhapura, Dambulla, Mahiyangana, Grandpass, and Maligawaththa were attacked and damaged completely or partially (Farook 2014b). An ancient Muslim shrine, *Dafther Jailani* at Kuragala near Balangoda, has been under threat by the same Buddhist extremist organizations for the last several years (Farook 2014b: 127–141).

But the most recent, most extensive, and most serious anti-Muslim violence since independence broke out in June 2014 at Aluthgama and Dharga Town, instigated by a BBS anti-Muslim rally that has been widely documented. Two Muslims and a Tamil ware killed, 88 Muslims were injured, 64 houses were completely damaged by arson, 126 houses were extensively damaged, and another 66 houses sustained minor damages; 40 shops were completely damaged and another 45 shops were attacked and looted; one mosque was completely destroyed and two others were damaged and 54 vehicles belonging to Muslims were burned. Most of the damages were done while curfew was declared and the police stood by passively. The total value of the damage was estimated at Rs. 400 million (Zuhair 2014).

However, astonishingly, 23 Sinhala Buddhist organizations, including All Ceylon Buddhist Congress, Government Service Buddhist

Association, BBS, Sinhala Ravaya, and SVV, jointly released a statement on "the truth about clashes in Aluthgama," putting the blame squarely on Muslims for the riot and asserting "the truth": that Buddhists were the most severely affected people in this riot. This absurd statement was published in *Ceylon Today*, July 10, 2014.

All of these incidents reveal the depth of the Sinhala–Muslim divide in Sri Lanka as it has been deepening over the years. As the Muslims are a thinly scattered and rather powerless minority with limited means to defend themselves, the damage that they have incurred has been heavy. Moreover, their inability to defend themselves indicates that there are no armed militant extremist groups within the Muslim community, as continuously alleged by some Buddhist groups and also by the LTTE in the past.

Islamism or Islamic extremism in Sri Lanka is not like the armed extremism in the Middle East or in Afghanistan. Sri Lankan Muslims are not fighting against foreign imperialist forces, or seeking to establish an Islamic state as in Iraq and Syria. The ground reality in Sri Lanka is certainly not favorable for the development of militant Islam as such in Sri Lanka, as Muslims are a scattered minority, surrounded by a Sinhala majority in the South and Tamils in the East. The Sri Lankan variety of Islamism, or Islamic extremism if it may be called such, is only an unarmed ideological extremism that propagates and promotes Islam within the Muslim community. There have been some violent clashes within the Muslim community, but these were not between organized militant armed groups. The International Crisis Group's Asia Report 2007 also supports this fact.

It is widely believed that the extreme Buddhist organizations, especially the BBS, have enjoyed political patronage from the ruling Sinhala regime under Mahinda Rajapaksa. These extremist groups operated with impunity. No action has been taken against them yet, despite the fact that Rajapaksa was defeated in the January 2015 national election. The immediate hidden agenda might have been to mobilize Sinhala voters and to marginalize the Muslim minority parties and their bargaining power in forming the government in the forthcoming elections. However, the Sri Lankan politics took a different turn unexpectedly in the Presidential election held in January 2015, an election that has eased the mounting tension visibly, at least temporarily.

Conclusion

It is a historical fact that the Sri Lanka polity and politics have been increasingly ethnicized during the past hundred years, especially after independence. All the political parties, including the left parties, carry the burdens of ethnonationalism or are under the influence of that ideology. The police force and the bureaucracy have been highly ethnicized from the 1950s and the army from the 1970s. All the religious and educational institutions have been ethnicized. A category of political Buddhism, as political Islam in the Middle East, has emerged in Sri Lanka as an overarching political force. Underdevelopment, economic competition, political opportunism, and 30 years of war have been the important factors impacting these developments.

Buddhism is often presented as a religion of peace, nonviolence, and compassion. So it is ironic that Buddhist nationalists, including some politically motivated Buddhist monks, actively participate in promoting hate and violence against minority ethnic and religious groups.

De-ethnicization of Sri Lankan society will be a major challenge for Sri Lankans to face. For this to prevail, Sinhala Buddhist hard-liners will have to accept the reality that Sri Lanka is a multiethnic, multireligious, and multilingual country. The overarching concept of pluralism within the context of equality for all, ethnicity notwithstanding, may be the only option for the future peaceful coexistence and development of all ethnic communities in Sri Lanka.

CHAPTER TWO

RETHINKING MUSLIM IDENTITY IN SRI LANKA

Dennis B. McGilvray

INTRODUCTION

The campaign of anti-Muslim agitation led by the Bodu Bala Sena (BBS) and other militant Sinhala Buddhist organizations starting in 2011 is only the latest manifestation of an underlying ethnic friction that has troubled Sri Lanka for over a century. Largely eclipsed by the Tamil versus Sinhala ethnic conflict in the postindependence period, an undercurrent of anti-Muslim sentiment has existed both in the Tamil and in the Sinhala communities of the island, posing a threat to Sri Lanka's most geographically dispersed and most widely visible minority community. In response to fluctuating political conditions and historical circumstances in the 20th century, the Tamil-speaking Sri Lankan Muslims (Moors) have embraced several different collective identities, each conferring cultural meaning and social prestige, but each entailing pragmatic political liabilities as well. The contemporary challenge posed by radicalized Buddhist monks and their Sinhala ethnonationalist supporters may require yet another readjustment of Sri Lankan Muslims' public image and sense of group identity.[1]

Muslims of Sri Lanka: A Brief Overview

Because the two main protagonists in Sri Lanka's contemporary ethnonationalist politics, the Sinhalas and the Tamils, justify their claims in terms of ancient settlements and control of territory, the Muslims—whose documented presence dates to "merely" a thousand years ago—are always at a historical disadvantage. Constituting 9.2% of the Sri Lankan population

(2012 Census), their origins are clearly connected to the maritime Indian Ocean trade between the Middle East and South and Southeast Asia that brought both Arab and Persian sailors as regular visitors to the island in the medieval period (Ali 1981a; Effendi 1965; Kiribamune 1986, Wink 1990).[2] Later, following Vasco da Gama's 1498 naval crusade against the "Moors" of Calicut, the Portuguese encountered Muslim traders in Sri Lanka who spoke Tamil, who had ongoing links with the Muslims of the Malabar and Coromandel Coasts of South India, and who had been given royal permission to collect customs duties and regulate shipping in the major southwestern port settlements under the suzerainty of the Sinhalese Kings of Kotte (Indrapala 1986; Abeyasinghe 1986). Commercial, cultural, and even migrational links between Muslim towns in southern India and Sri Lankan Moorish settlements are confirmed in the historical traditions of Beruwala, Kalpitiya, Jaffna, and other coastal settlements where Sri Lankan Muslims have lived for centuries (Casie Chitty 1834: 254–271; Denham 1912: 234). Like the coastal Muslims of South India and the Muslims of Southeast Asia, the Sri Lankan Moors are Sunni members of the Shafi'i legal school, a legacy of the south Arabian sea traders who first brought Islam to the region (Fanselow 1989). To varying degrees, the Sri Lankan Moors also preserve matrilineal and matrilocal family patterns, a legacy of the Coromandel and Malabar connection that has shaped Tamil social structure in Sri Lanka as well (Raghavan 1971: 199–217; McGilvray 1989, 2008).

Under Portuguese and Dutch colonial rule, the Moors were subjected to strict penalties and restrictions because of their Islamic faith and the threat they posed to the European monopoly of overseas trade. In the 17th century, many coastal Muslims migrated inland to the Kandyan Kingdom, where they engaged in *tavalam* bullock transport and a diverse range of other occupations (C. R. de Silva 1968; Dewaraja 1994, 1995). Ultimately, they settled throughout the Sinhala-speaking regions of the island, where two-thirds of them still reside today. The remainder, one-third of the total, are found in the Tamil-speaking northern and eastern regions of the island where they live as paddy farmers, fishermen, and merchants (see Figure 2.1 and 2.2). Taken as a whole, the Moors of Sri Lanka reflect a wide spectrum of socioeconomic levels

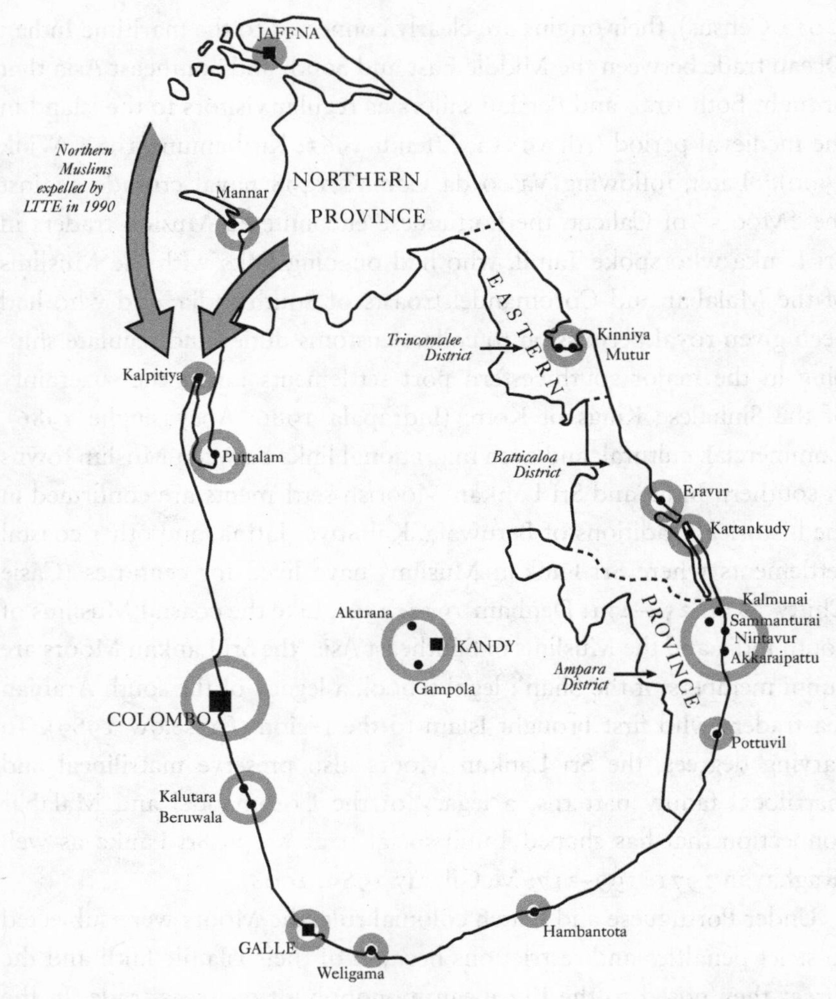

Figure 2.1 Important centers of Muslim population in Sri Lanka.

and occupational specialties, from wealthy urban business magnates and gem traders to rural farmers and fishermen; from textile and hardware merchants to restaurant owners and tea shop proprietors; from teachers and professionals to marginal smallholders and impoverished slum dwellers (Mauroof 1972). More recently, there are dispossessed "Northern Muslim" refugees who were forced from their homes and properties in Jaffna and Mannar in 1990 by the LTTE and who are

Figure 2.2 A Muslim merchant at his textile shop in Batticaloa.
Photo by Dennis McGilvray.

still living in IDP (internally displaced person) camps in Kalpitiya (Hasbullah 2004; Thiranagama 2011).

In addition to the predominant Tamil-speaking Moors—95% of all Sri Lankan Muslims—there is also a small Sunni Muslim community of Malays who are descended from Javanese soldiers and princes transported to the island by the Dutch in the 17th and 18th centuries (Hussainmiya 1986; Mahroof 1994; Ricci 2014) and who were historically concentrated in the Slave Island area of Colombo and in Hambantota. And finally, there are small numbers of Bombay and Gujarati Muslim traders—Bohras, Khojas, and Memons—who have prosperous business interests in Colombo. Recent anti-Muslim activism has not focused on these small Muslim subminorities but rather on the Tamil-speaking Muslims (or Moors, a term I will use interchangeably) who are the subject of the following discussion.

Anti-Muslim Sentiment in Sri Lanka

Muslims have often been the target of communal animosity and violence from the Tamil side, most harshly seen in the LTTE massacres of eastern Muslims at prayer and the forced expulsion and expropriation of Muslims from Jaffna and Mannar in 1990. However, the most traumatic case of anti-Muslim violence occurred in 1915 throughout the southern and central regions of the island when Sinhala mobs burned Muslim shops and homes in an outbreak of civil unrest that required the deployment of British colonial troops to restore order (Roberts 1994; Ali 1981b). When a leading Tamil statesman of the day, Ponnambalam Ramanathan, defended the Sinhala rioters against colonial justice, it deepened a rift that had already opened between the Tamil and the Muslim communities over the question of ethnic/racial group representation on the Legislative Council, further eroding Muslim confidence in Tamil leadership and strengthening Muslim loyalty to the British crown.[3] This was also the period when the influential Buddhist religious crusader, Anagarika Dharmapala, was preaching against Muslims and foreigners who were alleged to be weakening the integrity of the Sinhalese nation (Guruge 1965: 540). Nevertheless, when it became clear that the Sinhala ethnic majority would firmly control the democratic politics of Ceylon as independence approached in 1948, the urban Muslim leadership chose to align itself with the Sinhalese bloc instead of with the Tamil nationalist and federalist parties.

In the first four decades of independence, the Muslim leadership pursued a pragmatic, self-interested, and largely successful strategy of flexible coalitions and alliances within the two main Sinhala majority parties, taking advantage of their position as kingmakers and as foils against Tamil federalist agendas. Throughout this period, local anti-Muslim outbreaks occurred in both Tamil and Sinhala areas but never escalated to the level of community-wide concern. After 1985, when the armed Tamil Eelam conflict broke out, the Sri Lankan government took care, through concessionary tactics as well as covert subversive operations, to prevent the Muslims in the northern and eastern regions from joining the "Tamil-speaking" nationalist project. Despite these gestures from the Sinhala majority leadership, however, in the 1980s, the Muslims created their first political parties in response to the dangers they faced from the LTTE in the eastern region, signaling their intention to chart a more independent political course between the two ethnonationalist rivals, the Sinhalas and the Tamils.

Since the tsunami in 2004 and the defeat of the LTTE in 2009, the middle-class Muslims in Colombo and in the southern Sinhala-majority region of the island, as well as the Muslims in the Eastern Province, have prospered. Various rival Muslim "big men" politicians in Parliament representing major population clusters in Ampara and Batticaloa Districts have mobilized patronage networks that have delivered significant infrastructural benefits to their constituents, whereas the recovery of local Tamil communities, affected much more severely by the war, has lagged. In the northern areas of Mannar, Jaffna, and the Vanni, the reconstruction has been far slower under continuing Sri Lankan military occupation.

Politically speaking, the defeat of the Tamil Tigers and the diasporic departure of many middle-class Tamils from the north and the east led the Sinhala nationalist leadership under former President Mahinda Rajapaksa to feel they had less need to cater so assiduously to the Muslims, and some observers say this created an opportunity for Sinhala Buddhist xenophobes to focus on a neglected target (Imtiyaz and Mohamed-Saleem 2015). The absence of a unified clerical hierarchy among the Buddhist *sangha* made it possible for schismatic monks to create new organizations such as the BBS and to fabricate charges against Muslims and Christians that no one had heard before. Since 2011, an increasing number of anti-Muslim and anti-Christian incidents in Sinhala areas have taken place, starting with the demolition of a Muslim holy man's tomb in Anuradhapura and culminating with the dangerous Aluthgama riots of June 2014 (Centre for Policy Alternatives 2013; Sri Lanka Muslim Congress 2014; Haniffa et al. 2015; Secretariat for Muslims 2015).

The BBS ("Buddhist Strength Force") and its allies Sinhala Ravaya ("Sinhala Outcry") and Ravana Balaya ("Ravana Power") accuse the Muslim community of spreading a religion of jihadist terror, economic exploitation, black-veiled misogyny, and cruelty to animals. They argue that Islam is a foreign, neocolonialist religion like Christianity with no authentic roots in South Asian Indic civilization and one that allegedly, like Christianity, pursues "unethical conversions." They claim that Muslims are waging a secret contraceptive campaign (through tainted powdered milk and contaminated women's underwear) to keep the Sinhala birth rate low, while maintaining a relentless reproductive rate of their own that will demographically transform Sri Lanka into an Islamic nation within a generation or two.[4] They seek to demolish Muslim mosques and saintly tombs that have been built within the "sacred zones" of Buddhist temples and archaeological sites and object to the expansion or construction of new mosques in other areas (Amarasuriya et al. 2015, McGilvray 2016). They mock Muslim women's Arab-style *hijāb* (black outer *abaya* garment, plus head-covering scarf or wimple) and *niqāb* (full facial veil) as resembling a scary "gunny-sack monster" (*goni billa*), and they allege that hidden jihadi terror squads are poised to attack from within the Muslim community (Figure 2.3). They object to the success of Muslim-owned retail chains such as Fashion Bug and No Limit, which they claim are morally corrupt and exploitative. They decry the Muslim slaughter of cattle, despite the fact that beef is a widely consumed part of the Sinhala diet; and they claim, astonishingly, that the kitchen staff in Muslim restaurants are required by their religion to spit three times into the food before it is served to non-Muslim customers. The most successful achievement of the BBS campaign has been to remove the visible halal certification logo from supermarket food and toiletries sold to the general public, arguing that non-Muslims should not have to pay the extra cost for halal meat and merchandise (Haniffa 2016).

A number of theories have been proposed to explain why the BBS arose to prominence so suddenly starting in 2011 and why the Sri Lankan government of former President Mahinda Rajapaksa (2005–2015) did very little to silence its anti-Muslim slander campaign, even though it was humiliating to the Muslim members of his ruling United People's Freedom Alliance and risked alienating Muslim governments abroad with which Sri Lanka had vital trade

Figure 2.3 The *niqāb* veil portrayed as a female terrorist costume on the cover of a BBS publication in Sinhala entitled *Encountering the Demise of a Race: An Inquiry into Population Trends in Sri Lanka.* Image from Jones (2015: 148).

and diplomatic ties. The most plausible idea is that Rajapaksa, realizing he was unlikely to garner much Tamil or Muslim support for re-election to a fourth term, allowed the demonization of Muslims to increase the turnout of his rural Sinhala Buddhist voter base in the 2015 election. A less plausible theory is that Rajapaksa, desperate to block a United Nations human rights investigation into alleged military atrocities in the final stages of the Eelam War, hoped to provoke a violent reaction from Sri Lankan Muslims as proof of jihadi terrorism in the island, thus winning international sympathy and forgiveness for the brutal actions he took against the LTTE and Tamil civilians in 2009 (Harrison 2014). Predictably enough, international conspiracy theories also circulated: either the BBS was funded by the Pakistani intelligence agency (ISI or Inter-Services Intelligence) as a way to panic Sri Lankan Muslims into assisting their secret operations in South India, or the BBS was a tool of the Israeli Mossad and was funded by Norway as part of a global Zionist campaign against Islam.

Observers have been quick to notice that the BBS and its allies bear a resemblance to right-wing Hindutva organizations in India, such as the VHP (Vishva Hindu Parishad) and the RSS (Rashtriya Swayamsevak Sangh), who target Muslims and Christians and who espouse a narrow Brahmanical definition of the Hindu religious heritage. Recent developments indicate that the BBS aspires to emulate these militant Indian Hindutva groups by organizing a Sinhala Buddhist counterpart organization (Janardhanan 2015; Jones 2015: 60). They have already established linkages with the anti-Muslim "969" movement in Burma headed by the Buddhist monk Ashin Wirathu, who was invited to address a BBS convention in Colombo in September 2014. Especially worrying to many observers was that 2015 marked the 100th anniversary of the Sinhala–Muslim riots of 1915, suggesting that the Aluthgama riots might prove a precursor to even worse anti-Muslim violence. The democratic change of government in January 2015 from the leadership of Mahinda Rajapaksa to that of Maithripala Sirisena offers some hope that the danger of a widespread anti-Muslim outbreak can be reduced at this historic juncture.

Alternative Muslim Identities

Instead of focusing solely on the immediate causes of the crisis and the motives of the principal actors, it is important to consider the public image of the Muslim community as a whole vis-à-vis other groups in Sri Lanka's multicultural society, a collective identity that has shifted over time in response to British colonial rule, postindependence politics, and evolving global influences (Ismail 1995). Broadly speaking, there have been four major ways in which the identity of the Sri Lankan Muslims – that is, the Tamil-speaking Moors – has been conceived over the past 300 years, each offering advantages and disadvantages suited to a particular historical moment.

1. ENDOGAMY AND OCCUPATION: SRI LANKAN MUSLIMS AS A "CASTE"

Although it seems outlandish today, the precolonial identity of the Sri Lankan Moors would have placed them within a prevailing South Asian Hindu–Buddhist universe of hereditary castes: locally situated, endogamous, ritually ranked, occupationally specialized groups regulated by royal or chiefly authority. In 21st-century Sri Lanka, the idea of a Muslim caste identity is totally archaic and outmoded, yet one has only to look across the water to South India to see examples of Muslim subgroups today that have been deemed "caste-like" in their composition and behavior despite wide differences in Muslim versus Hindu perceptions (Fanselow 1996). Along the Tamilnadu coastline, one finds culturally distinct, semi-endogamous Maraikkayar Muslim settlements that proudly claim Arab descent and a seafaring tradition that connects them to Colombo, Penang, and Singapore (McGilvray 1998; More 1991; Raja Mohamad 2004; Vadlamudi 2016). In the North Malabar region of Kerala, the Malayalam-speaking Mappila Muslims recognize distinct caste-like social strata and local hereditary elites such as the Koyas of Calicut and the Keyis of Tellicherry (D'Souza 1973; Sebastian 2013). The Urdu-speaking Deccani Muslims of Chennai are an endogamous aristocracy unto themselves (Vatuk 2014). Recent scholarship strongly points to the influence of caste-oriented British ethnography on the 19th- and 20th-century creation and reification of these social strata among South Indian Muslims themselves, but they are nonetheless widely (if unevenly) recognized today (Tschacher 2014).

The early colonial history of Sri Lanka shows that Muslim traders and merchantmen were granted an occupational monopoly of trade at the island's seaports, and that later, in the Kandyan Kingdom, the caste-based service department for bullock transport (*madige badda*) was allocated jointly to the Sinhala Karava caste and to the Muslims (Rogers 1994, 1995; Dewaraja 1994, 1995). Dewaraja celebrates the integration of Muslims into the fabric of the 17th and 18th century Kandyan kingdom, but they were allocated their roles within a hierarchical caste-based Sinhala social order. In Tamil-speaking regions such as Batticaloa, ethnohistorical evidence indicates that local Moorish settlements were subject to high-caste Tamil chiefly authority and that Moors were allocated certain ritual duties in major Hindu temples in the same manner as Tamil castes (McGilvray 1982b, 2008). However, despite the existence of hereditary Muslim barber-circumcisers (*ostā*) and the saintly lineages of *maulana seyyids*, a differentiated set of Muslim "castes" did not emerge in Sri Lanka as they did in India. One factor influencing this outcome may have been the British colonial policy of enumerating Ceylon's population by native "races" rather than by a caste census as was done in India (Rogers 2004, Dirks 2001). Another factor is the diversity of livelihoods and economic adaptations in Moorish settlements across the island—from farming and fishing to trading and professions—that would have made a singular hereditary caste occupation and ritual rank impossible to define.

ANALYSIS

The universal equality of all Muslims before Allah is an obvious impediment to the creation of caste or hereditary barriers between members of the *ummah*, the community of all Muslims. Still, Sri Lankan Muslims have at times displayed group rivalries and prestige rankings that are not egalitarian, such as the early 20th-century disputes between Moors and Malays over administration of the Maradana mosque in Colombo (Asad 1993: 90; Nuhman 2007: 40–42). In the Ampara District, local mosques were traditionally administered by a committee of male trustees (*maraikkar*), each representing a different local matrilineal clan (*kuṭi*), and each clan ranked in terms of local status and prestige (McGilvray 2008). All such hereditary Muslim status differentials are gradually fading from memory now. However, the comparison with contemporary South Indian Muslim social divisions should not be ignored because a similar pattern could have arisen in Sri Lanka under different historical circumstances. Also, links between Sri Lankan and South Indian Muslim communities are still quite strong today, especially in the commercial sector.

2. LANGUAGE AND CIVILIZATION: SRI LANKAN MUSLIMS AS "ISLAMIC TAMILS"

In cosmopolitan areas such as Colombo, many younger generation Muslims attend school in the Sinhala medium, and they often study English for personal and professional advancement. There are a few mosques where the Friday sermon is nowadays delivered in Sinhala, and there are certainly some urban Muslim youth who can barely speak, let alone read, a word of Tamil (Nuhman 2007: chap. 3). However, the mother tongue, the spoken language of the home, for the overwhelming majority of Sri Lankan Moors remains Tamil. This is especially so in the North and the East, where Hindu and Christian Tamils live side by side with Tamil-speaking Muslims, but it is generally true as well in the Sinhala-majority areas of the South. Beyond the widespread popularity of Tamil cinema and pop music, there is a deep and continuing heritage of Muslim literature in Tamil, as well as an older corpus in Arabic-Tamil, which uses the Arabic alphabet to write Tamil phonetically (Uwise 1986, 1990; Nuhman 2007). Indeed, the strength and vitality of the Sri Lankan Muslim contribution to Tamil letters further underscores the paradox that the Moors in 20th century Sri Lanka have publicly rejected any identification as "Tamils," a group designation that is fundamentally linguistic in nature.

The question of whether the Sri Lankan Muslims are, like Hindu Tamils and Christian Tamils, simply "Islamic Tamils" (*islāmiya tamilar*) has been at the root of tensions between the Sri Lankan Tamil and Moorish leadership for over a century. High caste Jaffna Tamil leaders (some of them Christian) unsuccessfully tried to assert leadership over the Moorish community in the colonial period, utilizing colonial ethnography to support their argument that the Moors were actually Tamils in a linguistic and cultural sense (Ramanathan 1888). This occurred at a time when some conservative high-caste Tamils were loath to consider the untouchable Hindu castes as "Tamils" at all. In the early postindependence period, the Federal Party sometimes appealed to Muslims to unite under the banner of Sri Lanka's "Tamil-speaking peoples," but their political support was always contingent and temporary. The problem has festered ever since, resurfacing during the Eelam Wars in brutal LTTE vengeance against the Moors whom they regarded as traitors to the pan-Dravidian linguistic movement.

ANALYSIS

While working on a fieldwork project with me in Tamilnadu in 2015, my Moorish research associate from Colombo was surprised to find himself being introduced to Muslim friends in Chennai as a Tamil. A recent documentary film celebrates the strong Tamil ethnicity of Muslims in Tamilnadu (Anwar 2013). Although there has been some political polarization, including the creation of new Tamil Islamist political parties in Tamilnadu in the wake of the Babri Masjid incident, the majority of Tamilnadu Muslims still vote for the DMK (Dravida Munnetra Kazhagam), the Dravidian nationalist party founded by C. N. Annadurai in 1949 and led today by octogenarian M. Karunanidhi. When talking with scholars and intellectuals in Tamilnadu, both Hindu and Muslim, I found it difficult to convince them that Sri Lanka's Tamil-speaking Muslims should not be regarded as Tamils. The historic stone mosques in Kilakkarai and Kayalpattanam, carved in pure Dravidian style, seem to make the same argument architecturally (Shokoohy 2003).

This, of course, reflects the difference in linguistic demography between Tamilnadu, where the entire state is either monolingual or bilingual in Tamil, versus Sri Lanka, where 70% of the population speaks Sinhala. Muslims in Tamilnadu have had nothing to lose, and everything to gain, by embracing the Dravidian nationalist movement, which in turn welcomed them wholeheartedly as "non-Brahmins" (More 1993; Fakhri 2008). For the two-thirds of Sri Lankan Moors living in the central and southwestern Sinhala-majority regions of the island, on the other hand, asserting their identity as "Muslim Tamils" would be a severe liability, both at the ballot box and in terms of personal safety and economic well-being (O'Sullivan 1997). The situation would be different among the Moors of the North-East, where Tamil linguistic loyalties are shared with Hindus and Christians, but this could lead to a regional split within the Muslim community, something that Muslim politicians have tried to prevent out of fear of losing influence at the center. It remains an open question whether Moors in the postwar North-Eastern region will regain a feeling of shared linguistic nationalism with the Tamils, despite Muslim majority vulnerability in Colombo and the Sinhala-speaking South.

3. RACE AND ANCESTRY: SRI LANKAN MUSLIMS AS "MOORS"

As a counternarrative to the Tamil claim that the Moors are their benighted "Islamic Tamil" brethren, and as a way to earn a secure place on the official roster of "native races" in British colonial Ceylon, the Muslim elite at the beginning of the 20th century actively cultivated a racial identity as the descendants of Arab sea traders and pilgrims to Adam's Peak. The visits of Arabs and Persians to the island is well-attested in the historical record, but additional inspiration was provided by the arrival in 1883 of an exiled Egyptian revolutionary, Orabi Pasha, and his fez-capped entourage of followers. Orabi Pasha became a staunch colonial loyalist after arriving in Colombo, and his neo-Ottoman sophistication inspired new Sri Lankan Muslim fashion styles and projects of community self-improvement, including western-style schools for Muslim children.[5]

The colonial idea of native races, a concept long discredited by modern anthropology, is still alive and well in contemporary Sri Lanka. At the turn of the 20th century, it was the basis for indigenous representation on the Legislative Council in colonial Ceylon; and Muslim leaders hoped that the "Arab" Moorish race could stand on an equal footing with the "Aryan" Sinhalese, the "Dravidian" Tamils, the "Javanese" Malays, and the "European" Burghers. The term Moor is of Portuguese origin (from *mouro*, North African), a label the Portuguese applied to every Muslim they encountered between Lisbon and Mindanao. However, the closest term in Tamil and Malayalam is Sonahar (*cōṉakar*), meaning a person of West Asian or Arab origin, from Tamil *cōṉakam*, Arabia (Tamil Lexicon vol.3, p. 1679). This traditional ethnonym continues to be used in conversational Tamil by Sri Lankan Moors today.[6] For Sri Lankan Moors, Orabi Pasha and his

Figure 2.4 The library of the Moors' Islamic Cultural Home featuring portraits of past presidents and community leaders, most of whom are wearing a red Ottoman fez cap.
Photo by Dennis McGilvray.

supporters came to embody an ideal of Middle Eastern civilization and pan-Islamic solidarity, as later represented in the Khilafat Movement of the 1920s. His Ottoman sartorial taste inspired a legal "fight for the fez" in colonial courtroom etiquette while remaining a conspicuously loyal subject of the Queen (Thawfeeq 1972; Samaraweera 1977). The Moors' Islamic Cultural Home, founded in Colombo in 1944, remains today as the major cultural institution of the Sonahar community (Figure 2.4), comparable to the Dutch Burgher Union for Sri Lanka's Eurasian community (McGilvray 1982a).

ANALYSIS

The concept of an Arab Moorish "race" provides a simple and appealing origin story. However, at an ethnographic level, Moorish identity fails to reflect Middle Eastern Arab cultural norms in any way, apart from Islam. Moorish families are not strongly patrilineal or patrilocal; indeed, many are matrilineal and matrilocal. They forbid marriage with patrilateral parallel cousins (i.e., father's brother's son or daughter), which is standard practice in the Middle East. Instead, they endorse marriage with cross cousins, and they reckon family relationships according to a Dravidian-type classification that is virtually identical to the Tamil and Sinhala kinship systems (Yalman 1967, McGilvray 2008). Like the Burghers, many of whom bear little "racial" resemblance to their Portuguese and Dutch forebears, the Sri Lankan Moors are often indistinguishable today from the Sinhalese or the Tamils, apart from cultural markers of dress, language, and religion. This awkward point was acknowledged early on by Moorish boosters who nonetheless contended, following European genealogical rules, that even a few drops of patrilineal Arab blood from the 12th century would qualify today's Sri Lankan Moors as members of the Arab race (Azeez 1907). This obviously ignores generations and generations of intermarriage with Sri Lankan women, a cumulative maternal component that seems far more significant than any original Arab paternity (Ismail 1995). The only contemporary Moorish families who can specifically trace their ancestry to Arabia are the Maulanas (Seyyids), patrilineal descendants of the Prophet Muhammad and his companions, many of whom migrated from the Hadramaut and other districts of Yemen in the 18th and 19th centuries (Ho 2006).

Most Moors today know Arabic only as a language of prayer and Quranic recitation. Although today one sees many urban Moorish women wearing the black Saudi-style *abaya* and *hijāb*, this Arab form of dress has largely been adopted in the last half century (Nuhman 2007: 203–208). When I first began anthropological fieldwork in 1969, every Muslim women in the agricultural town of Akkaraipattu (Ampara District) wore an incandescently colorful sari, pulling the cloth across her face for modesty when necessary (*mukkādu*). Similarly, older Moorish men in Akkaraipattu wore a white or checked sarong, not a Gulf-style *thobe* or *jubba*. Moorish foodways are Sri Lankan, not Middle Eastern, with a preponderance of coconut-milk based curries and sweets.

Whereas the claim of Arab ancestry might have a grain of historical truth, the Sri Lankan proponents of Moorish identity have been silent about another, even more plausible, ethnic genealogy: migration and intermarriage from the Coromandel and Malabar Coasts of South India. This would also explain why the Muslim community speaks Tamil rather than Sinhala, the language that Moorish descendants would presumably have spoken if their Arab forefathers had wed Sinhala women they met when they landed along the southwestern coast of the island. When I spoke with Muslim Tamils in coastal towns of Tamilnadu such as Karaikkal, Kilakkarai, and Kayalpattinam in 2015, they considered Sri Lankan Muslim culture and history to be continuous with their own, citing a long history of family migrations and business dealings with Colombo and other Sri Lankan towns. Similar commercial and family connections with Mappila Muslims from Cochin and Calicut are well known in the British colonial period. Indeed, it has been argued that it was the sharp business practices and religious zealotry of so-called "Coast Moor" (i.e., South Indian Muslim) traders and shopkeepers in Sri Lanka that especially angered the Sinhalese rioters in 1915 (Ali 1981b).

Either way, whether "Arabs" or "South Indians," the Sri Lankan Moorish construction of a foreign racial or ethnic identity that was once useful under the British colonial regime eventually became a liability in the xenophobic postindependence era, just as it did for the Burghers. In the eyes of some, it could suggest that Sri Lankan Moors are self-proclaimed aliens, colonizers, and carpetbaggers rather than primordial inhabitants of Lanka whose ancestor descended on Adam's Peak.[7] The current influx of wealthy Arab tourists (and gamblers) from the oil-rich Emirates and Saudi Arabia further underscores the disadvantages of an Arab identity for the Sri Lankan Moors today.

4. RELIGION: SRI LANKAN MUSLIMS AS "MUSLIMS"

To escape the disadvantages and encumbrances of the prevailing language-based and racially based identities in Sri Lanka's ethnonationalist cauldron, some mid-20th-century Muslim leaders decided to opt for "none of the above." Although attachment to Tamil language and culture remains strong, and racial pride as Arab descendants still resonates widely, the primary identification of the Moorish community today has become simply "Muslim." By choosing to identify themselves solely by religion, the Muslims have done something no other Sri Lankan community has tried, or has been capable of trying. There are significant Christian minorities within both the Sinhala and Tamil communities, so their ethnicity cannot be reduced to Buddhism or Hinduism. On closer examination, even the "Muslim" label is complicated by the presence of ethnically distinct Malay Muslims and smaller Gujarati-speaking Sunni Muslim communities of Khojas and Memons. There are also wealthy Gujarati-speaking Bohras, a Shi'ite sect that maintains an elegant mosque in Bambalapitiya from which Sunni Muslims are excluded. In effect, the generic religious term "Muslim" has become an unmarked ethnic label specifically denoting "Tamil-speaking Sri Lankan Sunni Muslims": in other words, the Moors or Sonahars. To avoid ambiguity, all other Sri Lankan Muslim communities must be identified specifically by name.

ANALYSIS

When the idea of promulgating an island-wide "Muslim" identity was first proposed in the era leading up to independence in 1948, it may have been regarded as a more modern and universalistic label, possibly one that resonated with Muslim League politics in India, but it was not intended to mark out any Islamic sectarian agenda. Similarly, when the Sri Lankan Muslim Congress (SLMC) emerged in the 1980s in response to LTTE violence against Moors in the Eastern Province, it was not conceived as an Islamist party (Johansson 2016). In the decades since independence, however, the Muslims of Sri Lanka, like Muslims throughout the world, have experienced the effects of pan-Islamic reform movements, leading to significant changes in popular Muslim society and culture. Some of the visible shifts include the widespread adoption of austere Middle-Eastern-inspired *purdah* and *hijāb* attire by Muslim women; the wearing of Arab-style *thobe*s and *jubba* garments, and the concomitant display of henna-dyed beards and hair, by some Muslim men; the construction of many new well-funded mosques and madrasas; the stricter public enforcement of gender segregation rules; the marketing of meat and numerous other products with a halal-certified logo; and the growth of Islamic banks and financial institutions. In addition, some middle-class Muslim self-improvement organizations have urged a greater degree of social distance from non-Muslims in the interest of Islamic piety (Haniffa 2008). In some Muslim circles, participation in the Rotary or Lions Club is now frowned on because the non-Muslim members may consume alcohol.

Moreover, the very concept of Muslimness itself has been contested in recent decades by the polarization between traditionalist and reformist brands of Islam. I am sure that Muslim paddy farmers on the east coast of the island had no idea that their vow making and celebration of *kandoori* festivals at local saintly tombs was a "Sufi" practice when I first met them in the 1970s; but in recent years, fundamentalist opposition to such shrine-based Sufi devotion has become quite zealous, even violent (McGilvray 2011; Spencer et al. 2015: chap. 5).[8] A number of South Asian Islamic reform movements are now active in Sri Lanka, among them Jamaat-e-Islami, Tablighi Jamaat, and Towheed Jamaat (Nuhman 2007: 174–184; Osella and Osella 2013; Faslan and Nadine 2015). To distinguish themselves, adherents of the older and more customary forms of Muslim worship now actively identify as "Sunnattu Jamaat," that is, as Muslim traditionalists.

Sadly, the very Muslim religious identity that Moorish leaders had hoped would shield their community from Sinhalese ethnonationalism and Tamil linguistic chauvinism has now served to bring them directly into focus as a target of the BBS and similar militant Buddhist groups. An Islamic religious identity now makes the Moors vulnerable to accusations of having exogenous origins and importing an alien proselytizing religion into Dhamma Dīpa ("Island of the Dhamma"), the exclusive Sinhala Buddhist ethnonationalist vision of Sri Lanka.

Reactions and Concerns in the Muslim Community

Muslim reactions to the onslaught by the BBS have ranged from civil indignation and alarm to international conspiracy theories to collective community introspection. Although the most urgent issue was to find a compromise solution to the BBS campaign against halal certification (Haniffa 2016), there were soon broader community reflections about Muslim self-alienation from the rest of Sri Lankan society through unnecessary signs of religious piety. According to this view, the adoption of more stringent and visible markers of Islamic orthodoxy than were formerly the norm in Sri Lanka has alarmed and alienated the average Sinhala Buddhist citizen, thus drawing unnecessary attention to the Muslim community as a whole and generating sympathy for the BBS (Herath and Harshana 2015). Foremost among these changes is the Muslim women's black *hijāb* or *parda* attire, and the occasional full face veil (*niqāb*), both of which are nowadays frequently seen on the streets of Colombo and in major Sri Lankan towns (Haniffa 2005; Nuhman 2007: 199–208). Some Muslim commentators have argued that reverting to the customary colored sari would allow ample female modesty while honoring a local and familiar Sri Lankan sartorial tradition. Even changing the new-style *hijāb* to an attractive color, some say, would alleviate the negative symbolic connotations of the color black in the Sinhala cultural worldview. It has been noted that whereas Muslim women's *hijāb* may have helped to distinguish them from Tamils during the Eelam Wars, it now makes them highly visible targets of BBS fear campaigns.

Other concerns have been voiced from within the Muslim community, including a worry that rigid gender segregation, and the absence of women from mosques, could support fantasies about secret all-male business conspiracies and clandestine *jihādi* plots. In addition to the amplified call to prayer five times per day, a perennial source of non-Muslim complaint, there is the anachronistic uncertainty of Islamic holidays whose exact timing still relies on a human sighting of the new moon rather than on modern astronomical science. Another source of controversy and chagrin has been the planting of Middle Eastern date palm trees along the main street in Kattankudy as an expression of hyper-Islamic civic space (Ali 2012; Kolor 2015: 82–125).

Some of the most difficult issues in this debate are economic and governmental, and they have not yet been carefully addressed. For example, there are strong indications that economic rivalries and resentments have played a role in the anti-Muslim agitation. This was suggested most clearly by the mob violence and arson attacks against leading Muslim-owned retail clothing chains such as Fashion Bug and No Limit in 2013–2014. The restaurant sector, also heavily Muslim owned, could be vulnerable in the future. On the legislative side, the existence of a separate body of Muslim personal law, including Islamic inheritance rules and the (rarely utilized) right of plural marriage, is considered by some non-Muslims to be an affront to their civil equality before the law. Perhaps the least-recognized problem, and one that may take generations to solve, is the separation of Muslim schoolchildren from their Sinhala and Tamil peers as a result of Sri Lanka's national system of government-run Muslim schools, which also follows a different academic calendar (Figure 2.5). Promoted after independence by UNP politician Razik Fareed, and further implemented in the late 1960s under the leadership of the SLFP education minister, Badiuddin Muhammad, these schools were intended to remedy the historic educational disadvantages facing the Muslim community (Ali 1986; O'Sullivan 1997; Knoerzer 1998; Nuhman 2007: 146–148). Muslim schools today continue to perform well academically, but they also tend to keep Muslim children within their own community, reducing the likelihood of spontaneous face-to-face interactions and friendships with students from other ethnic and religious backgrounds, a trend that is seen also in the growth of private Muslim "international schools" in Colombo. In contrast, one sees throngs of schoolchildren in Chennai heading home after classes, Hindu girls in regular school uniforms holding hands with Muslim girlfriends in full or partial *hijāb*. Today's generation of Muslim adults may be the last to cherish lifelong friendships and informal acquaintances with Sinhala and Tamil school classmates. Even more worrisome is that the reverse is also true, and the implications for community "self-alienation" are profound.

Figure 2.5 A classroom at the A-Siraj Muslim School in Akkaraipattu, Ampara District.
Photo by Dennis McGilvray.

Conclusion

The most striking chromatic binary on the Sri Lankan street today is the saffron-robed *bhikkhu* and the black-shrouded Muslim woman in Saudi-style *hijāb*: a visual reminder of contemporary Sinhala–Muslim tensions. The emergence of the BBS and their allies poses once again the difficult question of group identity for the island's Tamil-speaking Muslim minority, a predicament vastly aggravated by media coverage of atrocities committed by al Qaida, Boko Haram, Taliban, and the Islamic State, not to mention the rise of Towheedi fundamentalist groups in Sri Lanka itself (Faslan and Nadine 2015). Although Muslim caste-like identity based on endogamy, occupation, and historic settlement still exists among some communities in South India, it is not a possibility in 21st-century Sri Lanka. However, three other familiar identities remain available, each with positive and negative implications: Muslims as "Arabs"—a community defined by ancestry; Muslims as "Islamic Tamils"—a community defined by language; and

Muslims as "Muslims" – a community defined by faith. All three refer to what social scientists call an "ethnic group," a community that typically shares a language, a religion, a biogenetic profile of some kind, a place of origin, and a historically constructed cultural heritage. By this definition, the Tamil-speaking Sri Lankan Moors are an ethnic group, as are the Sri Lankan Tamils and the Sinhalas. It is in relation to these ethnic neighbors—within Sri Lanka's economic and political arena—that a viable Muslim identity must be constructed.

Research has shown that ethnicity evolves over time in response to the political and economic environment, so it seems possible that Sri Lankan Muslim identity may adapt to changing circumstances. In the current xenophobic situation, the priority would presumably be to assert a more distinctively Sri Lankan cultural identity with deeper ancestral roots in the island and in the South Asian region rather than emphasizing itinerant Arab seafarers or a connection with global Islam. The primordial connection with Adam's Peak (Sri Pada)—sacred to Buddhists, Hindus, and Muslims—might once again become a key symbol of Muslim attachment to the island. It seems possible that a realignment emphasizing maternal intermarriage and shared Sri Lankan descent, and acknowledging their indigenous attachment to Sri Lankan Tamil, could become a more secure basis for Moorish identity. A revised version of the earlier Sonahar identity might serve this purpose, shorn of its Arab racial pretensions and its colonial ("Moorish") connotations, and celebrating its own Tamil literary heritage. Although these are only conjectures, it is clear that Sri Lanka's Muslim community will need to rethink its identity in the years ahead, just as it has, several times, in the past.

NOTES

1. Funding for this research was provided by fellowship grants from the American Institute for Sri Lankan Studies and the American Institute for Indian Studies. Research assistance was provided by Mr. Nilam Hamead and numerous other friends in Sri Lanka and Tamilnadu.

2. The possible impact of repeated visits to Sri Lanka of the 15th century Chinese Muslim admiral Zheng He (Cheng Ho) should not be overlooked. It has been proposed that he played a role in bringing Islam to Java and other parts of Southeast Asia (Aqsha 2010).
3. Support for the colonial power was first demonstrated when local Muslims aided the British in suppressing the Uva Rebellion of 1817.
4. BBS leaders have accused Muslim men—especially the employees of leading Muslim clothing chains—of seducing and raping Sinhala women with the goal of Islamic conversion. This resonates with so-called "love jihad" accusations against Muslims in North India (Gupta 2009; Jones 2015: 65–76).
5. Efforts to develop modern Muslim schools were already under way by then, led by M. C. Siddi Lebbe (Nuhman 2007: 104–107).
6. A variant of this term appears in the official Sri Lankan census as "Lanka Yonaka."
7. Sri Lankan Muslims today show little interest in Adam's Peak as a religious pilgrimage site. The bazaar town of Nallathanniya where the main trail begins does not even appear to have a mosque. Shifting religious identities of Adam's Peak have been analyzed by Premakumara de Silva (2014).
8. The religious violence is not entirely one-sided: in August 2009, the followers of a local Sufi shaykh in Beruwala attacked a neighboring Towheed mosque, killing two.

CHAPTER THREE

REFUGE IN THE STATE

Buddhist Monks and Virtuous Governmentality

Jonathan A. Young

Just before violence erupted between Buddhists and Muslims in the vicinity of Aluthgama during the summer of 2014, Galagoda Aththe Gnanasara, a leader of the *Bodu Bala Sena* (BBS), or "Buddhist Power Army," arrived and gave a rousing speech, accompanied by cheers from a sympathetic audience, in which he stated, "We say, in this country we still have a Sinhala police; we still have a Sinhala army! After today, if a single Muslim (*marakkalaya),* or some other foreigner (*paraya),* lays hands on a single Sinhalese person, let alone a Buddhist monk, it will be their end!"[1] As disturbing as such orations appear to those who aspire for a peaceful coexistence among the religiously plural population of Sri Lanka, there is a danger in tossing them aside as mere aberrations from a proper, pristine, and traditional form of Buddhism. The relationship between Buddhism and sociopolitical violence runs deeper and farther back in time than the advent of modernity; and if there is to be a successful challenge or critique of the potentially violent rhetoric of groups like the BBS, their activities and claims must be taken seriously.

To return to Gnanasara's speech, there is at least one noteworthy aspect of his remarks that encourages a closer look. The use of derogatory terms for Muslims (*marakkalaya*) and foreigners (*paraya*) along with the threat of annihilation couched in terms of their potential threat to an entire ethnic group (the Sinhalese) may seem like standard variety hate speech, but why reference the fact that the military and police forces remain "Sinhala," in Gnanasara's eyes? Clearly, the threat of retaliation has something to do with an expected backing by instruments of state-sanctioned violence. This relationship between the activities and aspirations of politically engaged Buddhist monks and the workings of the state offers a useful point of focus as one means of arriving at a richer understanding of the entanglement of Buddhism and violence, and it offers a unique case for assessing the broader problem of religion, politics, and violence in other settings. Despite the contemporary association of Buddhism with peace and meditative tranquility, the Buddhist tradition is not immune to interpretations that lead to the support of violent action.

When the monastic commentator who wrote the *Paramatthajotikā*, possibly but not probably the renowned Buddhaghosa of the 5th century CE, explained the meaning of the seemingly innocuous term "sarana" or "refuge," he emphasized the concept's active and violent potential. His text states the following:

> 'Refuge' means 'kills/destroys' [*himsati*]; by this very act of going to refuge, *refuge kills and destroys* [emphasis mine] fear, anxiety, sorrow, and the defilements produced from wrong livelihood.[2]

Such an active sense of refuge, whereby it is equated with the verb "himsati," from which derives the more familiar, negative term for nonviolence, "a-himsa"—popularized by Gandhian thought in the 20th century—enables one to conceive the one who bestows refuge as an agent capable of violence, albeit salvific and purificatory violence. Considering this notion of refuge in light of Weber's classic definition of the state as "the monopoly of the legitimate use of violence," a potential harmony between the two concepts, refuge and the state, is recognizable.[3] The state's responsibility to use violence in a legitimate manner mirrors the potential violence of the refuge toward the obstacles to Buddhist virtue. This renders the possibility of virtuous violence as a technology of virtuous governmentality.

The fact that Buddhists have endeavored to define virtuous governance throughout history is not surprising. Governmentality has a genealogic affinity with morality, and Buddhist agents have periodically worked to define and reinterpret proper governance within a Buddhist, moral framework. Thus, Buddhist monks have historically intervened in government in a variety of ways. For instance, the *Declaration of the Vidyalankara Pirivena*, well analyzed by Abeysekara, and works such as Walpola Rahula's *Heritage of the Bhikkhu*, each argue for the legitimacy of monastic engagement with governance.[4] However, the nature of this involvement has been a site of contestation regarding the legitimacy of monastic involvement in politics.

In 2004, nine members of the all-monk National Heritage Party, the *Jathika Hela Urumaya* (JHU), won seats in the Sri Lankan parliament, which was unprecedented, but only in scale. In 2001, as Deegalle has pointed out, a monk affiliated with leftist parties, Baddēgama Samitha, became a Member of Parliament; and earlier in the 20th century, monks contested and won elections for seats in municipal governments.[5] Thus, although the fact that nine, ordained, religious professionals stepped into office in the national government appears odd, perhaps threatening, from most secularist standpoints, I do not believe that the question of the legitimacy, or morality, of monastic politicians holds scholastic relevance.

Taking my cue from David Scott's assessment of scholarly debates about the historicity of Sinhala ethnonationalist identity, I maintain that here there is a similar need for "changing the problematic in which [our] questions [in this case of the political monks] have appeared to us natural, legitimate, or even imperative."[6] In other words, the debate over the legitimacy of monastic politicians is not capable of being satisfactorily resolved by historical inquiry itself. How, then, might a switch to a different problematic enable historical scholarship to develop a clear understanding of politically engaged monks at the turn of the 21st century without falling into the stale debate in which historical precedence somehow sanctions acts in the present?

I respond by examining politically active monks' conceptions and enactments of virtuous governmentality. In its simplest sense, I use a notion of governmentality to refer to "the mentalities of government," or the ways in which governance is thought, imagined, justified, and proscribed.[7] Thus, by "virtuous governmentality," I look to the discursive activities of individuals and groups who seek to merge governance and virtuosity. Attention to the ways in which Buddhist monks have historically imagined and sought to actualize virtuous governmentality allows us to breach the, often erroneously, assumed divide between politics and religion and to set aside the problem of whether monks should ever be politically active in favor of looking to questions about why they seek to become politically active in the first place.

In what follows, I examine trends in the conception and deployment of virtuous governmentality in Sri Lanka from two time periods: the late Kandyan kingdom and the first decade of the 21st century. In my assessment of each period, I address three questions: (1) how do monks cultivate the social capital necessary to empower themselves as potential critics of or participants in governance; (2) what interventions do the monks seek, or what types of transformations do they find necessary for the growth of virtuous government; and finally (3), who constitutes their target audience, or for whom do these monks act? Following this, I draw notes toward a further comparative analysis.

Before I proceed, I clarify that I choose to compare the politically active monks of the Kandyan period and the monks of the 21st-century JHU for at least three reasons. First, scholars tend to overlook the precolonial period when discussing monks involved in politics. Deegalle, for instance, writes, "[u]ntil the dawn of the twentieth century, Buddhist monks were passive agents in the political history of Sri Lanka."[8] Thus, I think it prudent to challenge such understandings of monastic political engagement as an entirely new phenomenon dependent on the developments of the 20th and 21st centuries. Second, when scholars do bring attention to the political activities of monks during the Kandyan period, it is largely to indicate the emergence of a trope of disengagement between Buddhism and the state. The Nayakkar dynasty, with its Tamil ancestral origins, is held up as a signifier of the loss of a truly Sinhala–Buddhist polity.[9] Yet, as my work will show, this is far too simplistic a reading of the history of the reigns of the last Nayakkar kings of Sri Lanka. Finally, I choose to focus on the monks of the JHU because two of the most vocal proponents of anti-Muslim activities in contemporary Sri Lanka, Gnanasara (noted previously) and Kirama Wimalajothi, were both members of the JHU prior to forming the BBS. Thus, a better understanding of the JHU's enactment of virtuous governmentality will prove helpful in understanding the contemporary Buddhist–Muslim conflict.

I do not intend for the monks whose careers I analyze here to be thought of as typical. The large majority of monks in Sri Lanka either do not seek such a strong engagement with politics or do not have sufficient social capital to have their voices proclaimed as loudly as the monks I discuss following. In fact, it is the uniqueness, the outstanding nature of the monks' involvement with politics, that draws my attention to their lives, projects, and aspirations. In other words, the fact that these monks maintain, or have maintained, such a privileged and atypical position in Sri Lankan Buddhist sociopolitical discourse allows them to be such suitable subjects for an inquiry of this sort.

The Elite Monks of Kandy

How do monks become actors capable of addressing governance? L. De Bussche, a captain in the British colonial army in Ceylon, describes the entrance of Kobbekaduwe Sri Nivasa, head of the prestigious Siyam Nikāya from 1811 to 1819, to an audience with Governor Brownrigg after the capture of Kandy in the following account:

> I cannot omit mentioning here, the manner in which the High Priest of Buddha ... was ushered in, and accompanied to the audience of the Governor. ... Near ten o'clock the noise of numerous tom-toms ... , some fifes, trumpets, and large whips announced the approach of this interesting personage, whose influence over the opinions of the Kandians was well known to us. The spacious courts on both sides of the great audience hall were perfectly lighted up by near a thousand torches, the bearers of which preceded and followed him. ... The whole hall, as well the ceiling and floor, as the beautifully carved pillars, were covered with white cotton cloth. In all these arrangements the strictest Kandian court etiquette was observed. The priests were all clad in large flowing robes of rich yellow silk; that of the High Priest was of velvet of the same colour;

> each held a kind of fan before him, which according to their different ranks of priesthood, was more or less covered with gold, silver, or coloured silk embroidery.[10]

The pomp and pageantry accompanying the *mahānāyaka*'s entrance exemplifies the performance of prestige, which was a vital component of elite Kandyan monasticism. Head monks sought to command respect through ritual displays of social capital. The musicians, palanquin bearers, and other members of the retinue were typically the inhabitants of monastic estates who owed fealty directly to the chief monks.

In a letter to the second governor of Ceylon, Thomas Maitland (1805–1811), the low-country *mahānāyaka* of the districts of Colombo and Galle, Mahāgoḍa Indesara, requested that the British government render assistance in enforcing the services and duties he believed were owed to him. His letter, through colonial British translation, requests Maitland

> to grant the petitioner that whenever he shall happen to go to the different Corles [Korālas] and Districts that Headmen of such a Corle or District shall assist and respect him and provide him with coolies for his expenses and farther permit your petitioner that he may pass in the palanquin by beating of tom-tom and carrying the Flag along with him without a hindrance of any person whosoever.[11]

The *mahānāyaka* must receive assistance from local headmen when travelling.[12] This includes laborers, or "coolies," the use of a palanquin, and an accompaniment of musicians and flag bearers.

Malalgoda notes the feudal nature of the *vihāra*s and the many types of services that the persons living on temple lands provided for the monasteries in the following description:

> Attached to temple lands there were different groups of Navandanno to build and repair temple buildings and to supply craftsmen and painters for temple decorations; people of the Baḍahäla caste to supply bricks, tiles and earthen vessels; Hunnō to provide lime and plaster for the walls and floors of monastic buildings; Radav to furnish clean cloth and

lampwicks for temple ceremonies; Berāvayō to provide drummers, pipers and dancers at festivals; Paduvō to carry goods and bear the palanquins of chief monks; and so on.[13]

We may conclude that the monks of the Siyam Nikāya constituted a powerful and prestigious segment of Kandyan society, one that demanded that proper respect be shown them through ceremony and ritual etiquette. Economically, the monastic temples, and the lands attached to them, functioned as feudal estates through which monks derived material subsistence, support, and other services of both necessity and luxury. The possession of these estates was guaranteed by the king, but the *sannasa* grants enabled a single, monastic lineage to maintain and control the estate in the manner in which they saw fit and, theoretically at least, within the bounds of the Vinaya regulations and the more explicit *katikāvata* regulations. What sorts of transformations, then, did these elite monks seek to make?

Elite monks of the Kandyan kingdom wielded considerable influence in the royal court. Take, for example, the monk Moratoṭa Dhammakkhandha, head of the Siyam Nikāya from 1784 to 1811. As Dhammakkhandha quickly rose through the ranks of the Siyam Nikāya hierarchy, no doubt aided by his reputation as a teacher, he impressed king Kirti Śrī Rājasiṃha with his abilities. As a result, he became the tutor to Kirti Śrī's brother and heir apparent, who would later become king Rajadhirajasimha. This king, Rājādhirājasiṃha, composed a Sinhala language poem, *Asadisadākava*, based on the *Asadisa Jātaka*, at the request of his tutor. Within this work, the king-to-be affectionately gives thanks to Dhammakkhandha as he writes:

> My best friend
> Teacher of many teachings
> Named Dhammakkhandha, shining
> The monk, like the moon, a mind with much compassion.
> Obtaining the fortune of liberation,
> Illuminating a deep teaching
> Telling [me] to create a poem,
> Happily by [his] invitation.[14]

Referring to Dhammakkhandha as his "best friend" (*iṭu mituru*) was a tremendous compliment demonstrating the closeness of their relationship and the fondness that Rājādhirājasiṃha felt for his teacher. Two *sannasa*, or land grants, one from Degaldoruva Vihara and the other from Selava Vihara, mention Dhammakkhandha's role as royal tutor, the former listing the texts that he used to instruct the king in the Dhamma (the *Dighanikaya, Upasaka-Jana-Alankaraya, Milindaprasnaya, and Mahawansa*).[15] Thus, the monarch himself becomes a site of transformation. Elite monks worked to cultivate the king as a knowledgeable Buddhist, thereby enabling virtuous monarchical governance. In time, as we shall see, the target of monastic projects for the production of political virtuosity would shift to the body of the nation.

Dhammakkhandha also engaged in ambassadorial communications with the Dutch and then the British colonial officials. It appears that the close ties with the royal house enabled him to serve not only as a teacher to Rājādhirājasiṃha but as an advisor to his successor, Śrī Vikramarājasiṃha, in certain affairs of state. In a letter from 1804, Dhammakkhandha replied to a message from the British Governor of Ceylon, Frederic North. The translation of this letter, found within records of the governor's correspondence, reads as follows:

> Buddha and [the] Four Gods watch over the island, and every foreign power that may wish to conquer the country will fail in the attempt. If foreigners desire to obtain any advantage from Ceylon they must employ peaceable measures and not violence—of the truth of which the fate of the Dutch is a proof.[16]

The defiance expressed in this letter reveals that Dhammakkhandha and the Kandyan court were quite confident following the failed military expedition of the British in the previous year.

Additionally, Dhammakkhandha exchanged letters with John D'Oyly, a British officer in charge of administering the Kandyan provinces, dealing with the release of a prisoner, Major Adam Davie, taken during the first conflict between the two powers in 1803. The thrust of

Dhammakkhandha's argument with D'Oyly was that the British must use proper ambassadorial etiquette, according to Kandyan customs, and deliver a formal letter to the king by way of an official embassy. His letter, through British translation, reads as follows:

> In former times when a Governor arrived at Colombo, a suitable Keydapana [formal epistle] is dispatched in a respectful manner to render that event acceptable to the happy lotus-like mind of the Divine Supremely Great King, the Ruler of Tri Sinhala. Ere this takes place it is impossible to think that the subject matter of this secret letter can have stability. Because heretofore there was not a Governor thus wise and just, many persons suffered loss of property and loss of lives. We have thought it a sentiment proceeding from sense and wisdom that the present Governor making mutual enquiry, negotiates for peace before the occurrence of such loss of property and loss of lives. If contrary to this hostile acts are committed, we shall make the necessary preparations.[17]

This exchange was primarily an attempt by Dhammakkhandha to assert the power of the Kandyan state and to demand that the British perform rituals of prestige. The issue was never fully resolved, and Major Davie died in captivity. This exchange of letters reveals that Dhammakkhandha sought a continuance of etiquette in foreign relations that would maintain the sovereignty and status of the Kandyan court.

Aside from Dhammakkhandha, the monk Kobbǟkaḍuvē Śrī Nivāsa was also said to have instructed king Rājadhirājasiṃha in several branches of learning.[18] This monk was the incumbent of the prestigious Lankatilaka temple, among others; and in a *sannasa* of 1794, Rājādhirājasiṃha rededicates the temple to him as his tutor.[19] The founder of the Kobbǟkaḍuvē lineage, Kobbǟkaḍuvē Medhaṃkara, held the post of *disāva* (or provincial lord) of the regions of Panama and Puttalam in the late 17th century.[20] According to Malalgoda, "he led the Kandyan delegation in their negotiations with the Dutch in 1688,"[21] and the history of his lineage as a whole reveals the tendency during this period for powerful families to monopolize the control of individual Buddhist temples.

For whom, then, did these elite monks seek the virtuous transformation of society and government? Perhaps the clearest evidence revealing the larger social contingent for whom the elite Kandyan monks acted is to be found in the decree issued during Kirti Śrī's reign that limited higher ordination (*upasampadā*) to monks from the Goyigama caste. Since the arrival of the Portuguese, the caste groups that were previously considered low ranking, within the coastal littoral, gained new opportunities for economic advancement. Particularly during the period of Dutch occupation, certain non-Goyigāma castes (the Karāva and Salāgam) gained considerable wealth and governmental power.[22] Despite the reforms made by king Kirti Śrī limiting higher ordination to Goyigāma candidates, well-to-do families in the south and west of the island desired to have that status for their monks who came from their own families. The admission to higher ordination was, after all, a precursor to temple incumbency; and monks from these castes were, therefore, precluded from gaining control over temple lands.

Thus, beginning in 1772, low-caste monks organized a ceremony of higher ordination (*upasampadā*) at Toṭagamuva temple and another in 1798 at Tangalla.[23] In response, Dhammakkhandha sent a letter addressed to Karāve and Durāve laymen in which "he accused the Salāgama monks of having bribed the 'sinful and impious Vagēgoḍa [Dhammakusala]' into presiding over the *upasampadā* ceremony at Toṭagamuva."[24] Despite the developments in the south and west, Dhammakkhandha sought to uphold Goyigama privilege.

In 1799, monks from the Salāgama caste who resided in the Välitara area of the southern coast traveled to Burma to receive higher ordination. Their journey was financed by a wealthy Salāgama patron, Haljōti Dines de Zoysa Jayatilaka Sirivardhana. When these monks returned to Sri Lanka, they began their own monastic institution, the Amarapura Nikāya. The chief monk in Burma at the time, the Saṃgharāja Ñānābhivaṃsa, wrote a letter addressed to Dhammakkhandha explaining the ceremony that the Burmese provided as well as the historical ties between the Buddhists of Sri Lanka and those of Burma.[25] The intent was to help provide the newly formed *nikāya* with legitimacy, but it did not sway Dhammakkhandha from his stance. Clearly,

Goyigama aristocratic privilege was a key component of the virtuous governmentality shared by elite Kandyan monks at this time. With this understanding of the elite monks of the late Kandyan kingdom in mind, I now turn to look at the contemporary emergence of monastic politicians, the monks of the JHU.

The Jathika Helu Urumaya (JHU)

Although the initial appearance of the JHU party was sudden, the monks of whom it consisted had a much longer rise in the public eye. Uduwe Dhammaloka, a general Secretary of the party, had gained a strong following due to his preaching abilities and his televised sermons. Following in the footsteps of Gangodawila Sōma, many monks of the JHU utilize forms of mass media (especially television and radio but increasingly the Internet) to make themselves heard and seen.[26] Another member of the JHU, Ellawala Medhananda, has made numerous television appearances, but he has also gained popular notoriety from his many books on Sri Lankan archaeology.[27] Medhananda's work focuses on proving the existence of Sinhala–Buddhist communities in the far north and east of the island, which had been claimed as the homeland of the Tamil ethnic minority.[28] The presence of these monks and their works in the popular media preceded their entrance into the JHU party, and many of the party's candidates in the 2004 election had already gained a high degree of notoriety.

Aside from popularity in the mass media, the academic credentials of the JHU monks stand out as a marker of credibility. As mentioned, Medhananda presents himself as a scholar with university degrees and many scholarly publications. Likewise, Omalpe Sobhita, the current head of the JHU, was educated at Vidyodaya and received a PhD from New Delhi.[29] Although the form of education has shifted considerably from the late Kandyan period, the monks of the JHU also drew on their ability to mark themselves as competent scholars as a means of gaining a legitimate voice in discourses of virtuous governance.

Perhaps the most puzzling thing about the monks of the JHU was the decision to formally enter the parliamentary race. Given the description of their popularity and their presence in the media, why was this not a sufficient platform from which to launch critical reappraisals of Sri Lankan governance? What made it necessary to transform the government from within? Here, I find Comaroff's idea of "lawfare" instructive. She writes the following:

> At a time when, under the sway of neo-liberal policies, many states have relinquished significant responsibility for schooling, health, and welfare—in short, for the social reproduction of their citizens—religious organizations have willingly reclaimed this role."[30]

Within this context, "the secular instrument of legality has become one of the principal means whereby members of faith-based communities attempt to secure the propriety and authenticity of religious rites."[31] The importance of entering the government, I suggest, is precisely because it affords the JHU monks the most direct route of initiating virtuous governance within a climate of globalization dominated by neoliberal policies. This is not to deny the use of other means for affecting change. Sobhita, for instance has performed numerous "fasts-unto-death" in opposition to the government's cooperation with the LTTE.[32] In August of 2010, monks gathered to protest animal sacrifice at a temple in Chilaw.[33] Other forms of transformative intervention are clearly available to the monks, and they utilize these modalities of protest often. However, it is the attempt to transform the government from within, to render it virtuous through direct, internal participation in government that marks the JHU monks as unique.

One of the more controversial bills that the JHU monks have sought to pass is the bill prohibiting "unethical conversions."[34] This bill targets evangelical Christian missionary groups—largely Pentecostal—who operate among the poorer segments of the urban population.[35] The monks claim that individuals who join the evangelical community are pressured, or enticed, to do so by the offering of gifts. Regardless of the accuracy of their claims, the proposal of this bill reveals a deep-seated anxiety regarding the future of the Buddhist population in Sri Lanka. This echoes fears put forth by Sōma, who often asked Sinhala-Buddhists to be more vigorous in their procreation efforts to stymie the tide of Muslim and Christian population growth.[36]

Other bills put forth by the JHU monks are less concerned with protecting the numbers of Buddhists in the country than with establishing virtuous conduct within the population. Such bills include the successfully passed Tobacco and Alcohol Act of 2006. Among other things, the bill limits the ways in which these products can be advertised. The monks followed this with the "mathata titha" campaign for a "full stop" to the consumption of alcohol, drugs, and tobacco. I also draw attention to the many campaigns against Valentine's Day, which the JHU monks have labeled as foreign and supportive of unethical sexual behavior. Thus, where monks of the Kandyan court sought the virtuous education of their monarch, the monks of the JHU have turned their gaze on the body of the Sinhala nation. For a democratic polity to govern itself virtuously, not only the politicians but also its citizenry must cultivate some semblance of "virtuosity." However, the means of achieving this, as is evidenced by the tactics of the JHU, lie in the realm of legal action and the political deployment of new bills targeting social ills. Is it, however, the nation as a whole for whom these monks seek to act?

Although the monks themselves come from a variety of regions throughout the country, most of them have rural roots. Yet, the JHU is most popular among the urban and suburban communities.[37] Their symbolic support base, Sri Vajiragnana temple in Maharagama, is located just outside of Colombo. Additionally, although there are some JHU monks with affiliations to each of the main fraternities, or *nikāya*s, the large majority belong to the Amarapura Nikāya, which is rooted in the non-Goyigama, urban and suburban middle class. Many scholars, including Deegalle and Frydenlund, have noted this.[38] The JHU does not claim a specific *nikāya* affiliation, but its independence from the prestigious Siyam Nikāya is visible from such cases in which the JHU monks deviate from the recommendations made by the *mahanayaka*s of Malwatte and Asgiriya. One such case is the 2005 "fast-unto-death" by Omalpe Sobhita, which the *mahanayaka* of Malwatte asked him to stop. Sobhita's response was that the *mahanayaka* should ask the president to stop destroying the country.[39] This ability to defy the monastic hierarchy of the older *nikāya* reveals that the JHU monks seek to represent a different sort of Buddhist community than that over which the Siyam Nikaya maintains its dominance. I argue that this is largely the urban and suburban middle class who do not maintain strong loyalties to the traditional monastic elites, the same monks who trace their lineages back to the elite monks of the Kandyan court.

Comparing the Performance of Virtuous Governmentality

What is to be gained from a scholastic endeavor that examines these cases of monastic intervention in politics comparatively? Following my first question, how do monks cultivate the social capital necessary to empower themselves as potential critics of or participants in governance, I note shifts in the cultures of prestige that were tapped by each group of monks. In the Kandyan case, prestige derived from the monarchy, a feudalist economy, and displays of Pāli-based education. In the case of the monks of the JHU, prestige was sought through the mass media and university-based scholarship.

Second, by examining the transformations that each group sought, we see that the Kandyan monastic elite endeavored to create a more secure kingdom at a time when the British and coastal elites were becoming an ever more serious threat. As a corollary, the Kandyan monks also sought to educate their king and to help him to become a proper Buddhist monarch. The JHU desired to ensure security, but in their case it was for a Sinhala–Buddhist ethnic community—their conception of a Sinhala national body—rather than a kingdom. Likewise, the JHU monks worked to produce an increased social virtuosity, which we may contrast to the Kandyan elite's focus on the body of the king.

Finally, when we look at whom each group sought to represent, we see that the Kandyan elite monks were particularly concerned with supporting the interests of the Goyigama caste and the Kandyan aristocracy, from which many of the Kandyan monks could themselves claim ancestry. The JHU, however, clearly represents the growing, urban/suburban, middle class. However, both groups of monastics exhibit a fear of the impending doom of the Buddhist religion (*sāsana*), and this is worth revisiting. What might be the significance of the resiliency of this trope of a tradition under siege? In what ways might the JHU draw on this discourse as a means to combat a type of neocolonial expansion of globalizing, Western culture, and how might this response be connected to the earlier struggles of the elite Kandyan monks with the Dutch and then the British?

Perhaps one of the more important conclusions I offer here is that there is no such thing as a "traditional Buddhist monk" except as a rhetorical device. Whereas various sides of politically motivated debate might make use of this trope of the "traditional monk," historical evidence suggests that the monastic role varied considerably from time to time, place to place, and among different peoples in the same historical moment. As we have seen, even premodern monastics entered the political arena of their day. Whether political intervention by monastic clergy is a desideratum is another question entirely. Regardless of whether they maintain political titles or offices, monks have always had the potential to engage critiques of government. How and why they do so at particular historical moments is what needs explanation. A comparative analysis of politically engaged monks, as presented here, permits us to notice patterns or traces running through each of our cases that help us to better explain the entanglement of monastics in politics in a way that moves us beyond the presumption that such involvement is a departure from tradition.

If we return to the speech by Gnanasara delivered at Aluthgama, we must begin to understand his, and the larger BBS's, anti-Muslim rhetoric as more than merely deviations from traditional Buddhism, however that might be conceived. Gnanasara, like the elite monks of the Kandyan kingdom and the monks of the early JHU, had been empowered by a segment of Sri Lankan society to engage in sociopolitically powerful displays of discourse on virtuous governmentality. The fact that these two monks abandoned hope for a change from within Sri Lankan government does not signal a break from interest in governmentality altogether. Rather, the BBS has invented new methods and novel tactics, drawing in many ways from the efforts of the early JHU, as they deploy messages through social media and publish books expressing their perceived threat of a Muslim rise in population.[40]

Although chastising monks like Gnanasara for their venomous rhetoric, or arguing against the involvement of monks in sociopolitical affairs, may be laudable actions taken to secure a more peaceful and tolerant society, I argue that a greater attention to the reasons why monks like Gnanasara become empowered as critics of virtuous governmentality in the first place may prove more helpful in the long run. For whom do Gnanasara and the BBS speak? Why have they perceived Muslims to be the new threat against Buddhism at this time, much like the Kandyans saw the British and the JHU saw evangelical Christians in their day? What global pressures and wider contexts have led the BBS to become the vocal spokesmen for politically engaged Buddhists when so many other monks have been unable to find the same level of power and influence in the country to date? Developing answers to these sorts of questions may enable us to find a new approach the problem of Buddhist–Muslim conflict: an approach that does not dismiss groups like the BBS as mere aberrations from tradition.

NOTES

1. Galagoda Aththe Gnanasara, "Bodu Bala Sena Meeting-Aluthgama," YouTube Video, 6:30, posted by Colombo Telegraph, June 15, 2014, https://www.youtube.com/watch?v=iOxPJzlXDJs.
2. Buddhaghosa, *The Illustrator of Ultimate Meaning (Paramatthajotikā); Commentary on the Minor Readings*, trans. Bhikkhu Ñāṇamoli (London: Pali Text Society, 1960).
3. Weber (1965).
4. See Abeysekara (2002) and Rahula (1974).
5. Deegalle (2004: 84). He also offers a helpful account of earlier attempts of monks to win seats in local governments beginning quite soon after independence.
6. Scott (1999: 105).
7. See especially Michel Foucault, "Governmentality," trans. Rosi Braidotti, in *The Foucault Effect: Studies in Governmentality*, eds. Graham Burchell, Colin Gordon, and Peter Miller (Chicago: University of Chicago Press, 1991), 87–104.

8. Deegalle (2004: 83).
9. Scholars have challenged the foreign, non-Buddhist characterization of the Nayakkars, and I agree with their assessment. See, for instance, John Clifford Holt, *The Religious World of Kirti Śrī: Buddhism, Art, and Politics in Late Medieval Sri Lanka* (New York: Oxford University Press, 1996). Yet, even here, the historical resistance to the Nayakkars by elite members of the Kandyan monastic institution and the Kandyan aristocracy receives some attention, and the ways in which the monastic elite worked together with the kings remains less discussed.
10. Capt. L. De Bussche, *Letters on Ceylon Particularly Relative to the Kingdom of Kandy* (New Delhi: Asian Educational Services, 1999), 45–46.
11. Pieris (1939: 167–168). There is no date, but Kitsiri Malalgoda speculates it to be ca. 1805 when Maitland first took office.
12. Kitsiri Malalgoda also notes how the monks of the southern province sought the backing of the local colonial government in receiving the honors due to a chief monk when travelling:

    A chief monk was entitled, in the first place, to command the obedience and respect of the other monks within his jurisdiction. His rights were not limited, however, to this purely religious sphere. He was also entitled, by virtue of his office, to such traditional honours as travelling in palanquins accompanied by flags and drums, and to such services as receiving aḍukku (cooked provisions) and coolies from the headmen of the areas he happened to pass through. The enforcement of these rights required the approval, if not the active support, of the effective political authority within the area concerned (Malalgoda 1976: 82).

13. Malalgoda (1976: 89–90).
14. Verses from the Asadisadākava taken from Sannasgala (1964: 506). The verses read as follows: *mā iṭu mituruvana/noyek dahamaṭa guruvana/damkanda nam sobana/yatindu sand sita nomanda kuḷunena// mok siri labana mena/gämburu damahak eḷuvena/kavikara kiyana mena/keḷen ārādanā satosina//.*
15. For the Degaldoruva Sannasa, see Lawrie (1972 [1896]: 138). For the Selava Sannasa, see H. C. P. Bell (1892: 89–90).

16. Pieris (1939: 76); included in CO 54/14, North to Hobart, September 30th, 1804.
17. Pieris (1939: 89); noted as "Moratoṭa to D'Oyly, 24th September 1805," included in CO 54/18.
18. John Davy (1821: 173) and Dewaraja (1995: 458).
19. Lawrie (1972 [1896]: 754).
20. See Wimaladharma (2003: 23) for a detailed chart of the Kobbākaduvē lineage.
21. Malalgoda (1976: 50).
22. Malalgoda (1976) discusses this; but also see John Rogers, "Post-Orientalism and the Interpretation of Premodern and Modern Political Identities: The Case of Sri Lanka." *Journal of Asian Studies* 53 (1994): 10–23.
23. Malalgoda (1976: 97).
24. Ibid. (97, n. 74). Also SLNA HMC5/63/8/(3).
25. See I. P. Minayeff, "The Sandesa-Kathā." *Journal of the Pāli Text Society* (1885): 17–28.
26. See Berkwitz (2008b) for a relatively recent study of Soma's career, including his use of mass media.
27. See, for instance, Medhananda (2005), which is also available in English translation.
28. Kahaṭapiṭiya (2008).
29. See a biographic article on Sobhita by Walter Jayawardhana for Sri Lanka Web News at http://www.lankaweb.com/news/items04/010104-1.html.
30. Comaroff (2009: 20).
31. Kapferer, Eriksen, and Telle (2009: 15).
32. See numerous articles in The Island newspaper covering this fast: "JHU MP monk begins fast against JM," June 7, 2005, <http://www.island.lk/2005/06/07/news1.html>, accessed 10/16/2010; "Fasting monk defies Mahanayake's command," June 8, 2005, <http://www.island.lk/2005/06/08/news1.html>, accessed 10/16/2010; and "PM, Malwatte Mahanayake visit fasting monk," June 9, 2005, http://www.island.lk/2005/06/09/news2.html> accessed 10/16/2010.
33. The Nation, "Animal sacrifice: An Act of 'barbarians'," September 5, 2010, <http://www.nation.lk/2010/09/05/newsfe4.htm > accessed 4/5/22016.

34. The full text of this bill is available in the appendix of the Christian Solidarity Worldwide Briefing (January 2010) at the following site: <http://www.cswusa.org/filerequest/1154.pdf>.
35. See Neena Mahadev, "Conversion and Anti-Conversion in Contemporary Sri Lanka: Pentecostal Christian Evangelism and Theravada Buddhist Views on the Ethics of Religious Attraction," in *Proselytizing and the Limits of Religious Pluralism in Contemporary Asia*, eds. Juliana Finucane and R. Michael Feener (Singapore: Springer, 2014), 211–235.
36. See Berkwitz (2008a).
37. See Rampton and Welikala (2005: 44–46).
38. Deegalle (2004), Frydenlund (2005).
39. See The Island "Fasting monk defies Mahanayake's command," June 8, 2005, <http://www.island.lk/2005/06/08/news1.html>, accessed 10/16/2010.
40. See, for instance, the many images posted and publications listed on the BBS website: bodubalasena.net.

CHAPTER FOUR

CONFIGURATIONS OF BUDDHIST NATIONALISM IN MODERN SRI LANKA

Benjamin Schonthal

Over the last five years, the Bodu Bala Sēnā (BBS) in Sri Lanka and the 969 movement in Myanmar have gone from being nowhere to being everywhere. Although the main spokespersons in each movement, Galagoda Gnanasara Thero of the BBS and U Wirathu of the 969, had careers as activists and monks beforehand, since 2012, the movements have burst forth into public prominence in a way that has surprised most, if not all, observers. The suddenness of this process and the often bellicose rhetoric associated with these groups has led many journalists around the world to describe the BBS and 969[1] as embodying a new and unprecedented style of aggressive Buddhist nationalism.

Looking at the violence linked to BBS and 969 in places like Aluthgama and Rakhine State, one is inclined to agree with the tone of shock and alarm indicated in these articles. Yet, how "new" is this kind of violence and how "new" are these groups? Sri Lanka and Myanmar have long been fertile ground for ethnic and religious chauvinisms. Indeed, in both places, there are documented incidents of violence between certain groups of Buddhists, Christians and Muslims extending back over a century. Religion-based rallies, riots, intimidation, chauvinism—these things are not new to Buddhist Southern Asia, nor is the jingoistic discourse of the BBS and 969 without precedent.

Focusing on the Sri Lankan side of things, in this chapter I examine the "newness" of the BBS's Buddhist nationalism[2] in historical terms. I argue that the BBS embodies not an entirely new and unprecedented type of Buddhist activism but a new *configuration* of Buddhist nationalism—a new variation of an older discursive template. The core of this template lays in the assertion that Buddhism in Sri Lanka is under threat. The BBS, like other Buddhist nationalists before them, insist that Buddhism is in danger of decay or extinction, despite the fact that 70% of the population identify themselves as Buddhists. This assertion finds canonical warrant in Pali texts such as the *Anāgata Vaṃsa* (the "Lineage of the Future"), which predicts that the *Buddha's sāsana*, or dispensation, has a limited lifespan and will gradually over time disappear from the world.[3] This assertion also finds validation in the observation that although Buddhists form a majority in Sri Lanka, from a regional or global perspective, Theravada Buddhists (and, more to the point, Sinhalese Buddhists) comprise only a tiny population.

The distinctiveness of the BBS lays less in its intensity than in the unique ways that it has configured Buddhist nationalism to reflect a new set of perceived threats and dangers. The BBS's configuration is the third major configuration to emerge since independence: the first dominated from the period of independence negotiations in the 1940s to the rise of militant Tamil separatism in early 1970s; the second dominated from the mid-1970s to the end of the civil war in 2009; and the third has emerged and gained prominence in the years following 2011.

In this chapter, I explore these three configurations by way of examining particular nationalist groups that embodied them, the Bauddha Jātika Balavēgaya (BJB), the Jātika Heḷa Urumaya (JHU), and the BBS. By focusing on single groups, I do not mean to suggest that Buddhist nationalist movements in any one historical period are identical or naturally aligned. As a number of scholars have pointed out, Sri Lanka's Buddhist nationalist groups have often disagreed and competed with each other.[4] Amid these differences, however, one can nonetheless identify particular leitmotifs that preoccupy nationalist thought in a particular period. In the first period (1940s to 1970s), one sees a configuration of Buddhist nationalism concerned predominately with Catholic agents, colonial legacies, and education; in the second period (1970s to 2009), one sees a configuration of Buddhist nationalism concerned predominately with Tamil separatists, "new" Western religious and aid organizations, and territorial unity; in the third period (after 2009), one sees a configuration concerned predominately with Islam and winners and losers in the island's postwar capitalistic economic climate.

A Colonial Precursor

This chapter offers a historical overview that begins in the 1940s. However, one cannot adequately address Buddhist nationalism without saying a few words about its colonial-era antecedents insofar as Buddhist nationalist movements from the 1940s inherit and build on ideas, arguments, and organizational structures that crystallize in the second half of the 19th century. Scholars refer to this period as an age of "Buddhist revival" because during this period, Buddhist monks and lay persons organized themselves on a national level to spread Buddhist teachings, restore Buddhist monuments and temples, create Buddhist educational institutions, and resist Christian missionizing.[5] The key figure here is Anagarika Dharmapala, the son of a wealthy furniture merchant, who would renounce his worldly ties for a life as a homeless "defender of the dharma" (a literal translation of his name). Dharmapala became the most important ideologue and exemplar of Buddhist revivalism at the turn of the century, authoring dozens of influential tracts and traveling all over the world giving speeches about Buddhism, colonial injustices, and grandeur of ancient Sinhalese civilizations.[6]

Consolidated in the Buddhist revival period, and particularly in the writings of Dharmapala, are a linked set of basic arguments that would form the foundation of Buddhist nationalism in the years to follow. The undergirding logic was impressively coherent (again, thanks largely to Dharmapala), involving conceits of an idyllic civilization lost. The basic features could be summarized as follows: Sri Lanka was originally controlled by strong Sinhalese Buddhist kings who ruled wisely over prosperous, healthy, educated populations in which monks and laity worked together to create a moral and peaceful society. The colonial occupiers of the Portuguese, Dutch, and British destroyed this paradise by overthrowing the Sinhalese kings; converting the people to Christianity; and introducing amoral, unhealthy, destructive practices such as drinking alcohol, eating meat, and gambling. Colonial occupiers, and the Christian churches that were supported by them, severely damaged Buddhism by destroying temple property, controlling temple lands, engaging in conversion campaigns, preferring Christians for government positions, and endowing a system of Christian schools that would not only serve as outposts for converting young people but would act as the key gateways for upward mobility and access to the prestigious professions, with the intent that the island's professional elite would gradually become Christianized.

Although this vision of paradise lost is clearly caricatured, it is not without some truth. Colonial occupation did do a lot of damage to Buddhist institutional organization; and one cannot deny that by the 1940s, a large percentage of the island's power elite consisted of Christians or those who attended Christian schools. Moreover, regardless of the realities of the matter, printed commentaries, newspaper articles, and records of public debates in Sri Lanka from the 1940s show that there was a widespread public perception that colonialism and Christianity had collaborated in disadvantaging the island's Sinhalese Buddhists. These feelings would come to animate the first configuration of Buddhist nationalism in independent Sri Lanka.

Configuration 1: Christianity, Education, and the Bauddha Jatika Balavegaya

The entire organization of the Catholic Action Movement has been extraordinarily active ever since Ceylon gained its freedom [in 1948]. It would appear that surreptitiously and imperceptibly the Catholic Action Movement has captured the key positions in the Armed Forces, the Police, and the Administrative Services as well as in Agriculture, Commerce, and Industry. By this means, it has succeeded in acquiring immense economic power in the land. It has gone even further. It has used its familiar technique to infiltrate into areas where Buddhism is a great force. On one hand, it has thrown ridicule on the practices that are enjoined by

> Buddhism; and on the other hand, it has put a high premium on the social habits, like the drink curse, that are alien to Buddhism. Designed as they are to undermine the hold of Buddhism on the lives of the people, these actions are most decidedly subversive of peace and goodwill in the country. By actions such as these, the Catholic Action Movement has set the stage to bring Ceylon under the suzerainty of the Vatican.[7]

With this paragraph, the *Bauddha Jātika Balavēgaya* (BJB, or Buddhist National Force) concluded its 1963 investigation of Catholic influence in Sri Lankan society published in a work entitled *Catholic Action: A Menace to Peace and Good-will*. In it, one can see an unusually strident and succinct version of the configuration of Buddhist nationalism that dominated Sri Lanka from the 1940s into the 1970s—one that, building on the writings of Dharmapala, linked together concerns about the influence of established Christian sects (particularly Catholicism) exercising influence and control over the highest levels of state power, sabotaging the interests of Buddhists and ushering in a new form of colonization by the church. The precise mechanism through which Catholics have come to acquire positions of power and influence is not mentioned in the paragraph, yet it is underscored extensively in the book. According to the BJB, education was the vehicle through which the Catholic church gained influence and through which it continued to maintain control over Sri Lankan society.[8]

The BJB was founded in 1963, only months after Sri Lanka's media exposed a coup attempt by a number of senior military leaders, most of them Catholic.[9] The group was set up by L. H. Mettananda, a principle at the island's oldest and most prestigious Buddhist secondary school, Ananda College. Although not the largest of the Buddhist groups of the period, the BJB was in many ways the most outspoken and campaigned publically for some of the most high-profile Buddhist issues of the time. The BJB called for the creation of a committee to investigate the secret activities of Catholics. It requested the revision of legislation to give greater land powers to Buddhist temples, and it advocated making Buddhist full- and new-moon days national holidays in lieu of the "Christian weekend" of Saturday and Sunday. It pushed for Sinhalese-language education and the end of Christian denominational schools. It also recommended greater government support for propagating Buddhist teachings throughout society through supporting Buddhist "dharma schools." The BJB's agenda was broad, everywhere bringing together desires to support Buddhism with concern over Christian influence.

Although distinctive in its large media presence and strident tone, the BJB's configuration of Buddhist nationalism remained very much a product of its time. Mettananda had been active in lobbying on behalf of Sinhalese and Buddhist interests for most of his life. He began his public career as a lobbyer in the 1940s when he spoke out frequently for universal free education for all Sri Lankan children. As a social goal, free education was a cause championed by the island's leftists and reformers. Yet the pursuit of free education also had an explicit Buddhist nationalistic element to it. In the 1940s, the act of nationalizing the island's schools was seen not only as a way to enhance the accessibility of education for all but also as a way to sever the close links between the island's elite professional classes and its English medium, Christian schools. This was to be done either by bringing these schools under the control of the government or by cutting off the flow of tax funds to them (a measure anticipated to reduce the power and influence those schools had, if not to lead to their closure directly). Mettananda, like other Buddhist nationalists at the time, hoped that a nationalized school system would eventually lead to the replacing of the island's Anglophone, Christian-school-educated elite with a new type of Sinhalese-speaking, Buddhist intellectual and professional class.[10]

The roots of the *Bauddha Jātika Balavēgaya* can be traced to Mettananda's involvement with education reform. In the 1940s and 1950s, Mettananda joined a broad Buddhist effort to defend the proposed education reforms against Christian opponents, led by the Catholic Church.[11] His coalition included lay Buddhist organizations such as the All-Ceylon Buddhist Congress (in which Mettananda had played an important role since the 1930s), Buddhist student organizations such as the All-Ceylon Buddhist Students Union, as well newly formed Buddhist monastic groups including the *Laṅkā Eksat Bhikṣu Maṇḍalaya,* which would become influential forces in monastic activism in the decade to follow. When Mettananda introduced his new group to the public in early

1963, he set the agenda in purposefully wide terms, hoping to attract the support of existing Buddhist organizations, provided they weren't too entangled with the interests of island's parliamentarians.[12] Membership in the BJB was open to anybody who was prepared to "dedicate his life for the establishment of a Ceylonese Buddhist society, to set up a social order that is traditionally Ceylonese [read: Sinhalese], to sever connections with political parties and to refrain from seeking power and prestige through the Balavegaya [BJB]."[13] The goals of the group included helping to unify Buddhists, to recover their "lost rights and privileges," and to spread the Buddhist *dhamma*. In all of this, the Balavegaya presented itself as struggling against silent enemies, described as "foreign" actors and "anti-national" forces. Yet, if one follows the BJB's statements over time, one sees that the group's main concerns clearly lay with the Catholic church and its associated networks.[14]

The BJB's publication of *Catholic Action,* cited previously, made a huge impact, provoking a book-length retort from the Catholic Union of Ceylon and engendering a considerably degree of controversy.[15] In its form—which had the appearance of an academic or government report—the BJB contributed to what was by then an established genre of "Buddhist reports" that had grown following independence. These ranged from the published findings of a government Buddha Sasana Commission in the late 1950s to the personal scholarship of wealthy Colombo elites.[16] Mettananda had, in fact, been actively involved in researching and writing the most well-known and influential of these reports, the All-Ceylon Buddhist Congress report of 1956.[17] Comparing the various reports, *Catholic Action* appears typical of the genre: it emphasizes the long history of Buddhism on the island; outlines the deleterious consequences of colonialism; and offers recommendations for improving Buddhism through modifying structures of law, government, civil service, and especially education. Here, as in other reports, the current Catholic threat to Buddhism appears as the moment of truth between a Dharmapala-like paradise lost and the independent possibilities of a newly sovereign Ceylon.

In its genre of publishing, its types of demands, its framing of the threats posed to Buddhism, the Balavegaya exemplified the first major postindependence configuration of Buddhist nationalism. This configuration took as its historical prompts the struggle for decolonization, anxieties over lingering colonial inequalities, concerns over historic Christian privilege, and fears over new or persisting international influences (Mettananda in particular worried about American interventions in Sri Lanka, similar to those of Vietnam). Christianity, particularly Catholicism, served as the natural object of menace not only on account of the much-discussed coup plot but on account of Christianity's obvious links with colonialism and privilege and international influence. Aside from the positive steps the state could take to support Buddhism (e.g., rebuilding temples and supporting monks), it was the reform of education that appeared most urgent insofar as it was through the mechanism of education that elite Sri Lankan society would be transformed from Christian influenced and Anglophone to truly Buddhist and Sinhalese.

Configuration 2: Separatism, Conversion, Nongovernmental Organizations (NGOs), and the JHU

Anyone who has followed Sri Lankan politics over the last few years will be familiar with the JHU, or National Heritage Party, a political party consisting almost entirely of Buddhist monks that formed and surged into politics in the 2004 general elections. The word *heḷa*, often translated as heritage, refers not to heritage in the general sense of inherited culture but to Sinhala culture in particular. In an interview from 2008, the JHU media spokesman explained to me that the party was formed to defend the rights of Sinhalese Buddhist people because they alone are responsible for "the country, the civilization and the culture" of the island.[18]

The JHU represent the fruition of a configuration of Buddhist nationalism that had been growing since the 1970s, in tandem with and in response to demands for the devolution of political powers to the Tamil-majority north and east of the country. Days after the election of nine of its monks to parliament in 2004, the JHU's then propaganda secretary (now leader), Ven. Athuraliye Rathana Thero, declared that the party had no loyalties to any of the island's political groups but would cooperate with whatever coalitions were willing to support its two paramount agenda items: "advocating a unitary state and supporting the Buddha Sasana."[19] In a newspaper interview, several weeks earlier, one of the key organizers of the JHU, Ven. Uduwe Dhammaloka Thero, explained:

> Our aim is to establish a "*Dharma Rajyaya*" [Dharmic state] based on Dhamma in this country . . . The country has become head-less (*arajika*). Therefore, it is up to us [monks] as the guardian [deities] to become the leaders. They say that there is an ethnic problem in this country. Only 5% of Tamils live in the North. 13% live among us. How can this be so if there is an "ethnic problem"? The terrorists claim that North and East is their "Nija Bhoomy" [homeland]. This is another fabricated story. . . . Thanks to the politicians, the terrorists woo the International crowd by spreading such falsehoods.[20]

From its inception until the end of the civil war in 2009, the JHU remained perhaps the most vocal and adamant critic of any territorial or political concessions to the Liberation Tigers of Tamil Eelam (LTTE) or other Tamil groups. For the JHU, militant Tamil separatism constituted the single most dangerous threat to Buddhism, both because it threatened to divide what they saw as an "island of dharma" and because foreign governments, NGOs, and missionaries—meddling and dangerous foreign interveners—were increasingly coming to the island under the auspices of helping deal with the war.

The issue of Tamil separatism and devolution did not, of course, emerge first in the 1970s. Proposals for a federal or quasi-federal political formation had been mooted since the 1930s. The largest Tamil opposition party, the Federal Party, had even staked its raison d'être to the creation of a federal structure for the island. The question of devolution came to a head with the creation of the island's two republican constitutions of 1972 and 1978, which declared in the first article that Sri Lanka would be a "unitary" state, a direct swipe at the Federal Party's previous efforts. During the 1970s, disenfranchisement among Tamils gave birth to a number of militant Tamil separatist groups that, through various guerilla tactics, began to engage in independent secessionist battles in the northern parts of the island. By the mid 1980s, one group, the LTTE, having killed or intimidated all other militias, began to engage in an active military conflict with the Sri Lankan armed forces.

From the late 1960s and into the 1980s, one sees a growing panic among established Buddhist organizations—such as the Young Men's Buddhist Association, All Ceylon Buddhist Congress, and others—about the issue of territorial unity. Like the issue of education in the independence era, the issue of territorial integrity and sovereignty would become the defining issues of Buddhist nationalism from the late 1960s. It was during this period that certain high-profile monks and prominent politicians began to mount their own campaigns to prevent any devolution of power to the Tamil-majority areas. In a forward to an anthology of speeches made by the parliamentarian Cyril Matthews, one well-known monk wrote:

> Sri Lanka is a Sinhala Buddhist Country although non-Sinhalese and non-Buddhists too have lived here for a long time. This fact should never be forgotten by the Sinhala Buddhists as well as by the non-Sinhalese and the non-Buddhists. For the non-Sinhalese even if they do not have Sri Lanka as their home, their races have other countries of their own. Hence these races will never get annihilated. But the Sinhalese have one and only one country, and that is Sri Lanka.[21]

In this paragraph, one sees all the hallmarks of the Buddhist nationalism that would dominate until 2009: the conflation of the island with Sinhalese people and Buddhism; the rationalization of this assertion both in terms of history and in terms of the global demographics (Sri Lanka is only place where Sinhalese exist); the idea of a tolerance within hegemony whereby non-Sinhalese and non-Buddhists were welcome provided they did not threaten the geography-ethnicity-religion nexus; and (in the background) the specter of the major threat to this, Tamil separatism.

In the 1980s, a number of groups embodied this configuration of Buddhist nationalism and directed their energies toward thwarting any attempt at decentralizing power on the island. A major catalyst for this growth was the arrival in Sri Lanka of a large Indian Peace Keeping Force (IPKF), sent from Delhi to broker and enforce an agreement between the government and the LTTE, which gave the island's provinces (including an amalgamated North and Eastern Province) greater powers of administration. Although the politics behind the agreement and the IPKF intervention are complex, the effects were predictable: those who were already concerned about the break up of the island into Sinhalese and Tamil areas were now also concerned about a large presence of Indian troops. In this context, Buddhist organizations protested in courts and in the streets, calling out for territorial unity and sovereignty. A number of new Buddhist groups formed during this period. These included lay-Buddhist-led groups such as the Representative Council of Sri Lankan Buddhist Societies (*Sri Lanka Bauddha Samiti Niyōjita Sabhāva*) and the Sinhalese Development Organization (*Siṃhala Saṃvardhana Saṃvidhānaya*). It also included a variety of monk-led groups including the National Front (*Jātika Peramua*) and the Movement to Protect the Motherland (*Mavbima Suraekīmē Vyāpāraya*, or MSV).[22]

The Buddhist nationalism of the JHU grows out of this period. As with the Buddhist groups in the 1980s, they favored a military solution and insisted Tamil claims to territory and autonomy were illegitimate. Yet, in developing their political platform, the JHU not only drew from the imagery and legacies of the late 1980s but from a variety of Buddhist movements that developed in the 1990s to argue against Chandrika Bandaranaike Kumaratunga's attempts to negotiate peace deals with the LTTE. Unlike the anti-IPKF movements in the 1980s, however, these movements showed significantly more organizational and ideological sophistication. By the mid-1990s, a National Joint Committee was created to link together 46 Sinhalese organizations that opposed President Kumaratanga's People's Alliance government (all of them were Buddhist in orientation, bar one).[23] From the Committee, a subcommission was appointed to investigate the grievances of the Sinhalese people. In a manner similar to the All-Ceylon Buddhist Congress and the BJB in the 1950s and 1960s, the subcommission produced a culminating report, known as the Sinhala Commission Report, which gave new visibility and ideological coherence to the antidevolution activists. It also inspired a new cohort of Sinhalese intellectuals who became increasingly outspoken in their calls for a new of "national thinking" (*jātika chintanaya*), which would both celebrate Sinhalese traditions of art, culture, science, and other domains as well as inoculate Sri Lankans against malicious new "Western" influences on society in the forms of global market forces, transnational NGOs and, most insidiously, new Christian evangelical organizations.[24]

It is in this second (anti-Western) part of "national thinking"—which was taken up with vim by the JHU—that one sees the other distinctive features of this second configuration of Buddhist nationalism. If Buddhist nationalists in the 1940s and 1950s viewed the Roman Catholic Church and vestigial British colonial links as the primary foreign threats, Buddhist nationalists in this second phase began to direct their attentions to other types of foreign threats, most important among them evangelical Christian organizations and international NGOs (and the local partners who worked with them). From the late 1990s to 2009, evangelizing Christians and NGOs became not only objects of scorn for Buddhist groups; they became objects of government scrutiny (in the form of presidential commissions of inquiry) as well as legal action (in the form of proposed bills to criminalize "forced" conversions and to limit the independence of local and international NGOs).[25] Following its promises to defend a unitary country and to fight for a Buddhist state, the JHU's 2004 election manifesto specified that, if elected, the party will render illegal the "unethical" conversions being undertaken by new Christian groups and will take steps to "control and monitor" the activities and bank transactions of NGOs.[26] In the logic of the JHU, the war constituted a breach into which proselytizing evangelical Christians and subversive NGOs could enter: missionaries could more easily convert vulnerable, war-affected civilians in their conversion campaigns; and NGOs could use humanitarian aid as a pretense for secretly supporting the LTTE or abetting Christian proselytism campaigns. In this second configuration of Buddhist nationalism, Tamil separatists, Christian missionaries, and foreign NGOs acted symbiotically to undermine the presence of Buddhism in Sri Lanka.

Configuration 3: Islam, Development, and the BBS

As one can see by now, Sri Lankan Buddhist nationalism may have had distinct configurations, but those configurations are neither cleanly bounded nor unlinked. Rather than neatly boxed eras of history, configurations of Buddhist nationalism grow out of shared sources, like branches emerging from a common trunk. Looking backward, one can see that fears of bottom-up evangelical conversion emerge from a deeper history of panic about top-down Catholic and Anglican conversions. Similarly, one can see how the maligning of Western influence associated with "national thinking" looks very similar to the maligning of the British seen in the independence era. The configurations of Buddhist nationalism that dominate during a particular phase of history also work alongside other configurations and anticipate configurations that come to dominate in the future.

Such was the case in 2008–2009 when, in the course of my dissertation research, I began to observe a new set of threats and grievances taking a front seat among Buddhist nationalist groups. It was during this period that I noticed the growing regularity with which Muslims were appearing in the rhetoric of groups like the JHU, along with the idea (mooted publically in newspapers) that Muslims were somehow quietly becoming more populous and powerful than the Sinhalese.[27] This was not the first time that Muslims figured as a threat in Buddhist nationalist discourse; one can point to instances from the speeches of Gangodawila Soma Thera in the early 2000s all the way back to the infamous 1915 Buddhist–Muslim riots. Yet this appeared to be the first recent time that Muslims figured as *the primary* threat.

It was a 2008 court case, initiated by one of the leaders of the JHU, which cast a real national spotlight on the idea that Muslims threatened Buddhist interests in Sri Lanka. The case involved a large housing scheme that had been built to resettle Muslims who had been displaced following the 2005 tsunami. The scheme was controversial both because the housing (funded largely by Saudi Arabia) was preferentially given to Muslims and because the scheme was built in the vicinity of the ancient Buddhist temple of Dighavapi. In the context of public outcry against the housing project, the JHU initiated legal action (eventually successful) to declare the scheme unconstitutional. Yet, the impact echoed far beyond the courts: in the publicity and controversy over the Dighavapi Case, one sees a key event in a new formation of Buddhist nationalism, one that constituted Muslims as greater threats to Buddhism than evangelical Christians and that concerned itself not just with conversion, separatism, and Buddhist values but with biopolitics and development. One can see instances of this formation in a number of cases of violence against Muslims following the Dighavapi case. In September 2011, a monk in Anuradhapura led a group in demolishing a Muslim shrine. In April 2012, a large mob led by Buddhist monks attacked a Muslim mosque in Dambulla. The culmination of this formation of Buddhist nationalism was achieved with the creation of the BBS, which formed shortly after in April 2012.

The BBS grew out of previous configurations of Buddhist nationalism in the same way as the JHU and the BJB. The Secretary General of the BBS (and its chief firebrand), Galagoda Aththe Gnanasara Thero, is a former member of the JHU, as is the BBS's founder (who has since withdrawn from the movement) Kirima Wimalajothi Thero.[28] Many of BBS's techniques and much of its discourse also seems to echo the JHU—even though the BBS has been very critical of the JHU (and particularly the idea of monks serving in parliament). The BBS even drew up its own twelve-point manifesto, echoing a similar twelve-point manifesto produced by the JHU in 2004.[29] One insight into the novelty of the BBS and its configuration of Buddhist nationalism can be seen in comparing the JHU and BBS manifestos. Although both underscore the importance of fostering a Buddhist society (*bauddha samājaya*) and in spreading the *dhamma* inside and outside of Sri Lanka, the two differ considerably on their vision for development and modernity. The JHU's manifesto reveals a more environmentally-minded vision of development, one that "should centre on the natural habitat, animals, and humanity" and should take seriously animal welfare, a stance confirmed by the JHU's public outcries against animal sacrifice and cow slaughter.[30] The BBS's manifesto, by contrast, has a much stronger capitalistic ring to it, devoting an entire section to the "development and protection of Buddhist business/entrepreneurship (*bauddha vyāpāra/vyavasāyakatvaya*)" in which they emphasize the importance of identifying and supporting Buddhist business persons, especially younger persons, and helping them to network and overcome any potential issues. In a section explaining their desire to "establish a Buddhist development fund," the BBS write that they intend to help establish a "Buddhist development bank." In fact, unlike earlier iterations of development-minded, Buddhist nationalist rhetoric (such as that associated with the Mahawaeli project)—which cast economic, industrial, and land development as a restoration of ancient hydraulic society (with its archetypical triad of water tank, paddy field, and Buddhist temple)[31]—the BBS discourse of development has a fully 21st-century ring to it. It invokes the buzz words of networking (*jālagata kirīma*), entrepreneurship, and business and even stresses the importance of technology and global outreach (particularly when discussing the revamping of monastic education). Part of this concern with technology and commerce comes from a key leader and spokesperson for the BBS, who has the title "Chief Executive Officer," Dilanthe Withanage, who was himself a specialist and teacher of information technology.[32] Moreover, unlike earlier Buddhist nationalist groups, the BBS participates in and is supported through a diverse and decentralized social media presence, with Facebook, in particular, at its center.[33]

One can see in the BBS's configuration of Buddhist nationalism many of the same grievances that one sees in earlier configurations but with Islam and Muslims configured as the most significant threats: concerns over education (Muslim privileges in education[34]), concerns over foreign influence (by Muslim-majority states and transnational Muslim organizations), concerns over conversion (this time, to Islam), even concerns over territorial unity in the sense of anxieties over Muslim-majority communities in the country's Eastern Province might become de facto Muslim polities. What is unique, however, is not just the target of the discourse—Muslims, as opposed to mainline Christians, Tamil separatists, evangelical Christians or NGOS (although all other groups appear as well, to a lesser degree)—but the strongly capitalistic tone to many of the BBS's grievances. For the BBS, Muslims threaten Buddhists, among other ways, by distorting and altering the patterns of production, consumption, wealth, demography, and industry in the country. If, in the first configuration of Buddhist nationalism, Christian professional privileges were thought to have been perpetrated through unfair practices in education, in this third configuration of Buddhist nationalism, Muslim economic privileges are imagined to be perpetrated through the manipulation of markets.

Take, for example, the issue of Halal certification, against which the BBS launched major campaigns in 2012 and 2013.[35] Although the issue was framed as a defense of Buddhists, the logic was pitched equally as a defense of free markets. The CEO of the BBS explained it as follows to me:

> [Muslims can receive] halal certification for the 9 per cent Muslims in this country. We [the BBS] don't have an issue with that. But why [should] they impose this [on non-Muslims]. . . . They go to Muslim areas and say "if it's not halal don't allow the Sinhalese business people to sell their products." So, Sinhala business people are forced to have halal certification. And not only that. They sometimes give a wrong interpretation. . . . They say that there's a huge halal market [overseas] and you can't sell without halal certification. Which is wrong. Now, in the world, we have 7 billion [people]. Only 1.5 billion are Muslims, that's less than 20 per cent. But they don't say that. . . . [The] non-halal market is 90 per cent![36]

The "threat" of Muslims is therefore not simply a cultural or territorial or political threat (as Christianity, Tamil separatism, and NGOs appeared to be): it is also construed as a threat on the logic and mechanics of free market economics, in terms of unfair business practices, the manipulation of markets, and the misrepresentation of consumer demand. As part of this, Buddhists are configured as victims, but their victimization lies also in their lack of ability to access and participate fully in the rapid economic development that has driven the country since the end of the civil war.

Although the neoliberal flavor of BBS nationalism appeared most strongly in the anti-Halal campaign, one sees echoes of it equally in the range of issues with which the BBS became involved. These include protests against the favoring of Muslim legal students, concerns over the treatment of Sinhalese migrant workers (particularly in the Middle East), against unfair practices in Muslim-owned business, and against the high "birth rate" of Muslims in Sri Lanka. The "threat" posed by all these activities, in the rationale of the BBS, is among other things the threat of unequal economic power as acquired through Muslim professional success (as lawyers), or Muslim exploitation of Sinhalese labor (in the case of Sinhalese migrant laborers and maids employed in Muslim-majority states), or Muslims' alleged monopolistic control of commerce (by Muslim retail and importing syndicates), or Muslims' increase in population (and therefore Muslim total powers of production and consumption). What's new about this current formation of Buddhist nationalism—one embodied not only by the BBS but by groups like the *Sihala Ravaya* and *Ravana Balaya*—is not only its aggressiveness, or its intensity, or even just its targeting of Muslims, but its ability to articulate threats to Buddhism in the language and framework of global market capitalism.

Old Wine and New Bottles?

The BBS clearly embody a new configuration of Buddhist nationalism. Yet the newness of that configuration must be contextualized within a longer history of Buddhist nationalism on the island. Examining the BBS in this light allows one to recognize both the profound similarities between the types of threats, grievances, and "solutions" proposed by the BBS and other groups (such as the BJB and JHU) as well as the ways in which each of the groups remains very much a product of its times. Taking the first point, it is clear that the BBS inherits from and models itself on earlier thinkers. One can see clear continuances from the 1940s to now in the BBS's concerns with Christianity, conversion, creating a Buddhist society, defending against "foreign influence," and so forth. These continuances are not simply accidents but (in many cases) deliberate attempts to revive and act on the ideologies of early Buddhist nationalist thinkers like Anagarika Dharmapala, which the BBS invokes regularly. (For example, in 2014 the BBS launched a large campaign to commemorate the 100th death anniversary of Dharmapala.) At the same time, the BBS's configuration of Buddhist nationalism also represents a clear break with earlier movements insofar as its major concerns lay less with Catholics or education or Tamil separatism or evangelical conversion than with Muslims and a particular vision of free market economics.

This observation—that the BBS embody the latest configuration of a rough but long-standing template of Buddhist nationalism—begs the question: was it inevitable that this new configuration of nationalism would have arisen with or without the BBS? If one looks at the central concerns of the BJB and the JHU, education and Tamil separatism, one sees that each of those concerns was (to a greater or lesser degree) resolved over the course of Sri Lankan history: education was eventually nationalized, with the exception of a small number of private schools; the LTTE were defeated. Examined in this light, this recent configuration of Buddhist nationalism may have gained prominence and support because, with the absence of vibrant mainline Christian churches or large evangelical populations[37] or separatist movements, Muslims may appear to nationalistic thinkers as the only imagined social collectivity that could actually constitute a plausible existential threat. A climate of pitched concern with Islamic extremism in the global news media certainly fed into the BBS's program, as do commentaries on Sri Lanka's most recent census figures that show an increase in the island's Muslim population from approximately 7.5 to 9.7% of the population between 1981 and 2011. Yet these facts may be beside the point: Buddhist nationalism requires the perception of threat; and, whether or not such a threat is imminent, one must be produced.

It is also no coincidence that the BBS have framed their grievances in the language of development, markets, and capitalism. Since the end of the civil war, Sri Lanka has undergone a rapid development boom with crony capitalists and entrepreneurs finding many new opportunities for profit, particularly through the development of property—frequently at the expense of the island's less-prosperous classes. By framing the Muslim threat—in significant ways—in economic terms, the BBS has successfully focused and mobilized for their purposes some of the most pressing anxieties of the day: the desire to make good on the "peace dividend" and to participate in the new economic boom. Just as education and territorial unity captured the emotions of people in the past, it is discussions of development and capitalism and the allure of prosperity that seem to capture emotions now.

The BBS is new in these ways. But perhaps it's less a case of old wine in new bottles than new wine in old bottles. Buddhist nationalism has always relied for its success on a seductive paring of threat and desire, resentment and utopia, paradise lost and regained. The discursive vessel is the same; it's the alarming and alluring contents that change.

NOTES

1. Properly speaking, 969 is more of a loosely organized and diffuse social movement, which tends to follow and gain inspiration from the speeches of U Wirathu; the more appropriate comparison with BBS might be the social and political activist organization called *Ma Ba Tha*, or *The Association for the Protection of Race and Religion*.
2. In referring to Buddhist nationalism, I am referring to a body of discourse (of words, images, signs, and songs) characterized by two features. The first feature is its deliberate and obvious invocation of signs, words, and persons that Sri Lankan audiences associate with Buddhism. What makes this discourse Buddhist is its display of dharma wheels, monks, bodhi trees, Buddhist flags, and so forth, and its use terms such as *dhamma* or *bauddha*. (The presence of saffron-robed monks also accomplishes this.) What makes this discourse nationalist is its regular conflation of Buddhism with the Sri Lankan people (as a nation, or *jātiya*), with the island of Sri Lanka (as a territory, or *raṭa*): Buddhist nationalist discourse assumes that it is Buddhists who constitute the proper Sri Lankan nation.
3. Alicia Marie Turner, *Saving Buddhism: The Impermanence of Religion in Colonial Burma* (Honolulu: University of Hawai'i Press, 2014), 28–34.
4. S. C. Berkwitz, "Religious Conflict and the Politics of Conversion in Sri Lanka," in *Proselytization Revisited: Rights Talk, Free Markets and Culture Wars*, ed. Rosalind I. J. Hackett (London: Equinox,

2008a). Ananda Abeysekara, *Colors of the Robe: Religion, Identity, and Difference* (Columbia: University of South Carolina Press, 2002).

5. George Bond, *The Buddhist Revival in Sri Lanka* (Columbia: University of South Carolina, 1988).
6. Steven Kemper, *Rescued From the Nation: Anagarika Dharmapala and the Buddhist World* (Chicago: University of Chicago, 2015). H. L. Seneviratne, *The Work of Kings: The New Buddhism in Sri Lanka* (Chicago: University of Chicago Press, 1999).
7. Bauddha Jatika Balavegaya, *Catholic Action: A Menace to Peace and Goodwill* (Colombo, Sri Lanka: The Bauddha Pracharaka Press, 1963), 117.
8. Ibid., 93, 144–150.
9. Donald L Horowitz, *Coup Theories and Officers' Motives: Sri Lanka in Comparative Perspective* (Princeton, NJ: Princeton University Press, 1980).
10. In an address delivered in 1956, Mettananda characterized the existing Christian-educated, Anglophone elite in government and the press as follows:

    "The sobriety, the restraint, the simplicity advocated by the Buddha are anathema to them. They stand for libertinism, sensuality and self—indulgence which are the keynote of the life in the decadent West. Lake House glorifies bookies, drunkards, dope dealers and other anti-social rogues while it loses no opportunity to ridicule national heroes, champions of temperance and defenders and promoters of Buddhism, Lake House is truly anti-national and anti-Buddhist." (*A Conspiracy Against Buddhism*, available at http://www.lhmettananda.com/wp-content/uploads/2014/02/A-Conspiracy-Against-Buddhism.pdf. Accessed January 5, 2015).

11. K. H. M. Sumathipala, *History of Education in Ceylon, 1796–1965* (Colombo, Sri Lanka: Tissa Prakasakayo, 1968), 313.
12. In this respect, the Balavegaya's position echoes that of many Buddhists following the assassination of the island's third Prime Minister, S. W. R. D. Bandaranaike, by a group of conspirators that included Buddhist monks. The position was that Buddhist groups should influence politics but not be directly involved parliamentary politics. This position would not endure. Donald Eugene Smith,

"Political Monks and Monastic Reform," in *South Asian Politics and Religion* (Princeton, NJ: Princeton University Press, 1966), 503.

13. N.a. "New Buddhist Union Formed," *World Buddhism*, April 1963, p. 16.
14. Ibid.
15. Catholic Union of Ceylon, *Catholic Action According to the Balavegaya* (Colombo: Senger Publications 1963). The BJB's publication was, in fact, a "reply" to an earlier publication put out by the Catholic Union, so one could also see this response as the third in a series.
16. Government of Ceylon, *Budha Śasana Komiṣan Vārtāva* [Buddha Sasana Commission Report] (Colombo: Government Press, 1959). D. C. Vaijayavardhana, *The Revolt in the Temple: Composed to Commemorate 2500 Years of the Land, the Race and the Faith* (Colombo, Sri Lanka: Sinha Publishers, 1953).
17. All-Ceylon Buddhist Congress, *Bauddha Toraturu Parīkṣaka Sabhāvē Vārtāva* (Colombo, Sri Lanka: Visidunu Prakāśanayaki, 2006 [1956]).
18. Interview May 3, 2009. For good general discussions of the JHU, see M. Deegalle, "Politics of the Jathika Hela Urumaya Monks: Buddhism and Ethnicity in Contemporary Sri Lanka," *Contemporary Buddhism* 5, no. 2 (2004): 83–103; Neil DeVotta and Jason Stone, "Jathika Hela Urumaya and Ethno-religious Politics in Sri Lanka," *Pacific Affairs* 81 (2008): 31–51.
19. N.a. "'JHU will not help any party to form new govt,'" *Daily Mirror*, April 5, 2004.
20. Shan Wijethunge, *Sangha Power! Discussion Led by Shan Wijethunge with the Venerables Who Registered for the Sri Lankan Polls on Feb 24, 2004* (2004), available at http://www.jathikahelaurumaya.lk/index.php?prm=subnews&snews=news_item_20040224. Accessed March 24, 2012.
21. Matthews, Cyril. *Diabolical Conspiracy* Dematagoda, Sri Lanka: n.p., 1980, 6.
22. See Sarath Amunugama, "Buddhaputra and Bhumiputra?," *Religion* 21 (1991): 115–139. P. Schalk, "Unity and Sovereignty: Key Concepts of a Militant Buddhist Organization in Sri Lanka MSV, Movement for the Protection of the Motherland," *Temenos* 24 (1988): 55–87.

23. K. N. O. Dharmadasa, "Buddhism and Politics in Modern Sri Lanka," in *Bhikshauwa Saha Lankā Samājeya*, eds. Maduwave Sobhita, Kamburugoda Sorata, and Mendis Rohandeera (Colombo, Sri Lanka: Dharmaduthasrāma Pirivena, 1997), 232.
24. *Jātika-chintanaya* intellectuals organized themselves through political organizations as well, such as the National Movement Against Terrorism and the *Sihala Urumaya*.
25. Berkwitz, "Religious Conflict."
26. Deegalle, "Politics of the Jathika," 95.
27. Dushy Ranetunge, "The Muslim Problem?," *The Island*, August 24, 2008, http://www.island.lk/2008/08/24/features11.html. Accessed January 14, 2015.
28. James John Stewart, "Muslim–Buddhist Conflict in Contemporary Sri Lanka," *South Asia Research* 34 (2014): 241–260.
29. http://www.bodubalasena.com/sinhala/daekma[daekmainSinhalascript]/. Accessed December 2013 (now defunct).
30. Deegalle, "Politics of the Jathika," 96.
31. N. S. Tennekoon, "Rituals of Development: The Accelerated Mahaväli Development Program of Sri Lanka," *American Ethnologist* 15 (1988): 294–310.
32. Interview with Dilanthe Withanage, January 9, 2014.
33. Samaratunge, Shilpa, and Sanjana Hattotuwa. *Liking Violence: A Study of Hate Speech on Facebook in Sri Lanka*. (Colombo, Sri Lanka: Centre for Policy Alternatives, 2014).
34. See, e.g., Edirisinghe, Dasun, "Law College Registrations Put Off by One Week," *The Island*, January 8, 2013, available at http://www.island.lk/index.php?page_cat=article-details&page=article-details&code_title=69977 (Accessed March 15, 2016).
35. For a thorough analysis of the BBS's neoliberal criticism of Sri Lankan Muslims, see Farzana Haniffa, "The Economy of Profit and the Economy of Merit: Halal Troubles in Post-war Sri Lanka," in *Religion and the Morality of Markets*, eds. Rudnyckyj D. & F. Osella (Forthcoming, Cambridge University Press).
36. Interview with Dilanthe Withanage, January 9, 2014.
37. Evangelical Christians only constitute a small percentage, perhaps 10%, of the island's Christian community less than 1% of the total population.

CHAPTER FIVE

GOSSIP, RUMOR, AND PROPAGANDA IN ANTI-MUSLIM CAMPAIGNS OF THE BODU BALA SENA

Kalinga Tudor Silva

The Bodu Bala Sena (BBS) evolved in the aftermath of the military victory of the Government of Sri Lanka over the Liberation Tigers of Tamil Eelam (LTTE) in 2009. In the backdrop of the Sinhala Buddhist nationalist triumph during the "war against terror," the BBS may be seen as a rabble-rousing effort aimed at targeting the Muslim minority, identifying them as a new threat to the economic, social, and cultural interests of the Sinhala Buddhist ethnic majority in the country. In spite of the social harmony that prevailed between Sinhala Buddhists and Muslims over a long historical period and the numerous social and cultural exchanges between the two communities (Dewaraja 1994), the BBS has managed to identify the Muslim community as a villain and a scapegoat because of their visible urban presence, particularly in trade, commerce, and religious landscapes and their apparent clannish tendency, inclination for residential segregation, and the newly adopted *hijab, niqab*, and *purdah* as distinctive dress codes among Muslim women. In this chapter, I analyze the propaganda that the BBS has deployed in mass public rallies and in electronic media such as Facebook; I also focus on the role of gossip and rumor triggered by the official propaganda of the organization in shaping ethnic hatred and promoting social tension and ethnic riots in postwar Sri Lanka. Although recognizing the crucial role played by the BBS in inciting the Sinhala Buddhist public, we cannot disregard a possible predisposition among sections of the Sinhala Buddhist public toward accepting these extremist views and believing some of the vicious rumors that have no factual basis whatsoever. Therefore, the BBS is not merely an isolated and opportunist actor playing on Sinhala Buddhist sensitivities but rather an extreme manifestation of ethnic and religious polarization in postwar Sri Lanka.

Bodu Bala Sena

The formal establishment of the BBS occurred on May 7, 2012.[1] Its leadership comes from certain Colombo-based Buddhist monks who also seem to have considerable international connections. The organization was reportedly set up by these monks following a visit to Norway sponsored by the Norwegian embassy in Colombo. During this visit, they apparently met some representatives of the Tamil diaspora in Norway, reportedly for bringing about reconciliation between war-affected communities in Sri Lanka. The actual orientation of the new organization, however, turned out to be totally antireconciliatory vis-à-vis ethnic and religious minorities in the country. Apart from one lay member who is also designated as the lay coordinator of the organization, all the other persons in the Executive Committee of the organization are Buddhist monks, typically with their origin in the deep south of Sri Lanka, a region well known for generating militant Sinhala Buddhist tendencies. Its composition is understood along traditional lines: *bhikkhu* (monks) and *bhikkhuni* (nuns), and *upasaka* (male lay devotees) and *upasika* (female lay devotees). Among its founding leaders are Rev. Kirama Wimalajothi and Rev. Galagoda Aththe Gnanasara who had broken away from the Jathika Hela Urumaya (JHU) on the grounds that it was not militant enough in protecting Buddhism. Thus, the BBS clearly represents a trajectory of political monks who have attempted increasingly to politicize Buddhism as a rallying point for the protection of the Sinhala Buddhist ethnic majority in Sri Lanka over the past several decades (Gombrich and Obeyesekere 1988; Seneviratne 1999).

The headquarters of the BBS, literally "Buddhist Defense Force," are located at Sri Sambuddha Jayanthi Mandira in Colombo. Sri Sambuddha Jayanthi Mandira is owned by the Buddhist Cultural Centre, an organization also founded by Kirama Wimalajothi. The center is replete with multiple facilities including a venue for conferences, modern offices for administration, and a well-stocked book store containing many publications from Sri Lanka and abroad about Buddhism. The center was ceremonially opened by President Mahinda Rajapaksa on May 15, 2011. Reportedly, the organization is funded by contributions from the Buddhist public. The organization has important links with Sinhala businessmen in Colombo as well as with Sinhala diaspora organizations in Australia, New Zealand, Singapore, Malaysia, Europe, and North America.

The demographic landscape of Colombo city is such that the central areas, including the central business district, is dominated by ethnic minorities, namely, Muslims and Tamils; whereas the expanding suburban areas such as Maharagama, Homagama, and Pilyandala are numerically dominated by Sinhala Buddhists who control much of public sector employment, professions, and some small businesses on the urban fringe. Sri Lanka may be seen as a classic case of the conflict between "market dominant ethnic minorities," such as Muslims, and a politically powerful ethnic majority, namely, Sinhala Buddhists. According to Amy Chua, in many cases, "[m]arkets concentrate wealth, often spectacular wealth, in the hands of a market dominant minority, while democracy increases the political power of the impoverished majority" (Chua 2004: 6). As can be expected the BBS, JHU, and other Sinhala Buddhist organizations have a greater presence in the Sinhala concentrations in the urban fringe.

Until the presidential election of 2015, the BBS avoided any direct involvement in politics. They did, however, support Rajapaksa as the presidential candidate in the 2015 election, claiming that the Rajapaksa campaign was more aligned with Sinhala Buddhist interests. The BBS, however, held the view that political parties are more interested in the short-term aim of gaining power for themselves rather than in long-term welfare of the Sinhala Buddhist majority in the country. Although they had strong contacts with the ruling political alliance at the time and some other political parties in and outside the parliament, they have had the freedom to criticize selected political groupings within and outside the ruling government, and they have taken some controversial polemical positions that they would be unable to take if they were part of the established political order. Whereas their campaigns are clearly political in nature, it is significant that they seek to posture themselves outside of existing political parties to avoid any limitations and strategic restrictions resulting from such affiliations. Ideologically and organizationally, the BBS has some affinities with Shiv Sena and Vishwa Hindu Parshad in India. There is, however, no evidence of any links between the BBS and such organizations in India.

The BBS convened its first national convention at the Bandaranaike Memorial International Conference Hall on July 28, 2012. The convention passed five resolutions that called for a ban on vasectomy and tubectomy operations in government health facilities, replacement of the various and diverse legal systems used in the country with a single legal system, preferential treatment in university admission for students who have attended Buddhism Sunday School classes, recruitment of monks for government schools to teach history and other classes, and the prevention of any proposed solution for the country's ethnic problem that is based on race or religion.

Structural Features of the BBS

From the preceding account, several important features of the campaigns by the BBS can be identified.

First, the BBS is illiberal or antiliberal in its orientation, as it clearly campaigns against multiculturalism, recognition of diversity, democracy, and human rights. Although some nationalisms can be liberal in outlook, as pointed out by Herr (2006), ethnonationalisms are typically illiberal, antiliberal, or nonliberal. From the propaganda and activities of BBS, it is clear that it identifies Sri Lanka as a Sinhala Buddhist country with limited political, social, and economic space for ethnic and religious minorities. It has taken an explicitly anti-Muslim posture in response to the rise of Islamic consciousness in recent decades, an Islamic consciousness largely due to the influence of the global rise of Islamic identity. Even though it has articulated some anti-Tamil and anti-Christian slogans as well, it has not felt the need to campaign against Tamils in Colombo and in other cities, given the low profile that Tamils have maintained politically, socially, and economically in the postwar era.

Second, the BBS presents itself as a moral police force with a responsibility for direct interventions whenever they feel there is reportedly immoral conduct or threats for moral integrity and monoculture of the Sinhala–Buddhist nation. They have been directly involved in raids of various kinds, sometimes with the participation of the police and media reporters. This shows that they have established some rapport and understanding with the police forces, making it difficult for any victims of these raids to seek protection from the police or to seek legal redress of any kind. Apparently through its highly publicized interactions with the President of Sri Lanka at the time and with his brother, the Secretary of the Ministry of Defense, the BBS gained a degree of immunity from possible interference from the police and other security forces, even when it engaged in the promotion of ethnic and religious hatred and acts of violence such as throwing stones at a foreign mission or violent anti-Muslim demonstrations in front of a Muslim business.

Third, a good part of its campaign has been directed against Muslim clothing shops while openly advocating Sinhala Buddhist customers to patronize only Sinhala-owned shops. The campaign has been not against "infidel brands," as in some Islamic countries (Izberk-Bilgin 2012), but against "infidel shops" identified as threats to Sinhala consumers. It has tried to reinforce the campaign against Muslim shops by spreading harmful rumors, such as these shops reportedly selling contraceptive laden panties or distributing free candy with contraceptive effects, all purportedly with a view to reduce the fertility of Sinhala women. Given the fact that a majority of customers in Muslim-owned shops are Sinhalese due to the demographic profile of the country, as well as due to the limited demand for fancy clothing sold in these shops from Muslim women who are compelled to adopt purdah, such campaigns can be expected to have a substantial effect on the sales in Muslim-owned shops. It is also significant that this campaign against Muslim shops started prior to the Sinhala and Tamil New Year in mid-April 2013, the period of peak sales for new clothing due to the practice of exchanging of New Year gifts and the customary wearing of new clothes by Sinhala and Tamil persons during and after the New Year festival.

Gossip and Rumor as Part of the Ideological Apparatus of the BBS

Gossip refers to interpersonal oral transmission of rumor that is unverified and potentially explosive information designed to differentiate, discredit, and demonize a perceived enemy. Gossip operates within existing social networks that validate and enhance its potency and at the same time limit its circulation to known parties. As Anjan Gosh claims, "Oral transmission is characteristic of rumor. Yet speech can also be embedded and embodied in print and other mediums" (2008: 1237–1238). With the emergence of Facebook, Twitter, mobile phones, and other forms of social media, gossip and rumor have received a new lease on life and an ability to fast-track the slow process of information flows typically associated with word of mouth. Whereas the public face of the BBS has been shaped by printed and electronic media, the movement has turned to gossip and rumor disseminated through word of mouth and social media in its efforts to influence and to provoke the Sinhala public vis-à-vis the Muslim minority in particular. In many ways, the BBS has transformed Sinhala Buddhist nationalism into a militant version of long-distance nationalism[2] transmitted simultaneously through word of mouth, print and electronic media, and social media in general.

Social-psychological investigations of the role of rumor in collective violence have highlighted how rumors are inherently generative of prejudices, negative stereotypes, and hatreds that, in turn, trigger outbreaks of collective violence in populations divided by race, ethnicity, and social origin. Allport and Postman go to the extent of stating that "'No riot ever occurs without rumors to incite, accompany and intensify the violence" (1965: 159). The rumors actually build on and intensify existing prejudices in a community in ways that provoke intolerance, hatred, and retaliatory violence. In a series of studies conducted on ethnic violence in Burundi, Congo, and Rwanda, it was found that rumors flourish in times of crisis, war, and moral panic in society (International Alert 2008). The buildup of negative stereotypes about the "ethnic other" is a precursor to, and at the same time an outcome of, violence. Based on the results of this study, International Alert argued that to promote mutual trust among various ethnic communities, the authorities must remove existing communication barriers between communities divided by languages, religious traditions, and political and spatial boundaries.

In contrast to the social-psychological perspective, the subaltern school has recently argued that rumors are generated by subaltern groups in their efforts to challenge the hegemonic world view represented by social elites (Gosh 2008). In Guha's words, rumor can be understood as "insurgent communication" (1983: 253). In analyzing peasant rebellions in colonial India, Guha argued that rumor served as an essential trigger and mobilizer of rebel action against colonial rule buttressed not only by heavily armed well-trained armies but also by official representations of reality in public statements, mass media, and religious interpretations. In this perspective, rumor has been identified as a weapon of the weak for the peasantry in their rebellions against ruling elites with entrenched interests in preserving the status quo.

The deploying of rumor by the BBS, however, is more in line with the social-psychological perspective in that it serves to promote hatred toward the "ethnic other" in the Sinhala Buddhist nationalist consciousness also driven and sustained by organs of a triumphalist state given to celebrate its military victory over the LTTE.

BBS Propaganda, Social Media, and Rumor

BBS official propaganda are carried out through widely publicized and well-attended public rallies, its website, printed publications, and raids on so-called anti-Buddhist establishments usually in front of television cameras. Social media, including Facebook and Twitter, are mobilized by sympathizers of the BBS to disseminate selected hate messages that usually target Muslims and evangelical Christian groups. The hate messages, especially those causing moral panic among people with Sinhala–Buddhist sensitivities, are often further intensified and made potentially explosive through gossip and rumor directly or indirectly triggered by BBS official propaganda. The transformation from facts to fantasies, from neutral information to ethnic prejudices and hatreds, and from mere characterizations to negative stereotypes can be exemplified by considering BBS propaganda in respect of selected issues.

BBS Concerns about Potential Demographic Threats Facing the Sinhalese

Fear of the potential extinction of the "Sinhala race" in light of what is perceived as a disproportionate natural increase and expansion of certain minority ethnic groups has been an important concern of certain brands of Sinhala nationalism for a long time (DeVotta 2007). This has resulted in various campaigns against the practice of family planning, conversion, and interethnic marriages among the Sinhalese. This theme was the focus of a BBS publication in Sinhala titled "Approaching the Extinction of a Race (*Wamsayaka Vinasaya Abimuwa*): Contemporary Population Trends in the Sinhala Land (Sinhale)" (Liyanage 2014). Attributed to the Educational and Research arm of the BBS, this publication sought to analyze population trends in the country from 1881 to 2012, using census statistics, essentially from a Sinhala–Buddhist angle. Through a highly selective reading of census information, anecdotal evidence of the researchers, speculative reasoning, and building on the legacy of the Anagarika Dharmapala,[3] this document highlights the slow population growth rate of Sinhalese as compared to the Muslims. Accordingly to the data presented, the proportion of Sinhala population in Sri Lanka increased from 66.91% in 1881 to 74.88% in 2012, with corresponding changes in Tamil population from 24.9% to 15.37%, and the Muslim population from 6.69% to 9.23%.

Through a questionable deployment of the percentage population increase, the document argues that the relative increase of Muslim population in the relevant period is more substantial when compared to the Sinhalese given their respective baseline situations. Completely disregarding the more substantial drop in Tamil population from 1881 to 2012, the publication highlights the reported increase in Muslim population as an unusual and alarming demographic trend. The national-level analysis of demographic trends is buttressed by selective analysis of district-level information that indicates a substantial increase in Muslim population in districts such as Ampara, Puttalam, Trincomale, and Vavuniya. What is not reported in this analysis is that there was an ethnic cleansing of Muslims from the Northern Province by the LTTE in 1990, compelling them to concentrate in certain districts for safety reasons. Further, the analysis of population composition of the Colombo Divisional Secretary area indicates that Muslims and Tamils together form a numerical majority vis-à-vis the Sinhalese. Anecdotal evidence gathered by the BBS researchers from selected locations further indicates an alarming population increase (*buruthpitin vadivenawa*) of Muslims in traditional Sinhala areas. The document finally claims, with no empirical foundation whatsoever, that Muslims may become the ethnic majority in Sri Lanka in time to come, paving the way for "the extinction of the Sinhala race."[4]

> Various opinions have been expressed to the effect that Musalmans will overcome the Sinhalese due to existing patterns of population growth in time to come. Some say it will happen in 2040 and others say it will happen in 2081. The population projections are not consistent in the way they forecast the future of the Sri Lankan population. *The basic truth is that Muslims are propagating at an unprecedented rate.* This miserable development and misfortune will not happen overnight. But we have to be alert to this possibility and the resulting political reality. (Liyanage 2014: 10; emphasis added)

Following this diagnosis, the BBS raided some family planning services and instructed the government of Mahinda Rajapaksa to prevent the NGOs from performing ligation and resection of tubes (LRT) on women, claiming that it is deliberately designed for reducing the size of "the Sinhala race." Subsequently, the government did indeed instruct the Medical Officers of Health to temporarily stop dispensation of permanent birth control devices in their respective areas (Wijenayake 2014).

The BBS declarations on population trends also triggered some vicious rumors directly targeting the Muslim-owned textile chains. For instance, one rumor held that certain Muslim clothing chains deliberately sell contraceptive-embedded underwear and freely distribute sweets with contraceptive affects to Sinhala women with the aim of making them barren and facilitating the extinction of the Sinhala race (Amarakeerthi 2013). Quite apart from the possible implications of this rumor for textile sales in the relevant business chains, this rumor also conveys the view that just like family planning NGOs, Muslim-owned businesses are part of an international conspiracy to bring down the Sinhala population.

Antipolitics of the BBS

The BBS has refused to identify itself with any existing political parties on the grounds that they have a higher goal than gaining power for themselves in their effort to fight for the rights of Sinhala Buddhists. In January 8, 2015, presidential campaign, they supported Mahinda Rajapaksa, confirming that the BBS had some understanding with the ruling regime at the time. This was further evident as the BBS activities seem to have been substantially reduced following the regime change in Sri Lanka. Muslim political parties were particularly targeted in the official propaganda of BBS. The document "Approaching the Extinction of a Race," for instance, argued that the Muslims followed a strategy of soft invasion initially by strategically aligning with mainstream national political parties. Later they established exclusive Muslim parties such as the All Ceylon Muslim Front and the Sri Lanka Muslim Congress that campaigned for Muslim rights within a unified Sri Lanka. The document argued that Muslim ministers who had a disproportionate power in coalition governments used their political power to reward the Muslims. For instance, when a Muslim politician became the Minster of Ports, it is alleged that he recruited some 12,000 Muslims as port workers. Similarly when a Muslim became the Minister of Justice, he reportedly recruited a disproportionate number of Muslim students to the Law College. BBS sympathizers also carried this information in their Facebook pages, giving wide publicity to this news. On January 7, 2013, the BBS stormed Sri Lanka Law College in Hultsdorf, Colombo, alleging that the admission examination results were being distorted in favor of Muslim students. The allegations were proved to be wrong, but the college was forced to delay new student registration by one week to investigate the allegations.

Selected Facebook entries circulated in 2013 targeting specific Muslim politicians are as follows:

45, Vijaya Mawatha Wattala land owned by Mahasangha being claimed by the Muslim mayor in the town by dumping waste in a low-lying area surrounding this land

Court-order obtained by Anti-Buddhist municipal authorities to demolish a structure owned by a Buddhist temple in Kolonnawa

Here is interreligious reconciliation! Muslim politicians in the East have distributed some 2500 acres of crown land among Muslims in the guise of resettling internally displaced.

Rishard Badiudeen [a Muslim cabinet minister in the Rajapaksa regime] engaged in clearing of a forest in Mulaitivu in the name of religious reconciliation.

I am unable to determine if these statements are true. Whether they are true or not, these statements have the effect of overgeneralizing and negative stereotyping of all Muslim politicians in the eyes of the Sinhala public. Further, they completely disregard the fact that there may be Sinhala and other politicians who are equally responsible for similar or greater misuses of power.

Among the political rumors disseminated widely by word of mouth, but nevertheless aligned with BBS propaganda, were those identified as "hard invasions" in the official documents of the BBS. For instance, the reported presence of armed Muslim groups in eastern Sri Lanka preparing for a LTTE-style separatist war had considerable traction in some Sinhala Buddhist circles. Similarly, Muslim politicians with links to the underworld and drug dealers were reportedly engaged in a viciously deliberate campaign to promote substance abuse among Sinhala and Tamil youth. This kind of rumor is likely to trigger ethnic hatred in the Sinhala community toward Muslim politicians and leaders of the Muslim underworld in general.

Campaigns against Market Monopolies of Muslim Traders

Even though the BBS presents itself ostensibly as a religiously inspired movement, Muslim business groups were the targets of many of its campaigns.

The significance of Muslims as a market-dominant, ethnic minority entrenched in selected urban centers in the South, including Colombo, may be partly responsible for this trend. BBS propaganda particularly turned against Muslim monopolies in the textile trade, financial markets, overseas employment and recruitment agencies, and the sale of electronic goods. Land grabbing by Muslims from Sinhala and Tamil owners and the refusal of Muslims to sell their property outside of their ethnic group were important concerns of Sinhala Buddhist nationalists for many years (DeVotta 2007; Jayawardena 1983). It is interesting how the official report of the BBS discussed earlier tried to connect the reported population expansion of the Muslim population to their expansion of trade monopolies:

> According to current population trends, the end result will be the Sinhalese becoming an inactive work force having sold their immobile assets to the Musalmans. With the help of overseas capital Musalmans will take control over the financial markets and business enterprises currently held by the Sinhalese. In the agricultural sector ownership of most of the paddy land and other productive lands will be transferred to the Muslamans. Muslims will gradually enhance their ownership of Rice Mills and Post-Harvest Technology. In the rest of the economy many of the processing industries and services too will be increasingly controlled by the Muslim entrepreneurs. (Liyanage 2014: 9)

The gossip and rumor disseminated by Facebook entries of the BBS supporters and sympathizers gave publicity to reported sexual abuse of female Sinhala workers employed in Muslim-owned enterprises. The BBS demanded that Sinhala women should not work in Muslim-owned establishments to preserve their self-respect. The Muslim-owned Fashion Bug clothing store in Pepiliyana, Colombo District, was attacked on March 28, 2013, by a mob led by Buddhist monks sporting mobile phones. Some reports suggested that the BBS was behind the attack. The BBS denied any involvement and condemned the attack. Prior to the attack, a rumor had spread that a Muslim boy employed in the establishment had raped an underage Sinhala girl working in the same establishment with whom he had a love affair; and this rumor had reportedly precipitated the attack. Later, some persons, including several Buddhist monks reportedly involved in the attack, were arrested and produced in court. An out-of-court settlement was eventually reached between the suspected attackers and the shop owners reportedly through the intervention of some Buddhist and Muslim leaders as well as the police to prevent any further escalation of religious tension.

The BBS openly advocated that the Sinhala customers should avoid patronizing Muslim shops. Incidentally, this coincided with the Sinhala and Tamil New Year period in 2013, the time of the year when new clothing is purchased by both Sinhalese and Tamils. These are some of the related Facebook entries:

> Sinhalese with uncontaminated Sinhala blood avoid patronizing the following Muslim dens (*tambi gubbayam*) for new-year shopping for cloths: Nolimit, FashionBug, Hameediya, Pallu, Glitz, Cool Planet!
>
> Visit Richlook which is a clothing shop run by our [Sinhala Buddhist] people

This campaign was expected to take business away from Muslim shops. Although this may have actually happened to some extent in 2013, this certainly did not force the relevant businesses to close down.

Protests against Cultural Invasions by the Muslims

The BBS attacked "cultural invasions" by Muslims on several fronts. The widespread building of new mosques, usually with overseas funding, was seen as one manifestation of the cultural invasion by Muslims. For instance, a report on "Approaching the Extinction of a Race" noted

> In a country where the Buddhist make up 71% of the total population there are only 9800 temples. On the other hand, 10% of the population who are Muslims reportedly have 6,300 mosques. (Liyanage 2014: 3)

In February 2013, a BBS leader, Rev. Kirama Wimalajothi, called for a ban on *burkha*s and the *abaya* identifying them as symbols of Islamic fundamentalism recently imposed on Muslim women by the Islamic establishment in Sri Lanka.

The widely publicized BBS campaign against halal food was yet another front of the campaign against cultural invasions by the Muslims. In February 2013, the BBS launched a campaign against the halal certification system in the country. In Sri Lanka, halal certification had been initiated by the All Ceylon Jammiyatul Ulama (ACJU), a group of Islamic clerics. The BBS initially threatened to take the ACJU to court. Later they threatened to launch a campaign of agitation against halal certification, stating "they [the Muslims] are trying to impose their ritualistic food products upon this country. The next plan is to bring about Sharia Law. Already there is a Muslim banking system in the country." At the public rally in Maharagama held on February 17, 2013, the BBS announced that it was calling for the abolition of the halal certification system, demanding that shops be cleared of halal meat by April. Further, it was claimed that halal certification that applied to various products other than food (e.g., paint brushes, clothing, and fancy goods) added to the costs of the products and that it was unfair that non-Islamic consumers too had to bear this additional cost. Also it was mentioned that the profits made through halal certification were used to finance Islamic fundamentalist activities in Sri Lanka and abroad.

In late February 2013, the ACJU offered to hand over the responsibility for halal certification to the government. This was flatly rejected by the BBS who called for the complete eradication of halal certification in the country. The BBS slammed the ACJU as "arrogant, corrupt, thieving, underworld thugs." The government also refused to take over halal certification due to the pressure exerted by the BBS.

Further expanding its moral policing functions, the BBS stormed a meat inspection facility in Dematagoda run by the Colombo Municipal Council (CMC) on March 1, 2013, alleging that young calves, pregnant cows, and water buffaloes were being slaughtered on the premises. The slaughter of calves is illegal in Colombo. The claim that the place was a slaughterhouse was found to be wrong. The premises were being used by CMC officials to inspect meat prior to its distribution around the city. Also, no concrete evidence was found to support the claim that the meat was from calves, pregnant animals, or buffaloes.

Through the mediation of some Sinhala and Muslim politicians connected with the government, meetings were held between the ACJU, the Ceylon Chamber of Commerce (CCC), and Buddhist clergy; and on March 11, 2013, a compromise was announced. The ACJU would stop adding the halal logo on products for local consumption but continue to use them for products being exported to Islamic countries where it is compulsory. This offer was also rejected by the BBS who continued to demand "the eradication of the entire Halal process." The BBS went on to attack those responsible for the compromise. They accused Milinda Moragoda, a former government minister, of "creating an unholy inter-religious alliance, and attempting to destroy our learned monks. These revered bhikkus are now in the grasp of infidels." They branded the Buddhist clergy as "pseudo Buddhist leaders who never stood against Muslim extremism and Christian fundamentalism." Further, they accused the Colombo Chamber of Commerce chairman for having a "Buddha bar" at a hotel he runs.

The government pronounced on March 13, 2013, that the ACJU had no authority to issue halal certificates and that a new way to certify halal products would need to be formulated. On March 17, 2013, the BBS finally declared victory in its battle against halal, saying it would not bring out the halal issue any longer.

The BBS gave wide publicity to allegations regarding encroachments by Muslims on historic sacred Buddhist sites in several locations in Sri Lanka, including Dighavapi,[5] Dambulla, Devanagala, and Kuragala. This was seen as a deliberate attempt by the Muslims to destroy the cultural heritage of the Sinhala Buddhist native sons of the soil. BBS activists sought to marshal a multiplicity of evidence, including folklore, historical consciousness, historical evidence, legal provisions, and archeological findings to protect these sacred sites against the so-called Muslim invasions. This can be illustrated by examining the dispute over Devanagala.

Devanagala rock is located 6 km from Mawanella town on the way to Hemmathagama some 14 km to the west of Mawanella. The rock, which is roughly about 20 acres in extent, has several Buddhist monuments including a *stupa, bodhi* tree, a pond, a rock cave, a monastery, a Vishnu *devalaya*, and a preaching hall. There are two inscriptions on the rock, one dating back to 11th century CE and the other from the Kandyan period. The inscription dating back to the 11th century Polonnaruwa period refers to the granting of a village by Parakramabahu the Great (r. 1153–1183) for one of his military chiefs in recognition of his success in a war fought by the king in Myanmar. The Kandyan period inscription also refers to a land grant in the village of Ruwandeniya by King Vimaladharmasuriya (r. 1592–1604) for a Buddhist monk who had helped the king to achieve kingship. The Buddhist temple at Devanagala, widely referred to as Devanagala Rajamaha Viharaya in the recent BBS propaganda,[6] was occupied by monks from time to time, but there were no resident monks in the temple in recent years due to the hardships faced because of its location on the top of the rock. The rock was declared by the state as an archeological site in 2004 by a gazette notification. Initially an area of 200 m from the boundary of the rock was declared as a buffer zone. The extent of the buffer zone was extended to 400 m from the edge of the rock in 2005. The boundary of this buffer zone, however, was not determined through a land survey and the formal establishment of boundary markers.

Devanagala rock is surrounded by several villages, some of which are predominantly Muslim and the others predominantly Sinhala. The upkeep of the temple on the rock has been under the custody of a Buddhist temple in nearby Ruwandeniya village. Following the declaration of the Devanagala rock as an archeological site and the accompanying declaration of a buffer zone, the Muslim and Buddhist residents adjoining the rock, many of whom had legal title to the land they occupied, came under the buffer zone, with the possibility of being evicted from the land they had occupied for many generations.

Traditionally Sinhalese and Muslims in the Mawanella area had many social, cultural, and economic exchanges between them. According to folklore, the Muslims had been settled in the area by the royal family in Kandy in recognition of their services to the palace, including transport services, medical services by traditional Muslim practitioners, and the establishment and maintenance of a royal orchard in the area. Muslim traders from Mawanella and Hemmathagama visited nearby Sinhala villagers for the collection of spices grown in the villages, and Mawanella became an important urban center largely controlled by Muslim traders who supplied commodities to small shops in surrounding villages. The Muslims also became important patrons of some of the leading Buddhist temples in the area, with there being mutual trust between the communities. Some ethnic tension, however, has broken out in the area from 1950s onward over issues such as love affairs across the ethnic divide, land disputes, and economic competition in general.

A major ethnic riot erupted in Mawanella in 2001 when some Sinhala ruffians with political backing attacked Muslim shop keepers when they refused to pay protection money demanded from them. The police aligned with Sinhala interests, and subdued by local politicians, did not investigate the matter swiftly. The resulting clashes led to one murder, many injuries, and the burning of Muslim-owned shops. The ethnic tension, however, was gradually diffused through the mediation of Sinhala and Muslim community leaders, including Buddhist monks and Muslim Mawlavis.

The BBS and three other organizations directly or indirectly affiliated with the BBS, namely, Sinhala Ravaya, Maitree Sahana Padanama, and Parakum Sena, became involved in the Devanagala issue from 2012 onward. Coming from Colombo and other outstations, they persuaded Buddhist monks in the area to demand the eviction of Muslim residents in the vicinity of the rock, but excluding the Sinhala Buddhists residents also within the designated buffer zone. Further, using a land survey conducted in 1876, Maitree Sahana Padanama claimed that the Devanagala site should actually be of 72 acres and 3 roods[7] in extent (*Maitree Sahana Padanama* 2013a). A new organization called the National Movement for Defending Devanagala was formed. This organization released statements to the press referring to an invasion of the Devanagala Buddhist sacred site by Muslims. A printed notice distributed by Maitree Sahana Padanama among local Buddhists and Muslims declared that "[t]he sinful Muslims who are killers of cows and eaters of beef should immediately move out of the Devanagala sacred Buddhist site" (*Maitree Sahana Padanama* 2013b). It also demanded patriotic Sinhala Buddhists to be ready to sacrifice their lives for defending their national heritage. These messages received wide publicity through electronic and printed media and Facebook. Due to pressure from these various lobbies, the Department of Archeology conducted a survey of Devanagala. The resulting report, prepared without consulting the Sinhala and Muslim residents in the area, recommended that the total land area of 72 acres and 3 roods should be demarcated and that the residents in the designated area should be relocated. This report had been released to the BBS and affiliated organizations, and they, in turn, used it for strengthening their campaign for the eviction of Muslim residents in the area, even though the report clearly included all residents in the demarcated area irrespective of their ethnicity and religion.

The Muslims in the area were deeply disturbed by these developments and sought the help of the local Muslim leaders including politicians to safeguard what they saw as their legitimate property rights. An organization called Mawanella Friendship Association was formed under the leadership of Sinhala and Muslim leaders for diffusing the situation. This organization conducted its own research on Devanagala and, based on the information that they gathered, argued that the 72 acres and 3 roods of land referred to in the report issued by the Archeology Department is in a nearby Ruwandeniya village and not in Devanagala (Gamage 2014). The Mawanella Friendship Association tried to involve the Maha Sangha and Muslim religious leaders for reaching a negotiated settlement; and as of 2015, such a settlement had not been reached. In the meantime, the Mawanella Friendship Association came under heavy criticism from the BBS, which identified the Sinhala leaders involved as traitors to the Sinhala nation.

Some rumors spread in the local Sinhala community claimed that the local Muslims had tried to blast the Devanagala rock. They used some white substance evident in cracks in the rock as proof of a Muslim effort to blast the rock. The Mawanella Friendship Association consulted a geologist on this issue, and his opinion was that the white substance was a chemical compound that is normally found in cracks in such rock formations. Similarly, it was alleged that some Muslims in the area had reportedly removed the moonstones in the rock and had planted them in their own houses.

This case illustrates how the involvement of the BBS and its affiliated organizations served to fuel and intensify ethnic tension in the area. It also shows how the state's actions, including declaration of Devanagala as an archeological site and the survey conducted by the Archeology Department, created space for BBS-like organizations to intervene and transform the situation in light of their nationwide campaign against Muslims, even though both Sinhala and Muslim people lived in the vicinity of the archeological site. If there is to be an invasion on this site, it is not a Muslim invasion on a Buddhist site, but rather it will be invasion by landless peasants in the area irrespective of their ethnic background. The information base related to this dispute, including the rumors, have emerged in a context where the state, the Department of Archeology, mass media, and the legal system in general appear to work in unison toward marginalizing ethnic minorities in their struggle for survival and the preservation of their separate identities.

Conclusion

BBS propaganda and related gossip and rumor examined in this chapter reinforce each other in ways that impact Sinhala perceptions vis-à-vis the Muslim community. Whereas many of the BBS assertions relating to demographic, political, economic, and cultural threats from the Muslims do not have a robust factual basis, as pointed out in this chapter, nevertheless they may further convince the already converted Sinhala Buddhists because of their existing prejudices, uncritical acceptance of the information presented, and a lack of access to alternative sources of authoritative information. The widespread acceptance of Sinhala–Buddhist nationalism as the official ideology of the state has enabled the BBS to plant its more biased statements in the imagination of certain cohorts of Sinhala–Buddhist nationalists. This, in turn, has triggered gossip and rumor that incite Sinhala mob reaction at the street level, targeting Muslims in particular. Thus the BBS is not an isolated development as such but rather a reflection of entrenched prejudices and misunderstandings in society. Its campaigns serve to harden ethnic prejudices and to convert them to ethnic hatreds and hostilities.

The emergence of the BBS in the postwar era in Sri Lanka indicates that ethnic polarization and hostilities in the country remain unresolved in spite of the end of the war. The victory celebrations of the state merely served to hype the triumphalist feelings in the Sinhala population without giving a chance for all parties to reflect on factors that gave rise to the war in the first place, as well as the challenges lying ahead for a war-torn society. The BBS took advantage of this situation to target the Muslim community, which itself was becoming increasingly visible and assertive in response to domestic and international pressures (McGilvray 2008).

The propaganda machine of the BBS cannot be easily countered due to its entrenched character and the sociopolitical environment in the country. Legislation making it unlawful to propagate hate messages as proposed by Vasudeva Nanayakkara, the Minister of National Integration at the time, may not be very effective insofar as gossip and rumor typically operate under the radar. A more effective approach may be to support and facilitate interethnic organizations and lobby groups such as the Mawanella Friendship Association (Gamage 2014). Legal interventions, however, may be essential for preventing organizations like the BBS from taking the law into their own hands by carrying out raids on Muslim-owned businesses and other establishments. Regarding inaccurate and biased information disseminated through social media, some mechanism must be developed for promoting social media that seeks to enhance mutual understanding and trust across ethnic and religious divides.

NOTES

1. This account of the BBS is largely based on newspaper reports about the organization in Sinhala and English media. This part of the chapter is adapted from a paper by the author on "Rival Nationalisms,

Collective Violence and Discourse of Entitlement in Urban Sri Lanka," presented in a workshop on "Violence, Insurgencies, Deceptions: Conceptualizing Urban Life in South Asia" May 6–7, 2013, organized by Asia Research Institute, National University of Singapore (Silva 2013).

2. Sinhala Buddhist nationalism propagated by BBS is a long-distance nationalism in the sense that it emanates from Colombo and that local issues embedded in specific circumstances are now interpreted in terms of an ideology that reinforces the ethnic divide and presents Sinhala Buddhist nationalism as a remedy for all problems.
3. Dharmapala was the first to explore the impact of a potential demographic expansion of Muslims in Sri Lanka (Guruge 1965).
4. Quoting Bandusena Gunasekera, the document states that the Sinhalese are among the 22 endangered ethnic communities identified by a world body of anthropologists. The source of this information, however, is not given in the document.
5. For a recent analysis of the role of political monks in the Dighavapi issue, read Jonathan Spencer et al. (2015).
6. Rajamaha Viharaya implies original land donation to the temple by the royal family and the deep historicity of a Buddhist temple.
7. A rood is equal to ¼ of an acre of land.

CHAPTER SIX

ADJUDICATING ANTIQUITY

The Politics of Historical Confrontation at Devanagala, Sri Lanka

Philip Friedrich

In the course of conducting research on the emergence of local and regional sources of political dynamism in Sri Lanka during the 12th through 14th centuries, I became interested in the history of a dramatic outcrop called "Devanagala," some three miles from the town of Mawanella in Sri Lanka's Sabaragamuwa Province. Devanagala evinces a complex, but poorly understood, epigraphic, archaeological, and literary legacy. Like many of Sri Lanka's archaeological sites, it is defined by a palimpsest-like quality: royal donative inscriptions from the 12th and 16th centuries mingle with an imposing stone-block structure of unknown provenance that seems to have been appropriated as the center of the famed Amaragiri forest hermitage by the 14th century. A later Kandyan stone-pillared Buddhist temple (*ṭämpiṭa vihāra*) occupies the same ritual circuit as a shrine (*devālaya*) to Visnu that, more recently, had been converted into barracks for two civil defense guards assigned to police the rock. Yet the way in which these seemingly disparate elements of Devanagala's past have been discursively linked and ordered at different moments militates against the notion that their configuration was simply the product of historical accretion, or the flow of successive presents from the past. The remaking of Devanagala in late-medieval and early-modern Sri Lanka was inseparable from the historiographical discourses through which the site was represented as an outpost of considerable political and religious authority. Competing agendas at various times were contested.

On the morning of March 1, 2014, I climbed Devanagala and was unwittingly confronted with the most recent appropriation of its history—one that, in addition to divergences in content, proceeded with rather different forms of thinking about the past and its relationship to the present. In the months prior to this visit, Devanagala had become a *cause célèbre* for a shadowy alliance of extremist organizations including the *Sinhala Rāvaya* (The Sinhala Roar) and *Pärakum Sēnā* (Parakramabahu's Army) that drew inspiration and public support from the *Bodu Bala Sēnā* (BBS). The BBS, by then, had entered the vanguard of an explicitly militant and outspokenly Islamophobic form of Sinhala–Buddhist nationalism. Claiming that the Muslim residences and shops that encircled parts of the base of the rock illegally encroached on an ill-defined "buffer zone" protecting antiquities and monuments at Devanagala, the alliance—then issuing statements as the Friendship Relief Foundation (*Maitri Sahana Padanama* [MSP])—formally called on the Department of Archaeology to conduct a proper survey of Devanagala's periphery to establish the archaeological site's legal boundary.[1] Simultaneously, the extremist groups conducted a vociferous campaign to intimidate Muslims in the villages abutting Devanagala: the imminent arrival of "an army of the *Sinhala Rāvaya* ready to die by suicide" to prevent the Muslim "invasion" (*ākramaṇaya*) was announced for December 23rd, 2013. Buddhist flags and a large banner proclaiming "Let the Buddha's Dispensation shine forth!" (*budu sasuna bäbalēvā*!) were erected above the entrance to a path leading to the top of Devanagala in the predominantly Muslim village of Katugahawatta (Mawanella People's Friendship Forum [MPFF] 2014: 8, 11). In both instances, attempts were made to carve out an exclusively Buddhist vision of the site's sacrality that was to be reinforced by the forthcoming ratification of its antiquity.

The degree to which these threats and provocations had mobilized some on both sides of the conflict into action was on full display shortly after we reached the summit of the rock. A young man approached our group from behind, running at full speed with a digital camera and visibly incensed at our presence. He did not introduce himself but claimed that he represented the interests of the head monk (*loku hāmuduruvō*) of the Devanagala Rajamaha Vihāra.[2] Should we wish to continue our visit to Devanagala, we would need to obtain the written permission of the head monk. On hearing that we had registered with the civil defense guard on duty—all that was procedurally required in view of heightened communal tensions—the man's tone sharpened. He clearly recognized a number of my travel companions as members of local civil society organizations that publicly opposed the BBS and, in response, had published a series of investigative reports into the "crisis" (*arbudaya*) at Devanagala, urging Muslims to counter claims to the site's uncertain periphery by furnishing legal documentation of the purchase and ownership of private land (MPFF 2014: 5–17). While taking photographs of us, he asserted that on account of the presence of Muslims in our party and swirling rumors of clear Muslim designs on more of Devanagala's land, we were not allowed to be there. Doing so, according to his logic, was to fulfill the duty of "protecting Buddhism" (*śāsanaya ārakṣā karanavā*). Its history was as a kind of constant exemplar for the present, displayed in the "facts" of Devanagala's royal inscriptions.

To call the exchange that ensued historical dialogue would be much too generous. What did transpire, however, was a fiercely antagonistic argument between the parties over what, precisely, "protecting Buddhism" entailed in the past as well as the utility of historical models of exemplary behavior held for a politically fraught present. Therefore, the encounter might be more accurately termed historical confrontation. It had eristic features in the sense that the critics of the BBS sought to subsume their opponent's arguments into expanded notions of what it could mean to "protect Buddhism." This was done with reference to professional historical scholarship. The earlier 12th-century inscription from Parakramabahu I was contextualized within the multireligious milieu of its production, where claims to political authority at Polonnaruva were frequently made using proclamatory discourses and a ritual grammar that spoke to Buddhist and theistic religious orders. The later 16th-century inscription from Vimaladharmasuriya I, despite making no mention of Muslims, was said to be symptomatic of a broader policy of *realpolitik* incorporation of religious others into decidedly cosmopolitan Kandyan sociopolitical structures—a point made clear, much to the chagrin of the BBS supporter, in Lorna Dewaraja's *The Muslims of Sri Lanka: One Thousand Years of Ethnic Harmony 900–1915* (1994). In both cases, the model of accommodative care for the *sāsana* furnished by historical precedent was forwarded as the preferred alternative to the BBS's exclusivism. However, the argument was also dialectical. Both parties worked to dialogically establish common points of agreement that permitted the confrontation to proceed, and, ultimately, the authority of their pronouncements about history was premised on anticipation and recoding of elements of the counterhistory. Most interestingly, all present believed that "protecting Buddhism" was desirable, and that to undertake such activities, however conceived, the Department of Archaeology needed to demonstrate the precise nature of the site's antiquity in a legally verifiable manner.

In what follows, I am more concerned with the kinds of political work that "history" is made to perform than evaluating the veracity of historical claims. Doing otherwise would be to posit an epistemologically privileged position over and above the field of authoritative historical knowledge that I seek to query. I take up questions raised by that initial encounter within the context of a public archive of materials produced during the ensuing social, bureaucratic, and legal entanglements between various interest groups and the Department of Archaeology at Devanagala. Under what conditions can history be invoked to authorize agendas of power in contemporary Sri Lanka? In a region for which history has been something of an "endlessly appropriable resource" (Ali 1999: 5) for the articulation of advantaged (and disadvantaged) ethnic and religious communities, what does the rather contingent quality of appeals to history at Devanagala say about the local operation of ideologies such as Sinhala Buddhist nationalism? Whereas much scholarship has ably demonstrated the way in which representation of Sri Lanka's past has been (and continues to be) structured by the agendas of nationalist politicians (Kemper 1991) and the limits of the modern nation-state and its prescribed forms of political community (Scott 1995), Sinhala–Buddhist nationalism did not hang over Devanagala like an ideological monolith, offering self-evident historiographical evaluations that correlated with positions on a grid of political affiliation. Instead, I argue that history and the generic forms, tropes, language, and evidentiary terrain that enable its narration were constrained by concerns about the conditions under which claims to antiquity could be made, and not the assertion, tout court, of a specific religious community's privileged relationship with the site (as one might expect from a controversy over a disputed sacred site). The acrimonious campaigns conducted by the BBS and their associates at Devanagala, as well as the strong emotional sentiments they evoked in both allied and opposed residents and local civic organizations, imbued bureaucratic and legal wrangling with the Department of Archaeology with a sense of urgency, indeed moral responsibility, that framed unfulfilled expectations of the Department of Archaeology—and by extension the Sri Lankan nation-state—as the prime adjudicator of ancient pasts.

The past, then, was something of a "scarce resource" at Devanagala (Appadurai 1981: 201)—although knowledge about it was frequently mustered to both contest and enable nefarious attempts to deny Muslim residents access to basic resources, its production was not unrestrained, proceeding in whatever way local actors pleased, or without cognizance of other statements about Devanagala.[3] Its invocation was a deeply social practice that, beyond enabling the definition and representation of religious communities, played an important role in the "expression and resolution of . . . conflicts" arising from their competing interests (Appadurai 1981: 206). As such, it became an important strategy for negotiating an asymmetrical field of relations that encompassed a range of civil society organizations, social groups, and state institutions operating beyond the pale of the usual suspects: Sinhala–Buddhist nationalism and populist political machines. Invocations of historical discourses that depart from grand, *Mahāvaṃsa*-inspired narratives trumpeted on national political stages in both their content and conditions of possibility are, then, worth studying for the way in which they index more subtle modes of local political organization, belonging, and critique.

The Production and Political Deployment of Historical Knowledge

Studies by anthropologists, historians, and sociologists have resulted in a body of scholarship that is unusually rich in its treatment of history and historiography as modes of discourse for interpreting the present in Sri Lanka. In the 1970s and early 80s, a series of academic conferences and publications organized within the foreboding context of hardening ethnic identities aimed explicitly to interrogate "the myths, misinterpretations and misunderstandings that have nourished their ideologies" (Social Scientists' Association 1984: i). The place of history in this critical intervention drew inspiration from then-current revisionist trends in ancient and medieval Indian historiography, such as the scholarship of Romila Thapar. Sri Lankan counterparts sought to formulate their critiques in decidedly historicist terms, meeting authoritative nationalist narratives on the same evidentiary ground and with the same terms of debate to challenge received interpretations.[4] As with the Devanagala controversy, upending the "facts" of Sri Lankan history was perceived as a traitorous slight by Sinhalas who envisioned themselves as ethnic, religious, and political homologues of past civilizational glories, and the debates provoked hostile reactions that spilled over into public domains (Serena Tennekoon 1990). Foremost among the contentious issues was the vexed question of the historicity of Sinhala consciousness. When early monastic chronicles and royal inscriptions used "Sinhala" as a marker of identity, did they do so in a way that would be intelligible to "Sinhalas" today—that is, as an ethnically cohesive "nation" of people? In an oft-cited exchange with K. N. O. Dharmadasa (1989), historian R. A. L. H. Gunawardana (1990, 1995) has argued against the seamless continuity of collective ethnic consciousness, and for a much more delimited social referent in earlier historical periods. Prior to the 12th century, when "Sinhala" came to refer to a socially heterogeneous body of Sinhala speakers, the term had a limited context of circulation as a marker of identity among "the ruling dynasty and its immediate socio-political base" (Gunawardana 1990: 78). Although Gunawardana's intervention did not challenge the basic premise that early historical precedents existed for ethnically Sinhala social groups (just that they were more circumscribed than Dharmadasa would have it), it did posit an uneven process of emergence in place of the unbroken historical thread that was central to cultural constructions of Sinhala–Buddhist nationalism. The anthropologist Steven Kemper (1991) has argued that these historiographical tropes of continuity and discontinuity were used to produce political and moral anxiety about the disintegration of the Sinhala people and Buddhism—both in the distant past and present. This condition allowed for political discourses on unity encountered in the *Mahāvaṃsa* to be poignantly transposed into nationalist pronouncements about the intrinsic relationship between the Sinhala people, Buddhism, and the Sri Lankan state. For Kemper, these decidedly historical discourses were "reexpressed" in ways that their "ancient" forms did not entirely anticipate but also diverged from the purported features of the modern nation-state (Kemper 1991: 42).

The debate between Gunawardana and Dharmadasa also occasioned deep reflection on the place of colonialist historiography in the production and mediation of knowledge about Sri Lanka's past. In arguing for a recent, 19th-century origin for modern ethnic identities, Gunawardana was quick to finger orientalist disciplines such as philology and ethnology as the prime culprits in propagating the fixed racial categories by which early nationalists interpreted seminal "historical" texts like the *Mahāvaṃsa*. Unlike India, where the "dream-like" quality of literary and textual production was said to preclude any kind of historical consciousness (Inden 1990: 7–84), orientalists and colonial bureaucrats in Ceylon heralded the island's tradition of monastic chronicles—although heavily redacted and shorn of irrational elements—as largely coterminous with "modern" modes of historical narration and thus particularly useful for explaining how contemporary social configurations came to be. These renderings of Sri Lanka's past, which John Rogers has demonstrated were "produced by the use of nineteenth-century Western historical ideas and methods" (1990: 102), had the paradoxical effect of galvanizing local Sinhala elites to contest the deleterious historical decline posed by colonialism, albeit with "ideas and methods" inherited and reworked from colonialist historiography. Indeed, sustained attention to the complex of agencies sometimes obscured in the assertion of mimetic correspondence between colonialist and nationalist historiographies has produced a more nuanced understanding of the historically uneven ways in which the past is made to inhabit the present.

Of particular importance to the topic of this chapter is the privileged relationship between archaeology and colonialist historiography that many scholars have cited as generative of the *Mahāvaṃsa*'s status as a properly "historical" source (Nissan 1985, 1989; Jeganathan 1995). Through the use of methods and technologies understood to be scientific and unerring—the measuring of "heights, widths, lengths, breadths, and related calculation of square areas and volume" and subsequent application of standard categories and classifications—an unruly landscape was, quite literally, disciplined to conform with a colonialist "regime of archaeological truth" (Jeganathan 1995: 123). Royal inscriptions were read as documents that recorded history in a positivist fashion, in turn providing colonial officials (who, at this point, doubled as archaeological experts) with a convenient template for mapping the chronology of the *Mahāvaṃsa* onto a material landscape that was simultaneously coming into being at Anuradhapura. Indeed, the overlap between the formalized archaeological practices and concepts that enabled the late-19th-century "discovery" of Anuradhapura and those that enabled the adjudication of Devanagala's historicity is startling. However, in the case of the Devanagala controversy, the lack of reference to the site in the *Mahāvaṃsa* has led to complex, locally sourced arguments for its antiquity. Many of these turn on technicalities related to the site's spatial properties and the orientation of monuments, and it is thus the Department of Archaeology's preliminary work (like surveying and the laying of boundaries) that is most contentious.[5] Rather than belabor the point that this set of practices and categories evinces a problematic colonial inheritance that has flattened the complexity of Sri Lankan pasts—a position that is certainly true and well-articulated by all the previously mentioned authors—in the following section, I take a somewhat different tack. I explore the political afterlives of such archaeological practices and concepts. Although certainly haunted by prior colonial impositions, particularly as they have been legislatively enshrined, they gain currency and importance through their strategic deployment in local confrontations. Here, questions of access to land, history, and religious space are blurred to the advantage of some and the disadvantage of others.

Finally, despite the rise of new, militant articulations of Sinhala–Buddhist nationalism following the military defeat of the LTTE in 2009, the issues raised by the seminal works on the political uses of history outlined previously have not been, on the whole, revisited with the same level of analytical depth, nor with the substantive treatment of earlier historical evidence.[6] This is, in part, justified given the overwhelmingly presentist orientation of former president Mahinda Rajapaksa's regime.[7] Seeking to divert attention away from the humanitarian disaster that accompanied the end of the war, as well as to stave off investigations by international bodies calling for scrutiny of this immediate past, a sharp historical rupture was posited through the declaration of a "postwar" periodization. The defining feature of this "new" dispensation was a regime that presented itself as markedly forward looking. It hedged its electoral strength on postwar triumphalism and the promise of forthcoming trickle-down benefits from large-scale infrastructure projects funded largely by the influx of private foreign capital—investment made possible, it claimed, only because of newly won conditions of "peace." Indeed, the prevailing situation, as it relates to the topic of this chapter, was one in which "history as a battleground for ideological agendas" (Ali 1999: 4) was effectively ceded to Sinhala–Buddhist nationalist parties allied with the Rajapaksa regime.[8]

In the absence of revisionist critiques of egregious abuses of history and historiography like one finds in the 1980s and 90s, as well as debates about the kind of political present implied by an understanding of history as a moral standard of evaluation, the deployment of historical discourses has increasingly been understood in vague terms of legitimation. That is, threatened by an inability to deliver on the economic promises of neoliberal development projects, the regime called on the monumental glories of the distant past to buttress a compromised form of state authority. Although this is no doubt true in a general sense, overweening emphasis on history's pliable legitimation of the present at the national level has foreclosed a more nuanced understanding of the local, socially embedded workings of these new articulations of Sinhala–Buddhist ideology. The Devanagala episode I now return to, although suffused with the expected tropes of ethnicized sacred space, turned on a contingent—but perhaps more insidious—invocation of "antiquity."

"Lithic Politics": The Local Afterlives of Archaeological Concept and Practice

"We have decided to initiate with a patriotic meeting the first volley in the historical battle (*aitihāsika saṭane*) of securing Devanagala's release (*Maitri Sahana Padanama* 2013b)."[9] By July 2013, public statements equating the historical confrontation at Devanagala with a militant struggle against a "Muslim invasion" appeared at regular intervals in villages at the base of the rock. Although the BBS carried out a very public campaign to intimidate Muslims on a national scale, its network of amorphous subsidiaries operating around Devanagala, like the MSP,[10] directed provocations at local Sinhala authorities it painted as "race traitors" (*jātidrōhi*) for their perceived inaction on the pressing matter of Muslim encroachment on Buddhist temple land. These included, among others, divisional representatives of the Department of Archaeology.

At the heart of the MSP's complaint to the Department of Archaeology was a disputed area of approximately 72 acres surrounding Devanagala rock, which, it claimed, had been granted to the Devanagala temple through a rather complex confluence of historical events and sources: the site's 16th-century inscription marking a land grant to a Buddhist monk named Ratnālaṅkāra who is said to have aided King Vimaladharmasuriya I's rise to power[11]; the "original draft plans" (*mul säläsma*) of 1876; and a series of ordinances and gazette notices issued through the Department of Archaeology between 1940 and 2005. Despite confusion resulting from these overlapping claims on history, their articulation does proceed according to a logic. As I discuss following, the presence of a pre-1815 evidentiary anchor was crucial to attempts to ratify the antiquity of the site. More to the point, because Devanagala's historical value had, in fact, already been acknowledged in published archaeological reports and gazette notices, the BBS and MSP demanded a long-overdue survey of the proposed 72-acre area by archaeological authorities. A physical boundary delineating the area protected under the Antiquities Ordinance of 1940 would be established as an outcome of surveying. However, the production of that boundary would have also actualized a precondition for the implementation of a 2005 gazette notification declaring a "buffer zone" (*pēraṇa kalāpayak*) of 400 yards from the edge of protected archaeological sites and monuments in which "no person shall erect buildings or carry on mining, quarrying and blasting operations on any land."[12] This was the fundamental legal pretext under which the MSP and BBS's campaign against Devanagala's Muslims operated: with Devanagala's antiquity authorized and emplaced on the site's physical landscape, it would then become "necessary to quickly remove those" whose presence within that 72 acres was not explainable by a historically verifiable means (*Maitri Sahana Padanama* 2013b).[13]

However, the Devanagala controversy did not proceed solely as a legal case regulated by attendant bureaucratic norms. It is also important to interrogate the rhetorical elements of the BBS and MSP's statements for the way in which they projected a manifest, emotionally laden historicity at Devanagala. Recognition of the qualities and features of history was, in fact, conveyed as a moral imperative for "good" Sinhala Buddhists that weighed heavily on the events at Devanagala, investing seemingly mundane bureaucratic wrangling with a sense of urgency that was not unlike the experience of other existential threats stoked by the BBS. These appeals to history were thus one particularly evocative strategy by which the intrinsic religiosity of Devanagala was publicly demonstrated by the BBS and their allies—an attribute that, as many commentators have pointed out, is frequently communicated in ethnically exclusivist terms (Kemper 1991: 148–160; Spencer et al. 2015: 68–89). For example, the MSP's "*Devanagala Haṭana*" ("The Battle of Devanagala") is framed with an explicit assertion of a rich Sinhala history at Devanagala unacknowledged because of a fundamental misapprehension of its medium of expression:

> To be sure, the historic Devanagala Rajamaha Vihāra is an historic sacred site that has been inscribed in the book of Sinhala history with golden letters. Commentaries and sub-commentaries are not needed. Though the *Pataranga Jātaka* is quite a book, there are [still] facts available in the history of Devanagala.[14] In whatever way the eight great pilgrimage sites and sixteen great pilgrimage sites [of Sri Lanka] are valuable to Sinhala Buddhists, Devanagala is just as important. (*Maitri Sahana Padanama* 2013b).[15]

In its disavowal of the superfluousness of canonical scriptures, as well as *Jātaka* literature known for its popular visibility amongst laity, the MSP's call to action posits a self-evident history at Devanagala—visible in its inscriptions and monuments—as the sine qua non for its status as a defensible religious site. Any religious reasons for that historicity, in "whatever way" they are thought of, are cast rhetorically as secondary concerns, to be debated as part of a separate discussion of Devanagala's place in a wider circuit of Buddhist pilgrimage sites in Sri Lanka. This is not to say that the religious has been wholly detached from the historical in the MSP's formulation, despite the MSP's rhetorical posturing as such. The opposition between the two is, in fact, complementary and serves an important discursive function. That is, appeals to history can function as vehicles for smuggling inflated concerns for Buddhism's "foremost place" among Sri Lanka's religions into conflicts with state institutions tasked with managing complex religious fields. Those institutions, somewhat paradoxically, must also balance attenuated commitments to secular liberal principles of governance in which the rights of all religious communities are to be safeguarded.[16] Indeed, it is precisely within this bind that the MSP's claims to a self-evident history at Devanagala were directed as a critique against the Department of Archaeology: "with even more authority than [they] need here" (*Maitri Sahana Padanama* 2013b), the Department of Archaeology was yet still ineffective in its duty to adjudicate over Devanagala's contested past.[17] The first salvo in the historical battle of Devanagala, then, was an incitement to archaeological action.

While in this chapter I highlight the importance of attention to local political circuits in which the discourse of history was deployed, there are two relevant national precedents involving the politicization of the Department of Archaeology to obstruct the material and religious interests of local Muslim communities. In both cases, the involvement of individuals and groups perceived to be "outsiders" re-signified the priorities of local stakeholders, amplifying "potentially local conflicts ... beyond recognition" (Spencer et al. 2015: 70). Although the BBS's attempts to portray the Devanagala controversy as the next "battle" in a clash of civilizations did not reach a comparable fever pitch at the national level, the local counterpart of its narrative did mobilize divisional offices of the Department of Archaeology into action in ways that evince interesting parallels with and departures from the earlier cases at Jailani and Dighavapi.

In the early 1970s, the presence of Brahmi inscriptions in the vicinity of a hermitage shrine to the Sufi saint Muyihadeen Abdul Qadir Jilani along the fringes of the southern upcountry, popularly known as Jailani, was used as historical pretext for the Department of Archaeology to uncover the site's purported prehistory as a Buddhist monastic complex.[18] Working at the behest of local Sinhala powerbrokers who extended their political influence through national patrons, the Department of Archaeology's historical preservation took the form of a provocative appropriation of foundational elements that gave Jailani religious coherence for Muslim pilgrims. Namely, in 1971, the Department of Archaeology began construction on a small *stupa* atop the cave where the Sufi saint is said to have meditated for twelve years. Although construction of the *stupa* was never completed, its half-formed presence—authorized, in fact, by a Department of Archaeology signboard proclaiming the 2nd century BCE origins of a Buddhist monastery of drip-ledge caves—continues to mark the very real effects of the deployment of spatialized religious histories to correct "seeming violations of the island's sacred geography" (McGilvray 2004: 286). In an apt turn of phrase, McGilvray demonstrates how trafficking in the symbolic currency of history's marks and traces was sedimented into kind of "lithic politics" at Jailani

(McGilvray 2004: 288). This practice persists nearly forty years later at Devanagala.

If the Jailani controversy more closely conformed to expected patterns of conflict over religious sites, where communities make competing claims to access, priority, and ownership, the more recent case of Dighavapi highlights how religious framings of conflict often mask a more complex set of local agents and their grievances over mundane concerns, such as access to basic material resources like land. Following the perceived encroachment of a resettlement project allocated for Muslim tsunami victims on an archaeological periphery of the Dighavapi *vihāra* complex, a fundamental rights suit filed in 2008 by a group of Buddhist monks was heard in the Supreme Court.[19] Whereas the main substance of the petition contested the legality of the Norichcholai resettlement project on the grounds of its ethnicized allocation of land and housing units, it presented these concerns alongside the question of "freedom of religion." A settlement of 500 Muslim families at the Dighavapi's periphery (albeit a distant 13 km), it was argued, had the "potential to limit the expansion of the Buddhist population" required to provide for the temple's material existence" (Spencer et al. 2015: 82). Meticulous analysis of the 2009 judgment in favor of the petitioners recently offered by Spencer et al. (2015: 81–84) has shown that its reasoning turned on an unacknowledged presupposition about the relationship between land, ethnicity, and religion. Whereas the Supreme Court's ruling contested the ethnicized manner in which state resources were allocated at Norichcholai, through its assent on the question of fundamental religious freedoms it simultaneously reinscribed an understanding of land as possessing an intrinsic religious connection to particular ethnic communities.

This goes some way in helping to understand the unstated assumptions that structured analogous arguments at Devanagala—namely, that the Muslim presence around the base of the rock infringed on Buddhist activities because of intrinsic, self-evident qualities that inhered in the site itself. An important difference in the case of Devanagala was that these were conceptualized through the discourse of history, whereas Spencer et al. argues that it was "religious issues

... that framed [the arguments]" at Dighavapi (2015: 83). As I suggested previously, the two very often operate as two sides of the same coin in populist political discourse. Yet, their divergence in these two relatively coincident, postwar deployments of notions of ethnicized terrain and space against Muslims is intriguing. A 2012 policy report produced in the wake of a series of attacks against mosques and *dargahs* perpetrated under the pretext of encroachment on "sacred areas" found that "the existing Sri Lankan legal framework does not provide for the declaration of 'sacred areas,' although there is regular practice of such terminology increasing the confusion" (Centre for Policy Alternatives 2012: 7). If the idea of "sacred space" is underdetermined by the qualities it is alleged to embody, and thus presents itself as a readily available resource for evocative political statements, why the notable reliance on the discourse of history at Devanagala and not blanket pronouncements of its sacrality? Moreover, if sacred space can be just about anything one declares it to be, what, then, can history be?

Although the criteria used for assessing historical sites is clearly defined by the Antiquities Ordinance of 1940, the conditions it sets for the ratification of a site's "antiquity" are capacious. As a result, concepts like history, the ancient, and antiquity tend to overlap and interpenetrate in matters governed by the Department of Archaeology without much regard for potential nuances that might distinguish the terms. In Part VIII, Section 17, entitled "Interpretation," antiquity is defined with reference to objects (i.e., antiquities) that fulfill the following conditions. They are

> (a) any ancient monument,[20] or (b) any of the following objects lying or being or being found in Sri Lanka, which date or may reasonably be believed to date from a period prior to the 2nd day of March, 1815:- statues, sculpted or dressed stone and marbles of all descriptions, engravings, carvings, inscriptions, paintings, writings, and the material whereon the same appear, all specimens of ceramic, glyptic, metallurgical and textile art, coins, gems, seals, jewels, jeweler, arms, tools, ornaments, and all other objects of art which are movable property.

More important than the myriad material forms antiquity takes in the Ordinance is the declaration of March 2, 1815, as a historical baseline of sorts. It is an act of periodization that marks 1815 as a point of rupture between what can count as history and what cannot count as history. Aside from creating a legal space from which "history" could be mobilized as an undifferentiated mass of facts, materials, and monuments today, the invocation of 1815 imposed a particular religious orientation and model for the state's management of historical sites. March 2, 1815, is, of course, the date of the commencement of the Kandyan Convention. This summit between Kandyan chiefs and colonial officials resulted in the transfer of Kandyan sovereignty to the King of England, with the important stipulation that protection and maintenance of Buddhism, which included "its rites, ministers, and places of worship," be guaranteed.[21] Popularly, the Convention has simultaneously come to signify the beginning of Buddhism's "betrayal" through the failure of the British to uphold the religious obligations of statecraft. The allusion to the Kandyan Convention in the Antiquities Ordinance thus highlights another postcolonial domain in which understandings of the state's proper relationship to potentially complex religious fields (like historical sites) came to be articulated using the reclaimed and repackaged idiom of royal Buddhist patronage.[22] Yet, ironically, it was a decidedly modernist vision of the state that was appropriated as "traditional"—one forged through the conceptual and material superimposition of bureaucratic structures of colonial governance on the fluid workings of Kandyan polity. The Antiquities Ordinance presents the Department of Archaeology as an extension of this hybrid state, one whose modern tasks of managing and regulating history were shot through with allusions to religious patronage. It was precisely this expectation that framed the encounters at Devanagala in which the Department of Archaeology was approached as the adjudicator of antiquity.

It is difficult to determine whether the Department of Archaeology was goaded into action at Devanagala through a sense of moral failure in fulfilling these expectations or direct collusion with the BBS and its allies at the local level.[23] Following deliberations between the

Department's divisional office in Avissavella and representatives of the headquarters in Colombo, surveying and boundary marking of Devanagala's periphery was to begin on November 28, 2013.[24] A team of Department of Archaeology research assistants, government surveyors, and police officers was amassed with the expressed aim of exploring the northern and eastern sides of the rock (where the construction of residences was heaviest) "to prepare a plan of encountered archaeological artifacts" (Department of Archaeology, Divisional Office 2013: 2). Preliminary boundary markers would be fixed, and the plan would then be used to determine (in consultation with Colombo) the legal boundary of the Devanagala archaeological preserve, beyond which a 400-yard "buffer zone" would extend.

Yet one gets the sense that the divisional office of the Department of Archaeology imagined their mandate from Colombo in amplified terms. As part of their "exploratory" activities, the Archaeological team also sought to collect details from 59 households surrounding the rock pertaining to ownership, land size, and deeds in possession of the householder (Department of Archaeology, Divisional Office 2013: 9–13). Fearing that this was the first step toward eventual eviction, a protest was organized by Muslims living in the vicinity of Devanagala in conjunction with a local civil society organization composed of Sinhala and Muslim community leaders—the MPFF. This group had recently begun to help Muslims legally demonstrate their claims to land by securing notarized deeds.[25] Suspicions of rapid confiscation of lands were given credence by ongoing seizures from politically and economically disadvantaged communities in the North, East, and Colombo in the name of national development and security. Traces of the opposition organized against the Department of Archaeology's perceived overstepping of its jurisdiction make their way into the divisional office's survey report: in the observations that accompany the data collected as a part of the teams "exploratory" activities, each of the fourteen Sinhala households approached are praised for showing "no protest related to the establishment of archaeological boundary posts."[26] Conspicuously absent are any details related to the ownership and deeds of the 42 Muslim families approached that day. Owing to the threat of open violence, an all-too-real possibility in light of entrenched memories of the communal violence perpetrated on Mawanella in 2001, the Mawanella Divisional Secretariat ordered a stop to the surveying activities. The Archaeological survey report ends by frustratedly applying the BBS's logic of the dangers of unchecked Muslim expansion to Devanagala: "if this zone is not declared an archaeological reserve . . . within a few days a concrete jungle will have been built on top of Devanagala rock."[27]

The survey report is noteworthy not only for the populist rhetoric that creeps into its narration of events but also for the way it responds to historical discourses that circulated around Devanagala in the months of the controversy. Although all parties turned to the Department of Archaeology as the authority by which "history" could be ratified—a position not without legal and historical precedent—its judgments did not cascade down from empyrean heights, as one might expect from a modern governmental state hanging above society. Rather, they were products of a dialectical relationship between central and divisional offices. The divisional office, as I have shown here, was entangled in relations of power that structured seemingly benign practices like gathering facts, figures, and measurements for the consequent production of verified historical truths. As such, the Department of Archaeology was an eminently local actor that articulated its concerns in ways not unlike other parties to the historical confrontation at Devanagala.

In the weeks leading up to the surveying and boundary marking of November 28, 2013, the evidentiary terrain for historical argumentation had shifted considerably. In response to the BBS and MSP's declaration that the 72-acre area mentioned in the inscription of Vimaladharmasuriya I encompassed the rock and thus belonged to the Devanagala Rajamaha Vihāra, the MPFF commissioned its own study of the inscription and survey of lands surrounding Devanagala (Mawanella People's Friendship Forum 2014: 12). According to its findings, the 72 acres donated in the inscription perfectly mapped onto a 72-acre area that, in the original draft plans of 1876, marked the boundaries of a village to the northwest of Devanagala rock. What was lawfully possessed by the Devanagala Rajamaha Vihāra, then, was not the rock but the adjacent village of Ruwandeniya and the products of its attendant service relationship (*rājakāriya*) with the temple. The MPFF claims that these findings were warmly received during a meeting in Colombo with high-level officials of the Department of Archaeology (Mawanella People's Friendship Forum 2014: 13). Consequently, as this historical knowledge began to circulate around Devanagala in the form of new arguments and counterarguments, the BBS and MSP changed their tack. In a public notice posted on August 4, 2013, the importance of the 72-acre figure for establishing an unbroken history of a Buddhist monastic presence is only mentioned in passing (MSP 2013a). Instead, focus was shifted to the remnants of a small stone wall that encircled the base of rock—running through the properties of both Sinhala and Muslim households—and demands were made for an archaeological survey in its vicinity. The notice invests this newfound boundary with an almost mythic importance: "the iron parapet protecting Devanagala, decorated by patriots who love the Sinhala race and *Buddhasāsana*."[28]

The divisional office's archaeological survey report reproduces the trajectory of these historical concerns in a mimetic fashion. Gone are references to the contested 72 acres, and in their place are unilateral declarations of the wall's antiquity. Throughout the report, the wall is frequently called "ancient" (*päraṇi*) without indication of the criteria that distinguishes these references from other descriptions of it as simply a "mound of stones" (*galgoḍa*). In fact, one of the few discernible patterns in the survey's evaluation of the site is the increased archaeological scrutiny that the properties connected to Muslim households were subjected to. Although "observations" of Sinhala households are limited to noting the lack of protest to the archaeological survey (as discussed previously), Muslim households inhabiting the same stretch of land around the base of the rock are admonished for building residences and various structures on top of the "ancient" wall and Devanagala rock itself.[29] The MPFF interpreted this discrepancy as the beginnings of an attempt to evict Devanagala's Muslims not on the grounds that they reside in a purportedly sacred area but because of violations to the 2005 Gazette Notification prohibiting the erection of buildings within the 400-yard buffer zone surrounding archaeological sites (Mawanella People's Friendship Forum 2014: 14). In response, the MPFF again made recourse to the original draft plans of 1876, claiming that the lack of any mention of the stone wall calls into question the Department of Archaeology's assertion of its supposed "antiquity"—the wall is, then, a more recent colonial construction. It is on this issue that the Devanagala controversy remains archaeologically stalemated to this day.

In this chapter, I have argued that the invocation of historical discourses and their political deployment in Sri Lanka are processes contingent on local relations of power and not simply predetermined by the ideological workings of Sinhala–Buddhist nationalism. I have simultaneously endeavored to demonstrate that historical discourse is a particularly important social domain—but certainly not the only one—for the articulation and representation of religious and ethnic communities in Sri Lanka. In this respect, historical discourse is one strategy by which communities establish a kind of political legibility; and, as such, historical confrontations tend to mask a more complicated set of claims to basic material resources, like land in the cases of Devanagala and Dighavapi. The chapter is admittedly thin on the historical discourses by which Muslims themselves represent their interests. Future scholarship will hopefully address this pressing lacunae. However, the omission is in part justified. By focusing on the weighted legal and political conditions under which claims to antiquity can be ratified, I have also tried to show that it is nearly impossible for Muslims to prove their historicity in the eyes of the Sri Lankan state. History and its constitutive generic features are, quite literally, disciplined into a particular religious orientation by the nation-state. This point, and the political violent exclusions it can entail, became painfully obvious as I scoured the annual reports of the Department of Archaeology for evidence of archaeological activities undertaken at Muslim historical and religious sites. In an ominous portent of the anti-Muslim violence perpetrated in June 2014, a 1997 request to explore and document the Zain Hassan bin Osman al Mosque and *dargah* in the Alutgama Division was met with this response: "This mosque was inspected at the request of the Secretary of the Ministry. It was found to be of no archaeological significance" (Department of Archaeology 1997: 15).

NOTES

1. For brief newspaper summaries, see Sarath Udagama, "The Devanagala Uproar," *Ceylon Today*, January 16, 2014 and K. Sanjiva, "*Devanagala Ginikandak Viya Häkiya*" ["Devanagala Could Become a Volcano"], *Rāvaya*, January 26, 2014.
2. Significantly, the monk who claims incumbency of the temple complex atop Devanagala resides in a temple in the nearby village of Ruwandeniya, thus leaving the monastic residences atop Devanagala vacant. This fact is frequently invoked as a rebuttal to the BBS's claims of an unbroken monastic presence at the Devanagala Rajamaha Vihāra.
3. The formulation is indebted to Marx's famous statement that "men make their own history, but they do not make it just as they please" (1972: 10).
4. For a critical evaluation of the utility of revisionist historiography as a form of political critique, see David Scott, "Dehistoricising History," in Pradeep Jeganathan and Qadri Ismail, eds., *Unmaking the Nation: The Politics of Identity and History in Modern Sri Lanka* (Colombo, Sri Lanka: Social Scientists' Association, 1995): 10–24.
5. This, of course, is not to suggest that survey missions have ever existed independent of monumental archaeological practices, or that colonial archaeological projects were somehow divorced from the practices the colonial state used to manage land, people, and property. Jeganathan (1995: 118) notes how early excavations at Anuradhapura were initiated in response to archaeological finds while constructing a road for migrant South Indian laborers to move from the island's north to plantations in the hills.
6. There are two important exceptions. One is a series of articles that appeared as part of the International Center for Ethnic Studies' (ICES) "Research Paper" Series. On the production of popular historiography that reinforces development-driven "heritage" projects,

see Wickramasinghe (2012). On new Sinhala–Buddhist ideological and political projects directed at the "conquered and occupied" Northern and Eastern Provinces, see Nirmal Dewasiri, "'History' after the War: Historical Consciousness in the Collective Sinhala-Buddhist Psyche in Post-War Sri Lanka." International Centre for Ethnic Studies [ICES] Research Paper 9. (Colombo, Sri Lanka: ICES, 2013). The other is analysis of the mytho-historical cult of personality that developed around Mahinda Rajapaksa in the weeks following the end of the ethnic conflict. These discussions, many occurring in the Sinhala press, were attentive to historical associations that Rajapaksa actively cultivated about his rise to power from the *Rohaṇa* region following a tsunami, and subsequent defeat of a Tamil "king"—much like the paradigmatic Sinhala hero king of the *Mahāvaṃsa*, Duṭugämunu.

7. I thank Dilshanie Perera for this point and for conversations on the topic.
8. One thinks, here, of the former parliamentarian and leader of the *Jathika Hela Urumaya* (JHU) Ven. Ellawalla Medhananda's popular articles and books on the Buddhist heritage of the eastern province as well as their mobilization in his legal complaint against Muslim housing projects around Dighavapi (see Spencer et al. 2015: 77–84).
9. "*Devanagala mudāgänīme aithāsika saṭane palamu veḍimuraya jātimāmaka hamuvakin ārambha karannaṭa api tiraṇaya koṭa ättemu.*" I thank the MPFF for providing me with copies of many of the public notices and pamphlets that circulated around the time of the Devanagala controversy. This paragraph is based on public written statements made in *Maitri Sahana Padanama* (2013a and 2013b). All translations are my own.
10. In this case, direct links between the BBS and the agitations at Devanagala can be established. In a January 16, 2014, interview with *Ceylon Today,* the chief incumbent of the Devanagala Rajamahavihara, and chair of the Devanagala Trusteeship Council, acknowledges, "we have talked to the 'Bodu Bala Sena' organization and they have promised to take necessary action" (Udagama 2014).
11. A published edition and translation of this inscription appears in Bell (1892: 87–88).

12. The buffer zone was initially measured at 200 yards according to a 2004 gazette notification, but it was expanded to 400 yards in 2005. Importantly, these were blanket provisions established by the Minister of Human Resources Development, Education and Cultural Affairs under the Antiquities Ordinance of 1940 (Chapter 188). They seem to have been produced and applied irrespective of local conditions or concerns about their implementation. Indeed, the earlier gazette of 2004 was applied to 56 archaeological sites across Sri Lanka.
13. "*ovunṭa vahā ivat kaḷa yutaya.*"
14. This statement is highly idiomatic and seems to have less to do with the content of the *Pataraṅga Jātaka* than popular understandings of it as a long and complex religious text. That is, even though it has been compiled as a single book, there are still important religious details it does not cover. These are to be gleaned from the history of Devanagala.
15. "*Aitihāsika devanagala rajamaha vihāraya vanāhi siṃhala itihāsa potē ran akurin liya vī äti aitihāsika siddasthānayaki. aṭuva, ṭikā aväsi näta. pataraṅga jātakaya taram potakaṭa vuvada devanagala itihāsayehi karuṇu äta. aṭamasthānaya, solosmasthānaya siṃhala bauddhayanṭa vaṭinne yam sēda epamaṇakaṭama devanagala vädagatya.*"
16. On constitutional precedents for the "compromise between secularism and Buddhist majoritarianism," see Schonthal's (2012: 218) history of the parliamentary debates that resulted in the 1972 Constitution's famed Section 6 (Chapter II).
17. "*purāvidyā depārtumēntuvaṭa ... mehilā aväsi pramāṇayaṭat vaḍā balatala äta.*"
18. The following account relies on Dennis McGilvray, "Jailani: A Sufi Shine in Sri Lanka," in Imtiaz Ahmad and Helmut Reifeld, eds., *Lived Islam in South Asia: Adaptation, Accommodation and Conflict* (New Delhi: Social Science Press, 2004): 273–289.
19. The following draws from recent work on the Dighavapi Supreme Court case by J. Spencer et al. *Checkpoint, Temple, Church and Mosque: A Collaborative Ethnography of War and Peace* (London: Pluto Press, 2015).
20. An "ancient monument" is likewise defined with reference to March 2, 1815, in the preceding clause.

21. The famous fifth clause of the Kandyan Convention is quoted in Malalgoda (1976: 109).
22. For a discussion of the Kandyan Convention's place in Constituent Assembly debates prior to the ratification of Sri Lanka's 1972 constitution, see Schonthal (2012: 215).
23. Allegations were leveled that divisional-level archaeological reports were given to members of the BBS prior to being forwarded to central offices in Colombo (Mawanella People's Friendship Forum 2014: 14). I have found no way of verifying this allegation.
24. This account was produced by reading the Department of Archaeology (DOA), Divisional Office's (DO; 2013: 1–6) version of events against the counterclaims of a local civil society organization called the Mawanella People's Friendship Forum (2014: 13–15).
25. The organization was initially formed as a venue for conflict dispute in the wake of ethnic violence between Sinhalas and Muslims in Mawanella in 2001.
26. "*Purāvidyā māyim kaṇu siṭuvīma sambandhyen virōdhatāvak nomäta.*" See households numbered 36–50 in Department of Archaeology, Divisional Office (2013: 11–13).
27. "*Mema kalāpaya purāvidyā rakṣitayak bavaṭa pat nokaḷahot . . . nobō dinakin devanagala gal parvataya mata konkrīṭ puravarayak idivenu äta*" (Department of Archaeology, Divisional Office 2013: 6).
28. "*Siṃhala jātiyaṭa sambuddha śāsanayaṭa ādaraya karana jātimāmakayingen sädumlat devanagala ārakṣā kirimē yakaḍa pavura*" (*Maitri Sahana Padanama* 2013a).
29. See, in particular, households numbered 3, 12, 16, 18, 21, 28, 29, 30, 31, 32, and 33 in Department of Archaeology, Divisional Office (2013: 9–13).

CHAPTER SEVEN

STORIES IN THE AFTERMATH OF ALUTHGAMA

Farzana Haniffa

The historic elections of January 9, 2015, that ousted incumbent president Mahinda Rajapaksa and brought about Sri Lanka's "democratic transition" promised a new era for the island. Although the supporters of the former president continue to be vocal, and Rajapaksa himself remains on public platforms, elements of the former regime's excesses are fading from popular consciousness. One such element that may be thus fading is the raging anti-Muslim sentiment that spread across the Sinhala-speaking areas of the island in 2013 and 2014 and culminated in the anti-Muslim violence of Aluthgama in 2014.

It is indeed a salutary development of the "democratic transition" that the anti-Muslim sentiment can now be thought about as in the past, or at most as yet another story of the excesses of a regime that was roundly defeated by citizen action. But as these self-congratulatory tales are being told, I pause to consider the manner in which the narrative of Aluthgama was constructed in its immediate aftermath. In doing so, I also want to consider the following questions: What is the status of Aluthgama today in the narrative of Sri Lanka's many "riots?" What is the place of Aluthgama in a country that has experienced countless struggles regarding its national narrative of suffering? And at a time when the country is finally asking questions about its past in a way that recognizes its multiethnic collectivity, what place will Aluthgama hold in the new national narrative?

The Event

On the 15th and 16th of June, 2014, mobs attacked Muslim homes and businesses in the southern Sri Lankan towns of Aluthgama, Welipanna, Beruwela, and Mathugama, destroying property and killing 3 persons.[1] This event culminated anti-Muslim sentiment that had been percolating for two years, instigated mainly by an organization called the Bodu Bala Sena (BBS). Those in positions of authority turned a proverbial blind eye to its increasing excesses. The experience resulted in shock, and in some cases devastation, for those who were subjected to the violence. For Muslims in other parts of Sri Lanka, it resulted in weeks of extreme stress and unease, as familiar neighborhoods became dangerous and tense, and the spread of violence seemed imminent. For many others of a certain age, both Muslim and non-Muslim, the anger and disappointment at what had occurred was compounded by its familiarity and seeming inevitability. The lead up to this antiminority (Muslim) sentiment that was evident in the media, on public platforms, around middle class dinner tables, in Sinhala-speaking classrooms across class, regarding the status of Muslims in the country, and the final culmination in physical violence against Muslims, was reminiscent of another such incident—July 1983.[2] The fact that the violence that many anticipated had finally occurred meant that Sri Lanka—despite the war's end in 2009—was yet to escape the cycle of devastating violence that the country had been trapped in for decades.

Just as in July 1983, the events of Aluthgama seemed to have been choreographed with the involvement of state institutions. Evidence of the choreographed nature included police permitting armed mobs to roam the streets when a curfew was supposedly in force; eyewitness accounts of organized groups with weapons gathered and waiting at places outside the area where the "trigger" incident of violence occurred, and the manner in which attacks in all the different areas of Dharga Town and Aluthgama began almost simultaneously. In the violence of July 1983, the attackers carried voter lists to identify Tamil houses.[3]

In this chapter, I will be concerned with the multiple narrative framings of "Aluthgama" in the aftermath of the event by those directly affected, by Muslims outside of the area, and by the country at large. For this analysis, I have compared Muslims' and their Sinhala neighbors' narrations of the event to the small group of us who arrived "from the university" to document its occurrence. I have also looked at the state's response, some commentators' references to Aluthgama, and its similarity to July 1983, as well as others' attempts to render it as a Jihadi conspiracy. I will conclude by speculating on what role these narratives played in the immediate aftermath of the event and what they now mean in a context that is vastly different and much more hopeful for all actors concerned.

> Storytelling is usually prompted by some crisis, stalemate or loss of ground in a person's relationship with others and with the world such that autonomy is undermined, recognition withheld and action made impossible. Storytelling is a coping strategy, that involves making words stand for the world and then by manipulating them, changing one's experience of the world. By constructing, relating and sharing stories, people contrive to restore viability to their relationship with others, redressing a bias towards autonomy when it has been lost, and affirming collective ideals in the face of disparate experiences. It is not that speech is a replacement for action: rather that it is a supplement, to be exploited when action is impossible or confounded. (Jackson 2007: 22)

Story #1: How It All Came About

This section is drawn from the tales of Muslim interlocutors in Aluthgama and members of the Muslim intelligentsia in Colombo. It is a narrative about attempts to stop the violence from occurring.

On Poson *poya* day (full moon day) in June 2014, a vehicle taking a monk from one temple to another in the Aluthgama suburb of Dharga Town was involved in an altercation with a three-wheeler taxi owned by some Muslims. On the narrow roads of Dharga Town, known to challenge commuters trying to pass one another, this altercation resulted in an exchange of words between the young Muslims and the monk's driver and then an exchange of blows between the men. The Aluthgama area was already tense; a month earlier a worker in a Muslim-run shop in town had been accused of molesting a (Sinhala) boy and the shop had been burned down one night. The *poya* day event quickly escalated, with the monk trying to lodge a complaint with the police and the police refusing to accommodate him. Some local individuals, aware of the prevailing tensions in the town, tried to calm things down by getting the young men to hand themselves over to the police.[4] The altercation was deemed by some Sinhalas as deserving of an intervention by the BBS. Anti-Muslim violence took place in the aftermath of an ensuing rally at which the main speaker was the Ven. Gnanasara of the BBS.[5]

Muslim activists, long active in trying to deal with anti-Muslim sentiment, were quite aware that not only might the holding of a BBS meeting lead to violence, but that such a meeting could be the excuse, the backdrop through which the space for violence might be created, and a "lesson" taught to the Muslims. Such events had taken place in the past in Aluthgama, and this particular manner of dealing with recalcitrant minority groups was well known in Sri Lanka.[6] In 2014, with the national level anti-Muslim sentiment rising, and with it various incidents of violence that had already occurred, the likelihood of violence erupting was high.[7] Hence, there were many attempts to get the authorities to stop the rally from taking place.[8] The state responded by promising security. Hundreds of Special Task Force (STF) personnel were mobilized to prevent violence. A group of traders from the Aluthgama Bazaar, whose shops were later damaged, stated that they had felt confident that this time things might be different due to the armed STF who were present on that day, *adiyen adiyet*—at intervals of a foot. They had informed politicians important to the area, including Anura Kumara Dissanayake of the Janatha Vimukthi Peramuna (JVP) and A. M. Fauzi, veteran of the SLFP (the Sri Lanka Freedom Party, the political party of the country's president), about the meeting and the threat of violence. Bazaar traders had been warned by customers that something was going to happen that day. Shops were closed, but many were confident that enough security had been deployed and that there should not be too much to worry about. Mr. M. N. Ameen, president of the Muslim Council, stated at a meeting in the aftermath, "Aluthgama looked like Jaffna, and I was relieved."[9] Nevertheless, the violence occurred.

For us, Muslim activists, the eruption of violence and the government's response to the event, the attempt to circumvent responsibility despite a security commitment (see following), revealed the fact that there was little we could legitimately do to stop Muslim persecution and victimization in the future. After Aluthgama, all of us who were engaged at some level with trying to bring about a halt to the public articulation of anti-Muslim sentiment and its consequent violence realized that there was very little we could do.

Story #2: My Narrative—An Analysis

The anti-Muslim sentiment that was cultivated under the Rajapaksa regime in postwar Sri Lanka must be understood as a manifestation of the martial logic of the regime: after the military decimation of the LTTE (Liberation Tigers of Tamil Eelam), they had endorsed the BBS monks' ideology of understanding minority identity as a threat to Sinhala hegemony (Haniffa et al. 2015). I have argued elsewhere that the monks, together with the regime, rendered the transitional Sri Lankan polity anew, and the new polity was Sinhala supremacist, militaristic, and did not tolerate what it understood as minority recalcitrance. For Muslims, it was necessary to combat this juggernaut, the racism of the regime, and its manipulation of the Buddhist nationalist movement for its own benefit. But after Aluthgama, we saw the fight not as an all-out battle but rather a constant negotiation against tremendous odds. The anti-Muslim agenda of the state, the monks, and what seemed then like the vocal majority of Sinhala society, could only be managed but not eradicated. After Aluthgama, it was clear that, for as long as the regime was in power, there would be no letup of the pressure on Muslims.

The Muslim leaders of the south, as I have discussed elsewhere, and others too have noted, have always anticipated violence from the Sinhalese. Arguably, after the anti-Muslim violence under the colonial regime in 1915, fears of attacks were foremost in the minds of the political leadership that had experienced violence. These fears affected the nature of their political engagement (Ismail 1995; Haniffa 2012). The manner in which the BBS monks had identified Muslims as the newly chosen "other" in postwar Sri Lanka and that had set into motion a national campaign to articulate this view, resulted in an unprecedented realization of this latent fear; however, its revivification occurred for a generation that had all but forgotten 1915.[10] Muslims have historically self-identified as the "good minority" that distinguished them from the recalcitrant Tamil. The postwar use of the old trope had a new twist; both the Muslim Council and the Shoora Council often referred to Muslims as "patriotic" and stated that if the Muslims had joined the Tamils, the Tigers might have won Eelam! The establishment's choice to constantly identify and vilify Muslims as possibly terrorists was therefore a matter of great consternation.[11]

Story #3: Another July '83?

Many commentators have equated Aluthgama and its anti-Muslim sentiment with the lead-up to the disastrous Sinhala riots against Tamils in July 1983. And certainly there are parallels. For instance, Nesiah has stated

> (T)he parallels between the anti-Muslim riots of June 2014 and the anti-Tamil pogrom of July 1983 are uncanny. . . . [T]he state, particularly the Police and other state institutions charged with maintaining law and order, did little to help or intervened [until it was] too late. In fact the impression created is that important sections of the state were as complicit in the riots in Aluthgama and elsewhere in June 2014, as in the island-wide pogrom of July 1983. In both cases the leadership was primarily politically motivated but used ethnic and religious prejudices as well as economic opportunism to promote the violence.[12]

As Nesiah correctly points out, both the state's complicity in the violence and the leadership's indifference to the suffering of the victims was similar to the aftermath of July 1983.

Pradeep Jeganathan's analysis of July 1983 has looked at the anthropological literature of the event in terms of "canonizing violence," a category by which Sri Lanka's could be measured in the aftermath (Jeganathan 1997). In that essay, Jeganathan suggests that anthropological engagement with the event has often rendered it as "politically incoherent." He argues that the event was "anthropologized" either as "culture" (Tambiah 1986, and Spencer 1990) or as "excess" (Daniel 1996), but not as "politics." Thirty years later, there has been much that has happened in Sri Lanka allowing us to understand the event as very much political in nature. It has in fact become defined as a watershed event that has impacted the nature of politics in the island ever since. July 1983 is understood by many, despite evidence to the contrary, as the point at which violent conflict began. It is also understood today—in a narrative that, again reductively, sees Sinhala nationalism as the sole cause of conflict—as Sinhala nationalisms' short-lived moment of triumph. Tamil nationalists see the event as a precursor to the inevitability of a separate state. How should the violence against Muslims as manifested in Aluthgama in June 2014 be understood? I argue that despite its similarities to 1983, June 2014 was a political act of a different order.

Although there are many similarities between July 1983 and Aluthgama 2014, there are significant differences that tell a very particular story about the latter event. The Tamil insurgency was emergent by 1983, and the pogrom was used by the regime to provide a lesson to Tamils for their political recalcitrance.[13] The Vadukoddai resolution calling for a separate state had been signed several years earlier, and the state and Tamil leadership were locked in a power struggle. In the case of the Muslims, there was really no such political background, and Muslims were far from being a political threat to the regime or the state; and there was no burning social issue other than the socially discernible and easily identifiable "difference" and "strangeness" of the Muslims, and arguably the reformist cultivated sense of Muslim superiority. I point out the difference in politics to note that in the aftermath of the military victory of 2009 over the LTTE, the popular purchase of Sinhala supremacist ideology was such that it was no longer necessary to have a political reason for seeing the minorities as "other." Simply seeing the Muslims as "different" fed amorphous and unverified statements about extremism and fundamentalism, and this was sufficient cause for violence (Haniffa 2016). As I will show later in relation to other stories, the violence itself, however, was also of a different order: perpetrated for political affect and economic consequences.

Story #4: The State Narrative

President Mahinda Rajapaksa, who was abroad at the time that the violence occurred in Aluthgama, visited the Beruwela Kachcheri (office of local administration) a few days after his return. He stated that there should be an inquiry and that law and order should be maintained. He also stated that "both parties" should look inward to try to understand why the event had taken place. Rajapaksa did not spell out who "both parties" were. However, in positing "two-parties," he was reproducing the religio-ethnic collective nouns of the BBS rhetoric. His brother, the ministry of defense secretary, would also use a similar narrative and extrapolate its categories to the entire country.[14] In this statement, the president was also not referencing local specificities—the attempts that had been made by civil society actors to bring the situation under control, to prevent the situation from escalating. President Rajapaksa later went on to state, in relation to a subsequent countrywide protest, or *hartal*, about the events that had transpired in Aluthgama—*sulu sulu de valata loku loku hartal*—"large protests for small things." "Some people asked why the military was not deployed." He stated at another public meeting. "Nothing requiring the intervention of the military took place in Aluthgama."[15] In continuing attempts to play down the significance of the violence, state representatives, the Inspector General of Police, the prime minister, and the state representative to the UN Human Rights Council stuck to one story at a variety of public fora.[16] State representatives steadfastly blamed the Muslims for the outbreak of the trouble and stated that it was Muslim attacks against monks in two different instances that led to the violence. Further, even as the violence was ongoing during the night of the 15th, state representatives stated that it had been contained. Muslims in Aluthgama and Beruwela told us that the attempt by the head of state and state functionaries to minimize the event was evidence not only of the state's complicity in the violence but indicative of the general place of Muslims in the current national dispensation, and the likelihood of continued harassment and violent attacks in the future.

In Rajapaksa's rhetoric, I also read the manner in which the regime was trying to deflect responsibility for inaction and unnecessarily "ethnicize" a distressing and complex event. However, I also read

Rajapaksa's comments as referencing a regime that was surprised by messages of support for the Muslims, messages of criticism for the state and the manner in which the event was being read internationally: as rampaging Buddhists attacking innocent Muslims.[17]

Story #2 (Again): My Analysis

Veena Das has described very powerfully how violence destroys lifeworlds and how survivors struggle to reconstruct the "everyday" in the aftermath of a violent "event" (Das 2006). In Aluthgama, we encountered multiple stories recounting the event and attempts to incorporate its significance into a common community narrative, one in which the sleight of hand by authorities gave attackers license for thievery and looting while misleading Muslims with promises of security. It was clear at the outset, however, that the stories were largely about oppositional politics and referenced the breakdown of personal lifeworlds, especially in relation to economic loss. Das narrates stories in relation to the violence against Sikhs in the 1980s and the violence of partition in 1948; the experiences in Aluthgama were qualitatively different from such events. Although narrating stories of huge economic losses, victims were very aware that their lives had been spared. Many were quite clear in making the distinction between threats to their lives and threats to their property.[18] As one interlocutor stated, "what was taken away was what God had given us—he gave it and he took it away, and he will give us again." South Asia has a troubling history of ethnopolitical violence of great brutality. Aluthgama simply did not involve bloodletting on the scale that was experienced in Delhi in the 1980s, during partition in 1948, in Gujarat in 2002, or even in July 1983 in Sri Lanka. The "remaking" of everyday worlds was called forth in the aftermath of the event, and many stories were constructed. But these stories were of Aluthgama Muslims' relationship to community, polity and material wealth.

In Aluthgama, unlike July 1983 when the violence was permitted to spread across the country, and where, according to official figures, 3,000 persons were killed, there seems to have been a concerted effort made to contain the violence to the area and to concentrate the violence on the destruction of property.[19] Of all the horror stories that we collected about the people's encounters with mobs, only one was about atrocities committed against the body. The fact that this was the case is borne out in the murders that actually *did* happen. There were two people shot and killed in the suburb of Welipitiya, and two teenagers who lost their limbs. In Welipanna, one security guard was killed on a farm—he was brutally hacked to death.

The potential for greater and more disturbing acts of violence, categorized today as "atrocities," was everywhere. The dehumanization of the other was also evident in the stories we heard. One from the Nagoda Hospital in Aluthgama is especially telling. Two of the teenagers shot in the melee in Welipitiya were transported by the police to Nagoda a little after midnight on June 15th. The hospital was soon overrun by a group of attackers, including a Buddhist monk, who told hospital staff and doctors "don't treat them; they are coming after attacking our people." At that point, attendants at the hospital had surrounded the bleeding teenagers and had begun to aggressively question them. No attempt was made to treat their wounds. Some of the attendants had slapped one of them and pushed the other into an empty corner room where he lost consciousness and where his bullet wound was left untreated overnight. The next day, after he was transported to Colombo, it was discovered that in addition to the one bullet wound, he had deep knife cuts on two sides of the leg.[20] He later lost his leg.

I relate this story because the possibility of the politically illegible "horror" that the many authors that reference, or violence as "excess" as Daniel posits it, was a potentiality in Aluthgama. It was a potentiality that was not permitted to realize itself, and there lies the political story of Aluthgama. Aluthgama, then, was an organized event that was not about suspending the rules of law and order for an orgy through which the brutalization of the body of the "other" could be indulged in; it was instead, I argue, the momentary and limited suspension of the rules of property ownership (Jeganathan 1997.

Muslim residents of Dharga Town accused the Special Task Force, who had been sent to provide security to the area, of virtually holding the Muslims captive in their homes during the curfew and permitting the mob a license to loot and burn. Two young Muslim men that we interviewed in the Seenawatte area stated that they were perfectly capable of defending themselves but were prevented by the STF from organizing themselves to do so. One man recounted that he was even prevented from crossing the street to reach the mosque. The other said that although he was confined to his house, he could see others driving around on motorcycles with complete impunity in the presence of both the police and the STF. One possible interpretation of the STF's inaction regards the culpability of the state and its failure to protect its citizens; the other is of course that the STF, after thirty years of training to fight a brutal war, were doing exactly what they were told to do with precision: what happened in Aluthgama was a precisely executed event. The Inspector General of Police stated, in fact, that if not for the interventions of the STF, the situation would have been far worse.[21] If Muslims fought the looters, the bloodshed would have been much greater; if the looters had engaged in hurting people, the death toll would have been higher.

Story #5: Victim's Tales about the Attacks, Looting, and Burning

In trying to understand the story about property in Aluthgama, two persons come to mind especially. One was a thirty-year-old-plus Muslim man, tall, clad in blue jeans and a T-shirt, who met us while we were at the Seenawatte mosque. He said that he was the owner of a small corner shop (*sillara kade*) and a pharmacy. He owned a house and two vehicles. The mobs had attacked all his assets. His van, parked on the street in Dharga Town close to the main mosque, was the first Muslim-owned vehicle to be set alight. Then the mob had broken into and burnt his second vehicle that was parked in his garage and not visible to the outside. The shop was looted and burned. All the stocks from his pharmacy had been carried off; and his equipment, storage shelves, and so forth were destroyed. They had also set fire to his house. He told us that he had no insurance, so he would recover nothing. He said he had worked hard all of his life to create a path toward a comfortable existence for his family. But this government, what they were telling Muslims, he said, was this: "You should not live well, you should not be successful. You should not prosper."

We entered a large compound on Military Road; the gates made of sheet metal had holes in them. It was then some two weeks after the violence, but the burned out husks of seven vehicles and two motorbikes were still to be cleared. The family's business consisted of leasing and renting out vehicles for the transportation of goods. Zaruk Haji, the owner, was a large and very dark-skinned man with reddened eyes. He greeted us with a nod and went on to relate the manner in which the mobs had forced themselves into his well-secured compound, despite the fact that he and his son had tried to fight them off. He talked about how the intruders had run all over his compound "like drunken mice" and how they hadn't left a thing untouched. They had looted and burned both buildings in the compound: his house and his office. He had begged them to spare his vehicles. He had tried everything in his power to dissuade them, he said. His mother was Sinhala, and he had even told them that he was actually Sinhalese, but they had not let up. They didn't even allow him to move the women and children out of the compound, he said. Their jewelry was stolen, their clothing, all their documents (land deeds, proof of ownership, marriage certificates, birth certificates, school certificates, etc.) were destroyed. The mob beat the two men for resisting. Zaruk Haji recalled the manner in which a mason he used to hire, whom he recognized, had swung a spade at him.

Story #2 (Continued Again): My Analysis

The stereotype of Muslims wielding considerable acumen in commercial trade had been internalized by many of the Muslim business people who had lost property in the looting and arson in Aluthgama. They felt that they had been true to the rules of the national economy, ensuring that their shops had fixed prices, refusing to participate in ripping off tourists, and providing more substantial services to their customers.[22] Middle-class Muslims in Aluthgama had taken their engagement with the state, and their position as good trader citizens, very seriously. The failure of state functionaries and institutions to deliver during their hour of greatest need, and the Muslim traders' feeling that these same state functionaries were, in fact, complicit in the violence, terrorizing them and inflicting damage on their property, was unacceptable to many of them. I read the situation in the same way as the affected Muslims—the state had failed to protect property. Within a neoliberal state, where the state is enjoined to protect property and to ensure the freedom of the market, the very premise for the state's existence was called into question (Harvey 2007). The state was no longer the protector of these Muslim merchants' right to do business. It was now perpetrating violence against Muslim competence, entrepreneurship, and trade facility. This sense of betrayal by the state, and more specifically the regime in power, was articulated very strongly by all of the people with whom we spoke. As Zaruk Hajji's son said to us, "If there had been at least one policeman actively present, the violence could have been stopped. But no one came." The event that terrorized them and destroyed their property also affected their expectations that their class position guaranteed certain privileges. After the event, the middle-class Muslim victims were compelled to radically question their relationship to both the state and the neoliberal economy.

Story #6: The Narrative of Class

The rhetoric deployed by the mostly middle-class victims of Aluthgama when referring to the perpetrators of violence is also significant. For instance, Zaruk Hajji was very clear that many of the people who attacked his compound were all known to him personally. When we visited him again in March 2015, he recounted a very interesting instance. "Among the attackers was a timber baas, whom we had paid close to Rs. 375,000 [@ $2,800] for his labour charge alone to install a timber staircase in my brother-in-law's house. He actually set fire to the staircase himself. The people who came and attacked us were not 'decent people' who have jobs, who are law abiding people who would not do such things." In this case, Zaruk Hajji was referencing not just income or class but caste as well. Many Muslims talked to us about the fact that the people who attacked them were *rasthiyadu karayo* ["lay abouts"]. Another statement we heard often in relation to the extensive and organized looting was that "they organised themselves to commit highway robbery. There was nothing 'ethnic' about this." Clearly a majority of those who were organized to participate in the violence were from the urban poor, engaged mostly in the sector of informal income-generating activities; they were identified as such by the middle-class gaze of their victims. Aluthgama Muslims understood the violence as state forces colluding with the underclass in terrorizing them and perpetrating violence against their property.

As a privileged middle class within a neoliberal economy, the Muslims affected had internalized middle-class expectations of the state so that it would enable their practices of accumulation and divert violence threatened by "riffraff." In Aluthgama, clearly this had not happened. The institutions of the state had, in fact, enabled the "riffraff" to destroy middle-class property. The neoliberal promise of state protection for middle-class success was radically skewed in favor of the Sinhala–Buddhist *rasthiyadu karaya*. In the case of Aluthgama, the "rationality" and "integrity" of the market was eclipsed by the ethnicity of the state.

Pradeep Jeganathan has noted the manner in which capital "dissolved" and disappeared in the riots of 1983. In that nuanced analysis of the manner in which a neighborhood flood in the 1990s and the violence of July 1983 had undermined principles of property ownership, Jeganathan argued that class enmities were worked out through the July violence in unanticipated ways due to the nonintervention of the state and the police. In the case of Aluthgama, there seems to have been a concerted attempt to let class enmities unleash themselves while representatives of state institutions mandated to control such violence ensured instead that no lives were lost.

Story #7: Terrorists in Dharga Town

In Welipitiya, the narrative was different. In that town at the northern end of Dharga Town, the people had gathered near the entrance to the village, determined to defend themselves and keep the attackers out. The mobs therefore encountered stiff resistance near the Welipitiya mosque by residents armed with sticks, stones, and glass bottles. Several persons sustained injuries and two lost their lives. The anger at the state had a different flavor among the Welipitiya Muslim community, given that the violence actually *was* perpetrated against persons. There the victims found state functionaries to be thoroughly "ethnicized" and complicit in the perpetration of violence. There was a strong sense that the state armed forces were involved in the violence committed against Muslims and in a cover-up of that violence. Specifically, there has been much speculation about how the industrial strength flashlights were shone in the pitch blackness of night where and when there was no power at all available in the area. And there has been further speculation about who might have been responsible for the gun shots that had caused two deaths and crippled two young men. Two young men who decided to speak to us from the area were both very articulate school teachers. When we asked them who they thought had fired the shots that had resulted in two fatalities and the injuries to two teenagers, one of them stated the following:

> The forces have a procedure that they follow: first they warn, then they use tear gas, later maybe rubber bullets, and it is only after that, if the situation really warrants, that there will be a use of live ammunition. If it was the forces, why didn't they issue a warning? Why didn't they use tear gas? They used it to disperse a crowd of 3000 near the main mosque in town? Why use live bullets on us—we were only about 50 people who were surrounding the mosque and protecting the people inside. Also when the shooting happened, the bottles and rocks were continuing to fall on us. So it's not as if they shot in the air to disperse the crowds; the attack continued from the people on that side. And if it was the STF that shot at us, why didn't they help us in the aftermath? And most of all, we were the ones being attacked. The forces should have been on our side of the road protecting us and our property. No, we don't think it is the forces that shot at us. We think it must have been a terrorist group.

This statement, full of irony, is a scathing indictment of the state and its treatment of Muslims. Here these young men invoke a conception of the state and its principled commitment to rules and procedures governing the use of legitimate violence. If not followed, then the suspect and illegitimate violence must mean the work of a rhetorical "other" of the state, that is, a terrorist group. These young men were mirroring almost exactly the rhetoric of a prominent state representative, Defence

Secretary Gotabhaya Rajapaksa's, regarding the possible presence of Islamic "extremists" in the country.[23]

It is interesting, then, to speculate about the state's response to Aluthgama. The president, as I mentioned earlier, constantly (and with visible anger) reiterated that "not much actually happened in Aluthgama." On one level, he was right. Not much did happen in Aluthgama in comparison to the many atrocities that were experienced by the citizens of Sri Lanka during thirty plus years of civil war. At the time that the Aluthgama violence occurred, Sri Lanka was under intense scrutiny by the United Nations Human Rights Council for alleged war crimes. A US-sponsored resolution calling for an investigation in to the allegation was passed in March 2014; and the investigation, which the government strongly opposed, was ongoing when Aluthgama happened. There were also several reports accusing the government of violence and human rights abuses in the north. Human Rights Watch had released a report accusing the police and the military of extensive crimes of sexual violence against Tamils. The violence in Aluthgama paled in contrast—buildings were burned and shops and homes looted and some people suffered injuries. Of those with serious injuries, two young men lost their legs. Three people died. The state's rehabilitation response to the Aluthgama violence was also unprecedented. The Sri Lanka Army Engineers Corps was sent in within a week of the violence to start cleaning up and to begin the rebuilding process. When we returned to Aluthgama eight months later, in March 2015, quite a few of the houses had been rebuilt and handed back over to residents. Some construction was still ongoing. Six Sinhala houses in Pathirajagoda had been attacked. These too had been rebuilt.

Story #8: "Sinhala" Stories

We talked to two Sinhala women in a large sprawling house full of beautiful southern antique furniture in the Dharga Town suburb of Sinawatte. The two women said they had first heard shouting and breaking glass and then had run out into the road. They saw the mobs running down the road brandishing weapons. Then they saw them trying to attack the houses of their Muslim neighbors and had shouted, asking them to stop. But they too were threatened. Then they also heard some Muslim boys who were chasing the attackers. It was then that the attackers fled, they said. If the Muslims had not come, then things would have been much worse, they said.

In addition to a discussion about what happened, we talked a little bit about why it happened. We were told that the Muslim boys should not have hit the Buddhist monk during the "triggering" event. *Api vadhinawane*—"we worship them/we pray to them." They should not have done that. And they said that, again if the Muslims had not thrown a stone at the parade [*perahera*], then the situation would not have escalated. They had seen the video uploaded on YouTube about how Muslims had started it. (This same video had been discussed among Muslims as indicating that the Sinhalese were responsible for initiating the confrontation!) For these two Sinhala women, the cause for this breakout of violence was Muslim provocation.

The stories that were circulated via short message service were to blame for the Sinhala people in the village becoming agitated. For instance, there was a story circulated that Muslims had killed two young monks inside their mosque and that Sinhala people had gathered together to retrieve the bodies for proper burial. Then, there was another story that young monks had been kidnapped and were being held hostage in a mosque. There was yet another that a young monk had been hacked to death. "It is natural for people to react when they hear stories like that," one of the women said. "That is really the reason for the violence spreading."

The two Sinhala women also said that they felt many Muslim neighbors were angry at them for not doing more. What were we to do?, they said.

> We had information from people who were in the [armed] forces who said that nothing like that—Muslims killing monks—had taken place. But there was nothing we could do. We didn't like the way in which that monk spoke [referring to Gnanasara Thero]. That also must be said. He should not have spoken like that. We are very close to the Muslim people here. When my brother was killed in the war, Muslims carried the coffin

> for part of the way. We had an ice cream *dansala* [food offering] for *poson* [the full moon day in June] and many of the Muslims contributed to it. But now they are very unhappy with us. We were so close with everyone. We were ashamed of what the Sinhala boys did that day. [By this time one of them was fighting back tears while the other was openly crying.]

In the suburb of Adhikarigoda, smaller, middle-class Muslim dwellings were also attacked. Among them was one Sinhala house. We spoke with a shirtless young man who came out of the house that was undergoing a renovation by green T-shirted and camouflage-pant clad soldiers. The young man described the attack, part of which he seemed to have witnessed and part of which he must have heard from others.[24] Signs of "Muslimness" and Sinhala–Buddhist identity were mobilized in his narrative. He said that he saw a crowd of *ape ayyala*, "our older brothers," running and shouting that there were Muslims, *hambayo* [derogatory term for Muslims], chasing them. He said that after the crowd had passed, he saw Muslims chasing them and throwing glass bottles of aerated water and perfume (because Muslims don't have access to alcohol bottles, he told us). He also stated later that it was pitch dark and people could barely see. He said he recognized some of the attackers by their voices as Muslims from the neighborhood, and that they talked in a derogatory and sexualized way about his cousin. Only those who knew them would have known her name, he said. Muslim neighbors say that their house was attacked by accident because the mob did not know that the house was owned by Sinhalese, he said. But the *Vesak Kudu*, or the paper lanterns hung up for *poson poya*, were used as fuel to set the house on fire; and the *Sivali Budhu Pilimaya*, the statue of the Lord Buddha, was also broken. Therefore, someone other than a Buddhist must have carried out this act of violence. He also stated that when the Sinhala mob heard that a Sinhala house had been attacked, they had come to help put the fires out.

Whereas the identity discourse of Buddhist/Muslim difference clearly demarcating "us" and "them" was maintained in the telling of the story, it soon started to break down. The young man blamed social media for the proliferation of hate sentiment and said that those who were active on Facebook about Muslims don't really know the "flavor" of living among the Muslims. Then he also talked about the fact that whereas the Muslims around his neighborhood were generally good and that Sinhalese got along well with them, there were other Muslims over the hill who were not so good. They were criminals and had been caught illegally transporting cattle for slaughter. "They were 'jihad,'" he said. It was they who would have attacked his house.

The tropes of "us and them," the "good" and the "bad," were worked into certain segments of this young man's narrative. However, it was extremely difficult to sustain it in the detailed description of the mayhem that he witnessed. For instance, in describing the attackers, the young man was quick to distance himself from those who had entered the area from elsewhere, regardless of the fact that these were Sinhala Buddhists. He said there were women wearing short pants using filthy language, *kunu harapa*, that he had not even heard before. He said people had been brought from outside, that a truckload of alcohol had been supplied to the crowds with the bottles to be used as weapons. He said that there were even "professional" people among them. (This we took to mean professional fighters, the military.) In talking about them he was not too eager to identify closely with them.

In the case of the two women, although provocation and rumor were understood as a factor in what made Sinhala Buddhists mobilize, everyday life becoming severely disrupted was also foremost in their minds. I saw the two women struggle with a need to acknowledge Buddhist identity and endorse the actions of the Buddhist community, even violence, in support of Buddhist preservation, regardless of the damage done thereby to the community of everyday interaction. However, it was also clear that the breakdown of everyday community was also strongly regretted. The young man from Adhikarigoda also reflected this distress. He stated that he was very unhappy with how things were at the moment. He was "fed up," he said, of the long faces of his Muslim neighbors. People that he had moved very closely with, who had shared food and things, were now turning their faces away. He was sick of it (*athi wela thiyenne*) and wanted to move away. He was angry with the neighbors and accused them even of claiming losses of gold, and so forth, that he was sure they never had. When he had known about the rally in Aluthgama and that there was a suspicion of tensions escalating, he had moved his family van that was usually parked in a Muslim lady's house to another place for safety. His Muslim neighbors think that this means he knew about the attack, and that maybe he had a hand in it, he said. The lady who owned the Muslim house was devastated by this act, we were told, when we inquired about this incident from other Muslims. She felt that it was because, as Sinhalese, they knew there were going to be attacks, and that is why the van was moved. Why didn't they tell her?, she wondered. To the Muslims this was evidence of their Sinhala neighbors' complicity.

Among the Muslims in the Adhikarigoda neighborhood, there was very little knowledge and minimal sympathy for the damages suffered by the Sinhala house. The Muslim houses had suffered much greater damage, they said. They had not gone to see the house, had never talked about it, and were not convinced by the stories of the damage, one of the Muslim neighbors told us. One person who we talked to even suggested that the damage may have been self-inflicted. The deterioration of relations and the ethnicization of the narrative of victimhood was such that neither group could see the other as anything other than essentially ethnic.

One woman stated that she had discussed the event with her Sinhala neighbor. In other neighborhoods, some Sinhalese had defended their neighbors from their fellow ethnics, she said. But in Adhikarigoda that didn't happen. This woman had told her neighbor that they should have done more to defend their Muslim friends. But the neighbor had said that as the perpetrators came with weapons, "we too feared for our lives." The Muslim woman did not accept her Sinhala neighbor's disavowal of her responsibility to defend her neighbors from the threat of her fellow ethnics. "They were their own people, they (the Sinhala neighbors) should have done something," she said. Her Sinhala neighbor's claim of danger from a fellow ethnic was not entertained or taken as legitimate by the Muslim woman. The Muslims were so completely interrelated in ethno-religious terms during 2013 and 2014 that the fact that this may not have been the case for other religious communities may have troubled some of them; that other allegiances may trump ethno-religious commonality could not even be entertained by this woman.

For the Sinhala interlocutors, the violence was shocking and difficult to come to terms with. And there was deep regret expressed at the breakdown of social relations. However, their very differently organized narratives speak to a dissonance in the understanding of the event between the Muslims and the Sinhalese that they all simultaneously experienced, one that indicates both the cultivated polarization prior to the event and its consolidation in the aftermath. The people in the neighborhood had lived in close proximity to one another while occupying vastly different realities regarding their most recent pasts.

Story #8: The Story of Muslim Extremism (the "True Story of Aluthgama")

The Sinhala Buddhist "establishment" was extremely agitated at the manner in which the Aluthgama incident became almost instantaneously internationalized to the extent that it was mentioned in the British parliament; at the UN Human Rights Council that was then in session; that there was a statement from the Organisation of Islamic Cooperation; and that several foreign missions, including the American Embassy and the European Union, released statements condemning the attack. The Sinhala establishment narrative saw the Sinhala anger that erupted in Aluthgama as legitimate and was distressed at the manner in which the "real" problem behind the violence in Aluthgama, in fact the problem to which the BBS was a solution, was not being articulated in any substantive manner.[25] Although there were many voices that articulated this particular position, that of legitimate Sinhala anger, a Jathika Hela Urumaya parliamentarian Champika Ranawaka who was a cabinet member in the Rajapaksa government, and is now cabinet member under Maithripala Sirisena, was perhaps the most vocal and most visible proponent of this position. He also fleshed out and intellectualized the problem articulated in openly racist terms by the Rev. Gnanasara in ways that only a few other Sinhala intellectuals have done.[26]

Just days after the violence, a video was uploaded to YouTube portraying the damage done to six Sinhala homes in the Pathirajagoda suburb of

Dharga Town. The video is entitled "The True Story of Aluthgama." At the beginning of this film, parliamentarian Champika Ranawaka makes an extensive statement to the media. The focus of Ranawaka's intervention was on setting the narrative of the events "right" by introducing "new information" regarding the Aluthgama violence that had been "suppressed" by the media. Ranawaka stated that the violence occurred because there was a meeting of Jihadists spreading hate sentiment in Dharga Town and that it was these individuals who first attacked the Sinhalese. It was in response to this violence that the Sinhalese became angered and the subsequent troubles had started in various places in Aluthgama and Dharga Town. He accused Muslim ministers of misleading the public and especially foreign embassies in Colombo. He stated that this entire event had been part of an international conspiracy to isolate Sri Lanka and to further bring down the reputation of "our armed forces" (under scrutiny for war crimes at that time) in the international arena.[27]

I am, of course, most interested in the manner in which Muslim Jihadism in Sri Lanka is framed by Ranawaka:

> What happened in Aluthgama was a response. What was the real problem to which this was a response? And there *is* a "real problem." The problem is that there is a small jihad group that is operating inside the Muslim community and they are trying to introduce a separatist ideology into the Muslim community and take them on a journey towards extremism.

And then, later on:

> What they are doing is that they are building up Taliban cells. We tell Madame Cisson [American Ambassador] about their responsibility. America nurtured the Taliban in Afghanistan and they attacked New York. In the same way these Taliban cells that you are feeding in Sri Lanka will come to Washington and kill your children! [28]

In between the two statements, Ranawaka produces a litany of complaints that include seeing how Muslims' transformation toward greater piety during the past thirty years or so is indicative of the emergence of extremism. He specifically names transformed dress practices and the demand for halal labeling as indicative of this social separatism (*samaja bedumvadaya*) of the Muslims. Then he makes the leap to linking this "social separatism" to the possibility of violence, that the Muslims of Sri Lanka are transforming themselves into "Taliban cells" that will kill American children.

Story #2 (Yet Again): My Analysis and Conclusion

This jump from practices of everyday piety, dress, and food to militancy is a consistence rhetorical move made by all proponents of action against "Islamic extremism" in the country. Linking Muslims newfound piety to stories of militancy for political purposes has a history that predates the BBS and Champika Ranawaka in Sri Lanka. During the time of the LTTE too, it was regular practice to mention "Jihad" groups in relation to the Muslims of the east. For Ranawaka too, then, the justification for Sinhala anger was the emergent "Jihad" groups.

As I have argued elsewhere, reformists did actively cultivate social distancing, and not just through dress and food practices. However, what seems to escape most commentators, racist or liberal, is the fact that the reformists in Sri Lanka have concentrated almost exclusively on everyday practices of personal piety. The discourse of political Islam has been virtually absent from the country. (An engagement with an Islamic discourse that includes the state is emerging, but this is Fiqh Al-Aqalliyyat, the discourse on jurisprudence about Muslims living as minorities in non-Muslim majority countries.[29]) The reformist group most successful in Sri Lanka, the Tablighi Jamaat, has been explicit in its embrace, in other contexts, of a nonpolitical position (Metcalf 2002). Identified Muslim political parties, such as the Sri Lanka Muslim Congress (SLMC) and the All Ceylon Makkal Congress, were ideologically concerned with the representation of Muslims as a community group and in garnering Muslim votes. There is no publicly expressed affinity to any Islamic ideology of the state by these parties. Those who have researched the "Islamic" nature of the Muslim congress have argued that the SLMC was quick to distance itself from being considered an *Islamic* party (Knoerzer 1998; McGilvray and Raheem 2007). Additionally in Sri Lanka, Muslim political representation has been mostly with the larger national political parties; that is, the constituencies of the Muslim parties have been fairly marginal when compared with the entire Muslim voter population of the country. These facts are not well known in the country; and few have looked at what political claims Islamic militancy, if it were to emerge, would make in the Sri Lankan context.[30] In Aluthgama, Ranawaka argued that the possibility of militancy emerging was reason enough for the violence.

The lessons that Aluthgama holds, then, are many. In the aftermath of the attacks, anti-Muslim sentiment was at its highest point. We attempted to put together a team to do the fact-finding exercise in Aluthgama, but getting another scholar/activist to join me and other Muslims proved to be an uphill task. Several agreed and then pulled out. We were told by other colleagues to make sure that we were sensitive to "both sides." The fact that the progressive community members were urging us to follow what had become the narrative of a repressive state whose culpability was speedily becoming apparent was disturbing to say the least.

Stories are created in conversations with interlocutors and audiences in mind. The stories about Aluthgama, regardless of the clarity that many had as to the manner in which an ethnic community was being held hostage to the dynastic ambitions of one family, the Rajapaksas, were not always uniform. The seething anger against social, ethnic, and religious others, inevitable perhaps in a ethno-religiously plural polity such as ours, was mobilized to excellent effect in what was a relatively short time. Politically, there was an attack on Muslim property in a vein that was familiar to Sri Lanka. As an angry Rauf Hakeem (SLMC leader) stated at a press conference in the aftermath of the Aluthgama attacks, this was the Muslims being taught a lesson. In the aftermath of "the lesson," the state steadfastly stood its ground regarding the issue of Muslim culpability for the attacks. Additionally, the state imposed a news blackout on the national media that meant that few had much information about the incident. This was not lost on all political commentators in Sri Lanka, and thankfully some record and analysis of the event remains.[31] But the general response was worrying. In the melee of competing stories regarding the event, the Muslim narrative, the state narrative, the Buddhist national narrative, and the international condemnatory rhetoric, it was perhaps difficult for citizens of the country to come to an understanding of the issue.

Muslims should heave a sigh of huge collective relief that Aluthgama was no worse than what it was. As stated earlier, Sri Lanka has been the location of countless atrocities for which redress is yet to be found. People in Aluthgama, thankfully, are moving on. It is important also that perspective is maintained regarding Aluthgama and the nature of the lesson that Muslims were taught. The manner in which Muslims were targeted, with an emphasis on the destruction of property, leaves many important unanswered questions. What does it say about who is being mobilized for political work in this country? What class enmities are being ethnicized and for what purpose?

Aluthgama also holds a lesson for the manner in which stories of hate, belonging, supremacy, and legitimacy become normalized in this age of social media and irresponsible governance. When Maithripala Sirisena first defected from the folds of the governing coalition and accepted the role of presidential candidate, he caused a huge crack in the dominant narrative of the regime's postwar success. This opening up of a space to critique what many found appalling about the excesses of the Rajapaksas made possible a rewriting of the dominant narrative regarding Muslim hate as well.

We have some clarity today regarding what we can talk about and how we can talk about ethnic relations. The Ven. Gnanasara's particular brand of minority vilification no longer has the legitimacy that it enjoyed under the Rajapaksas. The president has stated publicly that there is no place for racism in Sri Lanka's transition. Many continue, however to speak disparagingly of Muslims referencing the tropes made popular by the BBS. However, the fact that there is no longer state sanction for such speech—and that the national mood, at least of the governing party, is, in fact, completely against such rhetoric—means that the likelihood of such speech becoming part of legitimate, collectively formulated stories becomes less and less. It is very likely that problems will continue in a multiethnic polity such as ours; therefore age-old rules regarding how we live with one another need to be rethought and reformulated. There is much talk about reconciliation these days. But no one seems to have quite defined what this may mean. It could be as simple as reimagining the social rules of engagement and reciprocity through which we tell our collective stories as different ethnic and religious communities.

NOTES

1. The fieldwork on which this chapter is based draws from three trips to Aluthgama with a team from the Law and Society Trust (LST) to formulate a fact-finding report. The report is entitled "Where Have All the Neighbors Gone? *Aluthgama Riots and Its Aftermath: A Fact Finding Mission to Aluthgama, Dharga Town, Valipanna, and Beruwala*" (Haniffa et al. 2015). I thank the LST for permission to use the material. Further, in this chapter I do not refer in too much detail to the event itself. Please refer to the report for additional details.
2. July 1983 is an iconic event in the history of the Sri Lankan ethnic conflict where Tamil homes and businesses across the island were attacked by organized groups of thugs. Many in fact regard it as marking the beginning of the conflict.
3. S. J. Tambiah, "The Colombo Riots of 1983," in *The Sri Lanka Reader*, ed. John Clifford Holt (Durham, NC: Duke University Press, 2011), 643.
4. Interview with local Muslim provincial councilor, July 2014.
5. LST report on Aluthgama: *Where Have all the Neighbors Gone? Aluthgama Riots and Its Aftermath* (Haniffa et al. 2015).
6. There have been many attacks against small Muslim communities that have been sparked off by individuals falling out with each other.
7. See Secretariat for Muslims, "Anti-Muslim Sentiment in Sri Lanka: Hate incidents of 2014." (Colombo, Sri Lanka: Secretariat for Muslims, 2015).

8. Muslim activists also emphasized that they were told by the Deputy Inspector General, Mr. Anura Senanayake, that there were orders from "higher up" to not stop the BBS meeting.
9. The comment begs an explanation as to the curious relationship between Muslims activists and Tamil nationalism. I have explored this issue at some length elsewhere in "Conflicted Solidarities? Muslims and the Constitution making process of 1970–1972" (Haniffa 2012) and in "Competing for Victimhood Status: Northern Muslims and the Ironies of Sri Lanka's Post-War Transition" (Haniffa 2014). See also "The Quest for Redemption: The Story of the Northern Muslims," (Report of the Citizens' Commission on the Expulsion of Muslims from the Northern Province by the LTTE in October 1990) Law and Society Trust (2011).
10. There have been other clashes at different times and different places. For instance, Puttalam in 1976, Galle in 1982, Mawanella in 2001, and Aluthgama in 2006.
11. And needless to say, a source of amusement for some Tamil commentators.
12. Devanesan Nesiah, "The Riots of June 2014 and the Pogrom of July 1983." http://groundviews.org/2014/07/04/the-riots-of-june-2014-and-pogrom-of-july-1983/ (July 4, 2014). I have taken out the following sentences from the middle of this quote. "In both cases there were many Sinhalese families and individuals who incurred much cost and great risk in helping individuals and families attacked or under risk of attack to escape. Several institutions helped but few found it possible to openly confront the attacking mobs." In fact, there were very few Sinhalese families who actually tried to help; we encountered only two such stories in extensive conversations with affected Muslims. In fact, our report ("Where Have All the Neighbours Gone?") reflects what was *different* about Aluthgama was precisely the fact that neighbors were reluctant to help out.
13. There are many references that can be cited in relation to description and analyses of July 1983. A possible start is Michael Roberts' 2008 piece on July 1983, "Looking Back in Anger and Despair 25 Years on," in *Groundviews*. http://groundviews.org/2008/07/25/july-1983-looking-back-in-anger-and-despair-25-years-on/. For

a powerful and poignant personal account of that time and some important insights into what the political elite was doing during those days, see Devanesan Nesiah, "On the 30th Anniversary of the Pogrom of July 1983." http://groundviews.org/2013/08/02/on-the-30th-anniversary-of-the-pogrom-of-july-1983/

14. "I Deplore any form of Extremism; Gota," *Daily Mirror*, Thursday, July 4th, 2014.
15. This was despite the fact that the army was called in on the 16th of June to dispel the mobs.
16. See "Where Have All the Neighbors Gone?: Report on Aluthgama Riots and Its Aftermath."
17. See, for instance, Dharisha Bastians and Gardiner Harris, "Buddhist-Muslim Unrest Boils Over in Sri Lanka," *The New York Times*, June 16, 2014, http://www.nytimes.com/2014/06/17/world/asia/deadly-religious-violence-erupts-in-sri-lanka.html?_r=0. Also see Dharisha Bastians, "UK House of Lords Raises Aluthgama Riots," published in the local *Financial Times*, July 4, 2014, http://www.ft.lk/2014/07/04/uk-house-of-lords-raises-aluthgama-riots/
18. Drawing attention to this distinction does not in any way intend to minimize the experience of the victims. But it is an important distinction for analytical purposes.
19. See Michael Roberts, "Looking Back in Anger," on July 1983, and the Law and Society Trust report on Aluthgama (Haniffa et al 2015). In Aluthgama, the violence was experienced in the Dharga Town suburb of Welipitiya. There, the people gathered at the mosque and waited for the inevitable arrival of mobs and prepared to defend themselves with household implements, rocks, bricks, and bottles. When the mobs arrived, they had started attacking one another by throwing stones and bricks at each other. It is in the deterioration of this situation that shots had been fired from among the attacking mobs, killing two men, crippling two boys, and injuring several others.
20. There was some controversy regarding the shooting deaths in Welipitiya; the Government Medical Officer's report stated that one of the fatal wounds were from a knife cut and not a bullet. Much was made of this claim, and the government was accused of trying to cover up military involvement. See, for instance, Saman Indrajith,

"Aluthgama Mayhem: Ranil Alleges Cover-up," *The Island*, July 8, 2014, http://www.island.lk/index.php?page_cat=article-details&page=article-details&code_title=106471.

21. See "Where Have All the Neighbors Gone?: Report on Aluthgama Riots and Its Aftermath."
22. See also Qaudri Ismail (1995) on the Muslim trader elite's self-representation.
23. In fact, the Ven. Gnanasara had called Dharga Town "a hot bed of extremism" in the speech that many feel incited the violence in the first place.
24. He told us later that while the violence was occurring, he had gone to find his aunt who had promptly locked him inside her house.
25. https://lrrp.wordpress.com/2014/07/10/23-sinhala-buddhist-organizations-reveal-the-truth-about-clashes-in-aluthgama/
26. See, for instance, the post-Aluthgama commentary by Chandraprema in *The Island* newspaper of June 21st, 2014. In this commentary Chandraprema explores why Muslims may want to become militant in the context of Sri Lanka and concludes that they do not have sufficient reasons for doing so. He states "Muslim extremism does not pose a danger to this country the way Tamil separatism did. The Muslims never asked for a separate state and given the distribution of the population such will be impossible. Muslim extremism will mostly be a state of mind and nothing more. Even if Muslim extremists start a terror campaign in this country, what will that achieve other than getting themselves killed?
27. Much of this same information was articulated in a media statement released by 23 Buddhist organizations that bemoaned the action taken by the Information Department to suppress press coverage of the incident, which meant that only one side of the story was made available internationally. According to the statesmen, "Sinhala Buddhists were condemned for the whole world to see as religious bigots who were against other religions, such as Islam, Christianity and Hinduism. We were greatly pained by these developments and register our extreme condemnation of premeditated action by the authorities which could harm the country's image internationally." The statement can be found at https://lrrp.wordpress.com/2014/07/10/23-sinhala-buddhist-organizations-reveal-the-truth-about-clashes-in-aluthgama

28. *US Creating a Taliban in Sri Lanka: Champika. DailyMirror* online, June 20, 2014, http://www.dailymirror.lk/48702/tech
29. Said Fares Hassan, *Fiqh Al-Aqalliyyat: History, Development, and Progress* (New York: Palgrave MacMillan, 2013).
30. One exception is Chandraprema in *The Island* newspaper of June 21st, 2014.
31. See, for instance, Darisha Bastians' excellent reporting on Aluthgama and related events in the *Financial Times*: "Alas Aluthgama!," June 4, 2014, available at http://www.ft.lk/2014/06/16/alas-aluthgama/; "The Agony of Aluthgama," June 17, 2014, http://www.ft.lk/2014/06/17/the-agony-of-aluthgama/https://www.colombotelegraph.com/index.php/aluthgama-a-game-without-winners/

CHAPTER EIGHT

A RELIGIOUS SYNTAX TO RECENT COMMUNAL VIOLENCE IN SRI LANKA

John Clifford Holt

INTRODUCTION

While on a Thai International Airways flight from Bangkok to Colombo on Monday, July 25, 1983, I fearfully read the lead story in the *Bangkok Post*: a violent imbroglio at Welikada Prison had occurred the previous night in Colombo, Sri Lanka, and consequently at least thirty-five Tamil prisoners had been killed in the mayhem. What I didn't know at that moment is that the prison murders were but a tiny portion of the chaos then unfolding in the country, what eventually amounted to a six-day riot throughout the southern Sinhala regions of the island that claimed the lives of an estimated two to four thousand Tamil people and resulted in a massive destruction of business and personal property. Indeed, I saw and heard much destructive havoc firsthand during the five days that followed my arrival. On my first night on the island, following a hair-raising, eye-opening foray into burning Colombo, the hotel next to mine was torched, completely burned out, its occupants and workers sent fleeing for their lives amidst a menacing crowd of rowdy young men. The next day on the way to Kandy, I saw groups of Sinhalese thugs stopping buses and vans searching for Tamils. That night in the hills above Kandy town, I could hear from down below the sounds of shattering glass; people shouting in Sinhala and Tamil; and men, women, and children shrieking. In the following three days, the retail heart of Kandy town was looted and burned out while Peradeniya town was also torched by thugs who arrived in lorries with cans and barrels of gasoline. After six days of bedlam ended with a 72-hour curfew, I traveled about upcountry Sri Lanka for several days and saw town after burned-out town: Nuwara Eliya, Welimada, Badulla, Bandarawela, Kegalle, Matale, and so forth, all sights of great devastation and death. Indeed, over the years that followed, July 1983 became a benchmark in Sri Lanka's history for many: it galvanized Tamil militant resistance such that the situation in the country eventually devolved into what became twenty-six years of intense civil war. Following 1983, an avalanche of scholarship and journalism was undertaken in attempts to ferret out not only the litany of events leading up to the riot per se but root causes of what became an extended armed conflict as well. Although I remained on the island after the 1983 riot for two years and paid close attention to local and international assessments, I kept quiet publicly about my own thoughts, even though I disagreed with the consensus of general appraisals: that what was unfolding was a war between religious antagonists. In addition to much of the scholarship, the international media almost always framed the sprouting civil war as a conflict between Sinhala Buddhists and Tamil Hindus, this despite the fact that the Liberation Tigers of Tamil Eelam (LTTE) went to great lengths to proclaim that they supported no religious causes whatsoever and that their aim of an independent state of Tamil Eelam was solely political in nature.

Moreover, from my own personal experiences in Sri Lanka, I hadn't seen much of what I would call religiously based, or religiously incited, violent behavior at the time of the 1983 riot, although the violence in Colombo purported initially broke out at a cemetery in Borella where a crowd had gathered to observe the funerals of thirteen Sinhalese soldiers who had been blown up by a land mine days before.[1] (I will return to the significance of this type of ritual occasion shortly.) To the contrary, almost all of the Sinhala Buddhists I had known and had spoken to extensively about the riots had expressed great chagrin and remorse about the ethnic violence that had occurred. Frankly, many were quite embarrassed that such violent pandemonium had occurred in their country. I also heard many stories about how some Sinhalas had heroically protected Tamil victims during the riots, and I keenly followed the proceedings of a greatly trumpeted, all-political party and all-religious communities conference that had been convened in Colombo ostensibly to help find ways to ameliorate the conditions of the postriot situation. At the time, it had seemed to me that religion, or religiously generated sentiments for communal concord, provided more of a hope for the solution to the ethnic conflict than its cause. The religious factor, in my view, was potentially a constructive one that could contribute necessarily to a healing process. Although it was gradually revealed later that sections of President J. R. Jayewardene's government were complicit in the pogrom victimizing Tamil people in July 1983, I had taken his own words seriously, words broadcast over the Sri Lanka Broadcast Corporation on the afternoon of Thursday, July 28, the fifth day of riots, that what had occurred was truly a "crisis in our civilization." Based on my own experiences and interactions with Buddhist people, admittedly mostly university academics and monks at a nearby neighborhood temple, I believed that what had transpired was certainly an anomaly and that the deeply rooted causes in play were primarily economic rather than religious in nature. I reasoned that although religion is without doubt a constituent element of ethnic identity, there was a fundamental difference in this case between the emergence of distinctive ethnic *identity* on one hand, part of which may be due to religious affiliation, and ethnic *alienation*, caused more fundamentally by an increasingly uneven playing field for economic opportunities, access to education, and the right to use one's mother tongue in public discourse.

I finally wrote about my views regarding causes for the ethnic violence many years later.[2] I argued that although it was true that in the aftermath of July 1983, and in the years of civil war that followed, as Buddhists tried to articulate reasons or rationales for the continuing violence, reasons that generally had to do with the necessity of preserving the nation for the sake of the religion, I remained unconvinced that religion itself was a primary reason or motive for the conflict. To support this view anecdotally, I recalled the specific circumstances in which the hotel next door to me had been burned down on my first night in Sri Lanka in 1983. Subsequently, I had come to know that the mob responsible for that incident was made up of young men who were all Christians. (The hotel was located in the enclave of Negombo, a town that is roughly 90% Roman Catholic, the remaining 10% being Buddhist and Muslim.) Finally, I had also written an article, focused on the events of the second Janatha Vimukthi Peramuna (JVP) uprising in 1988–1990, in which I had argued that ritual articulations in public could be considered more often a sign of the abatement of violence, a return to civil social normality, than either an occasion for the instigation of violence or a functional surrogate for violence itself.[3] In effect, in retrospect, I had continued to view religion as a positive construct that could ameliorate conflict.

In any case, this extended preamble leads to my first point that given the communal events of violence in Sri Lanka since 2012 that have been instigated by Buddhist nationalist groups, I have now reconsidered my views about how religion, more specifically religious culture, is implicated in violence between communities in Sri Lanka. I would now argue that it is just impossible not to consider the religious factor as central to what has been transpiring, especially when considering how moments of ritual observance, its venues and its temporal occasions, and predominate symbols of religious identity have figured in the unfolding dynamic of contestation. In this chapter, I will explain why I have shifted my perspective.

Rites and Symbols Are Not Merely Indexical

I begin by citing a passage taken from Leonard Woolf's diary written in 1911. Leonard Woolf is better known as the husband and Bloomsbury group publisher of his wife's work, the writings of Virginia Woolf. Before he married Virginia, Leonard Woolf served for over six years in the Ceylon civil service, living for about two years each in the Tamil dominated northern Jaffna peninsula, in the upcountry Sinhala–Buddhist dominated Kandyan highlands, and then in the Sinhala low-country scrub jungle region around Hambantota where, in each instance, he was the assistant government agent, or the principle judicial and administrative representative of British colonial power. Leonard Woolf's only novel, *A Village in the Jungle*, written during the year following his return to England in 1912 and his resignation from the civil service, was eventually turned into an award winning commercial film in Sri Lanka by the acclaimed filmmaker Lester James Pieris. (As a result, in his old age, Woolf attained something of an iconic status in Sri Lanka after the film's spectacular success for the manner in which it profoundly explores the desperate and sometimes sinister worldviews of exceedingly poor and vulnerable rural Sinhala peasants of the time.) Woolf's diary provides an excellent point of departure for my own reflections about how religious culture cannot be separated out from the dynamics of Sri Lanka's recent interethnic violence:

> May 12, 1911
> Holiday.
> At 5 p.m., I was just going out when a messenger arrived to say that there had been a riot going on in the town. The Buddhist procession had, he said, been stopped by the Mohamedans when passing the mosque and a large number of persons were fighting with sticks and stones. I went at once to the mosque but the fighting was over. Eight men were more or less injured including Mr. Amerasingha, Gansathawa clerk, who lives near and had tried to stop the row when it had begun and been hit in the face by a stone. The story at first told to me was that the Mohamedans attacked the Buddhist procession first with sticks. I was therefore not a little surprised to see 6 or 7 Mohamedans wounded and covered with blood and only one Sinhalese. I got hold of 3 or 4 non-residents who had been present and began Police Court proceedings at once. They were all Sinhalese and their evidence very soon showed that the row had started by the Buddhist procession tom-toming before they passed the mosque. Some Mohamedans tried to stop this and the Buddhists fell upon the Mohamedans, the latter being severely handled. The Mohamedans in the Bazaar hearing of this rushed to the spot in large numbers tearing up the fences to provide weapons. The Buddhists seeing they would be overwhelmed sought sanctuary in the police officer's house where they were soon surrounded by a crowd of angry Mohamedans.
>
> This was, of course, not quite the story as told by the Sinhalese, but as they had no time to prepare evidence, they very clearly gave it away. After recording sufficient evidence to make it clear, I adjourned.[4]

Woolf's diary entry turns out to be prescient. As he has indicated at the outset, May 12, 1911 was a holiday. But it wasn't just any holiday; it turns out to have been the ritual occasion of Vesak, the full moon day (or *poya*) that since the late 19th century Buddhist revival, led in part of by the American Theosophist Col. Henry Steele Olcott, had become the celebratory occasion marking the birth, enlightenment, and *parinibbana* (final attainment) of the Buddha. By the early 20th century, Vesak had become arguably the most sacred of ritual days for many Sinhalese Buddhists throughout the country: not only a festival of lights, when most Sinhala Buddhist families create paper lanterns to hang above their doorsteps, sing devotional songs (*bhakti gee*), and observe the basic fivefold moral precepts[5] but it had also become a prime occasion for the performance of *perahara*s, public processions affirming a Buddhistic sense of prosperity and the enduring hierarchical character of both the local social order and the traditional Buddhist nation-state.[6] *Perahera*s are at once both very noisy affairs (to which Woolf's mentioning of "tom toming" is a reference) and decorous public affirmations of Sinhala–Buddhist communal or national identity. I have recently written a chapter for a new book, *Theravada Traditions*, on how the relatively recent prolific spread of *perahara*s throughout Sinhala Sri Lanka quintessentially expresses the increasing specter of Sinhala Buddhist nationalism in a time of political uncertainty and perceived political vulnerability.[7] May 12, 1911 was also a Friday, and Woolf tells us that the timing of the fracas that occurred was in the afternoon, which means that the local mosque, at that time, was likely ending its weekly ritual prayers and sermons. What helped to give rise to the melee at the time, then, was a veritable collision of two ritual occasions of central importance to both religious communities, a collision of competing conceptions and expectations for sacred time and sacred space. The intrusion of one on the other was read not only as an act of intrusion but one of subordination, an existential threat. In other words, for the Muslims of Hambantota, it was a matter of Buddhist-dominating public space articulated by the *perahara* procession impinging on their sacred space (mosque) and time (Friday afternoon prayers). For the Buddhists, it was a matter of expressing their majoritarian entitlement to public space and public time while in the process asserting the dominance of their religious identities. What is prescient, as I have said, about Woolf's account is the fact that it preceded, by exactly four years (again on Vesak), the breakout of a massive communal riot in the upcountry Kandy region between Sinhala Buddhists and Muslims, a riot so serious in nature that the British declared a period of martial law that lasted for some four years. That is, in 1915, the most serious conflict between Muslims and Buddhists in Sri Lankan history occurred when a Vesak *perahara* passed by a mosque on a Friday while observant Muslims were engaged in ritual observances.[8]

When one reflects on the Sinhala–Buddhist and Muslim clashes of 1911 and 1915, it is possible to conjecture that what transpired was not a consequence of strategic planning on the part of the Buddhists; although in retrospect, the conducting of a consummately noisy procession in front of a mosque during times of ritual prayer may have been provocative indeed, it may not have been orchestrated precisely to rile up a response from Muslims, who in turn may have been spontaneous in their reaction to the disruption. In either case, whether intended or not, planned or spontaneous, the result was the same: simultaneously in play definitive ritual occasions and venues provided a perfect catalyst for communal violence.

These events are instances that reflect a religious syntax in political play. By religious syntax I mean to highlight how elements (symbols and rites) of religious culture can transcend their specifically religious connotations and assume significations that have definitive political denotations. (Invariably, religious culture and political identity are extremely difficult to separate out in South and Southeast Asian societies.) But what interests me here specifically in this context is how factors of ritual time, ritual space, and specific symbols can function as catalysts for the potential outbreak of intercommunal violence when they are deployed, targeted, or exploited for not only religious purposes. I use the term "syntax" because elements of religious culture sometimes occasion a syntactical structure, a rhetorical catalytic channel, or an emotional, transitive stimulus for the outbreak of intercommunal violence. Ritual and symbol, in these instances, do not so much signify a transcendent reality pointing to a trans-social or metaphysical reality as much as they can constitute or signify veritable existential social and political articulations.

Rites and symbols, particularly as they have been understood in Euro-American contexts, are sometimes regarded as formally orchestrated actions meant to signify the presence or reality of *something else*. They often function commemoratively for primordial events of the past, or function as a means of symbolically maintaining a consecrated order or identity. But in this context, I mean to indicate that they can also be regarded as occasions existentially constitutive, potent moments or designations that are not merely indexical.

A History of Desecration

Violent attacks at and on sacred places of religious worship became an all too frequent marker of intercommunal violence in the 1980s and 1990s in South Asian nation-states. Perhaps the most spectacular instance of this nature occurred in 1984 when Indian Prime Minister Indira Gandhi sent the Indian Army into the Sikh's revered Golden Temple premises in Amritsar where the Sikh revolutionary leader Bhindranwale had holed up with his militant cadres who had recently declared their intentions of establishing an independent state of Khalistan. In a ghastly firefight between Indian government troops and Sikh militants, over four hundred people were killed, including Bhindranwale himself. And seemingly, from one perspective at least, as an act of karmic retribution from the Sikh perspective, Mrs. Gandhi was subsequently assassinated by one of her Sikh bodyguards for having perpetrated such a desecration on this holy site. At the time of these events, I was still in Sri Lanka, and I remember not only feeling very disturbed when hearing about such a spectacularly violent invasion of a religious sanctuary but worrying about how the invasion of the Golden Temple and Mrs. Gandhi's assassination might set a very dangerous precedent. I was right to worry. Within months, an LTTE commando force stormed the premises of the Sri Mahabodhi sacred area in Anuradhapura and massacred 135 people, many of which were *dasa sil mata*s (Buddhist "nuns"). Sri Mahabodhi is believed to be the 2,500-year-old graft of the original *ficus religiosus* in Buddha Gaya in Bihar, under which the Buddha purportedly gained his original enlightenment. According to the Theravada Buddhist monastic chronicle, the *Mahavamsa* [XVIII–XIX], although the great Indian emperor Asoka's son, Mahinda, had established the monastic *sangha* in the 3rd century BCE in Lanka, it was Asoka's daughter, Sanghamitta, who had brought a sapling to symbolize the implantation of the *sasana* in Lanka for perpetuity. Sri Mahabodhi remains, along with the Dalada Maligava, a most sacred place of pilgrimage for Buddhists on the island today, and it has also been venerated by pilgrims internationally at least since the time of the 5th century Chinese monastic itinerant Fa Hien.[9] It remains a symbol of the Buddha's dispensation in Sri Lanka. And so it became a strategic target by the Tamil militants.

Unlike the riots sparked off by the Buddhist–Muslim collision of ritual cultures, the attacks on the Golden Temple and Sri Mahabodhi were, of course, premeditated—as was the attack by Hindu militants in India on the central Muslim mosque in Ayodhya in 1992, militants who erroneously claimed that the mosque had been built over the remains of a temple devoted to the very important Hindu deity, Rama. (In the epic *Ramayana*, Ayodhya was the site of primordial *brahmanical* kingship.) The semiotics of such attacks on sacred places can be interpreted in a very straightforward way. They are blatant desecrations of symbols and ritual venues that normatively reflect the highest religious values and visions that bind a religious community together. In other words, these violent attacks are acts of profanity meant to wound the identity and to desecrate the integrity of a religious community. As if to underscore their aim, within months of the Sri Mahabodhi attack, a busload of thirty Sinhala–Buddhist monks traveling near Arantalawa in the Eastern Province were unceremoniously offloaded by another squad of Tamil Tigers before their throats were slit and their bodies left strewn about the roadside. In the same way that many Buddhist nuns had been massacred at Sri Mahabodhi months earlier, so these other monastic incumbents wearing the saffron robe had been selected to be murdered as a symbol of their Tamil enemy's determination to desecrate the ideals of Sinhala–Buddhist religious culture.

Although the Tamil Tigers perpetrated many spectacular terrorist hits on prominent public places—including Bandaranaike International Airport, the Central Bank of Ceylon, and the central bus stand in downtown Colombo—as well as the assassinations of prominent government officials including defense ministers and the country's president (Ranasinghe Premadasa) in 1993, perhaps the most psychologically traumatic terrorist attack occurred in early 1998 when the Dalada Maligava, or Temple of the Tooth Relic, in Kandy was bombed. The *dalada*, or tooth relic of the Buddha, had become, at least by the 12th century, the palladium of Sinhala Buddhist kingship. Since that time, no temporal ruler was considered legitimate without claiming its custodianship. Indeed, a visit to Kandy and the Dalada Maligava is still regarded today as among the most important items of protocol for all newly arriving international diplomats on the island. It is also the ritual symbol celebrated and venerated during the annual *asala perahara*, the most famous of all public ritual pageants in Sinhala–Buddhist religious culture. The Dalada Maligava, like Sri Mahabodhi, is an internationally significant pilgrimage site for Buddhists all over Asia, not just for Sri Lanka and Theravada Southeast Asia. An attack on the Dalada Maligava, like the attack on Sri Mahabodhi, was a calculated assault on Buddhist religious culture, especially on how Buddhism has traditionally functioned as a legitimator of the Sinhala nation-state and insofar as Sri Lanka's current constitution (of 1978) provides that Buddhism will be given "the foremost place" among the country's religions. The attack was widely regarded in Sinhala circles as nothing less than naked aggression against the Sri Lankan nation-state per se.

The practice of desecrating sacred places, and what they stand for, was hardly monopolized by Tamil Tigers during the civil war. Sri Lankan government security forces often did not respect the sanctity of Hindu or Christian sacred places in the country's Tamil regions of the north and northeast. One need look no further than the violence in late 1980s and early 1990s that occurred at Nallur, the largest and perhaps most sacred Hindu temple in Jaffna, a venue sometimes referred to as the "heartbeat of Jaffna."[10]

The specifically South Asian religio-cultural and social significance of these historical events of terrorism are well kept in mind when we try to address the grammar of communal violence occurring in Sri Lanka recently, especially in the years following 2012, which witnessed unprecedented attacks by militant Buddhists on Muslim mosques and Christian churches. These attacks were also aimed at wounding and insulting, physically and psychologically.

The "Syntax" of Militant Buddhist Aggression

In June 2012, three years after the demise of the LTTE and the effective end of the civil war, troubles began for a small and modest mosque located nearby the historic Dambulla Rajamahavihara in the Central Province. Following an attempted firebombing that had occurred on the previous night, which led to the deployment of police and the army in the mosque's vicinity, an enterprising and well-known monk—who had arisen to notoriety in the 1990s for breaking away from the orthodox Siyam Nikaya sect and by leading protests, on environmental grounds, against the construction of a nearby five-star hotel—Ven. Sumangala Thero, addressed a large crowd on his temple premises, including many from the notorious chauvinistic Sinhala Ravaya ("roar of the Sinhalas") who had arrived on the scene from out of town. According to a well-placed British anthropologist who witnessed the events that then unfolded, Ven. Sumangala exhorted the crowd by asserting

> that Muslim terrorists are wiping out the Buddhist heritage in the whole of Asia. The crowd . . . had been gathered to protest the presence of a mosque that had been 'illegally' developed in an apparently exclusively Buddhist sacred area referred to as *Puja Bhumiya*. When Sumangala finished his caustic diatribe against Muslims in Dambulla, Asia, and the world, he led the march to the mosque. The tone set by his opening address was continued by the protestors as they proceeded down the road chanting, *may Sinhala, apigay ratay*—this is the country of us Sinhala people.[11]

The claim that Muslims were somehow usurping sacred areas or temple lands recalls the halcyon days of the Ven. Gangodawila Soma, an extremely popular and media-savvy *bhikkhu* who rose to fame as a self-proclaimed "modern monk" in the late 1990s and early 2000s. Soma led campaigns aimed at the elimination of deity veneration within Sinhala–Buddhist religious culture on the grounds that most deities worshipped by the Sinhalese are of Indian and Hindu origins and therefore not indigenous to Lanka. Indeed, he was correct in this assertion; but deities such as Natha, Visnu, Kataragama and Pattini, and so forth have been thoroughly "Sinhalized" over the past 800 to a thousand years. Indeed, each is regarded, as Gananath Obeyesekere has pointed out,[12] as a future Buddha or *bodhisattva*. (Natha is regarded popularly as a penultimate form of Maitreya, the next and future Buddha, whereas Visnu enjoys a reputation as the guardian of the *buddhasasana* in Lanka.) In any case, Soma was famous for preaching against both Christians and Muslims, to which he attributed a conspiracy to undermine Buddhism and take over Sri Lanka. For Soma, Sri Lanka was under a dangerous siege. The Muslims, in particular, had to bear his charges that they were overpopulating the country because of a lack of birth control practices, distorting the economy by aligning themselves with Middle Eastern financial interests (including the sending of their men and women to Persian Gulf states who allegedly would return to Lanka with exotic and extreme forms of understanding Islam), and their supposed insatiable desires to take over Sinhala lands. In one famous campaign, Soma cited how, over the centuries, Muslims had encroached on lands previously deeded by Sinhala kings to the Dighavapi sacred area, only recently (in the 1970s) rehabilitated by the state archaeology department. Dighavapi is regarded in Sinhala lore as one of the sixteen sacred places of pilgrimage associated with the Buddha's three visits to the island mythically narrated in the *Mahavamsa* monastic chronicle. This was a famous case in point that had served to highlight the general claims of a Muslim conspiracy to take over endowed Sinhala–Buddhist lands. And it was a claim that had been recently re-enforced in a court case brought against Muslims who had been resettled in the area about 13 km from Dighavapi following the 2004 tsunami, a settlement funded by a generous grant from Saudi Arabia. The court had ruled that the scheme to resettle Muslims only, and not to include Sinhalese, was unconstitutional. In Dambulla, Ven. Sumangala was tapping into and reviving the emotions of xenophobia generated by these controversies. The issue of Muslims being intent on commandeering sacred Sinhala–Buddhist land was further parlayed by radical Buddhist monks at a large public gathering of the Bodu Bala Sena (BBS) in Kandy in March 2013, when the assertion was made by a prominent monk that Muslims typically slaughter animals, then chant something he called the "Bismullah mantra," which allegedly has the effect of releasing *preta*s (ghosts) from the dead meat of the animals who then infest land, thereby making it uninhabitable by Buddhists.[13] Making fantastical claims like this became a hallmark of BBS propaganda.

As in the case of the Dambulla mosque, the threat of losing sacred space or sacred land is the prompt or rationale for engaging in communalistic contestation. And by invoking the sacrality of temple space, Ven. Sumangala provided the syntactical religious structure for advancing a political and economic cause. Luke Heslop, the British anthropologist I referred to earlier, assessed the Dambulla incident in the following manner:

> 'Preserving' a sacred area in Sri Lanka is at once performing a religious responsibility and inescapably at the same time, the pursuit of a Buddhist political project. . . . By staking the claim to a 'sacred area' and evoking the language of religious responsibility for the development of the town, Sumangala has carved out an effective way to wade into the murky waters of "the political."[14]

The Dambulla incident in particular raised consciousness of a Buddhist/Muslim conflict to the national level. Within months, a series of events attracted attention throughout the nation and made Buddhist extremist groups such as the Sinhala Ravaya and the now infamous BBS ("Army of Buddhist Power") household names in Lanka.

During a period of two and a half years from 2012 through mid-2014, according to a document prepared by the then Sri Lankan Minister of Justice Rauf Hakeem (a Muslim) for submission to the United Nations Human Rights Council, two hundred and forty documented perpetrations by Buddhists against Muslims exacerbated ethnic relations. In February 2013, the BBS engaged in public agitations urging a Buddhist boycott of Halal food, alleging that its unfettered sale results in unfair trade practices to the detriment of Sinhala merchants. Dilanthe Withanage, the lay "CEO" of the BBS, publicly alleged that sales from Halal have been used to fund the terrorist activities of Al Qaeda and Hamas.[15] The campaign against Halal then morphed into a boycott of Muslim clothing stores, including the largest clothing retailer on the island, Fashion Bug. One of Fashion Bug's stores in the southern coastal town of Kalutara was subsequently looted and set afire. The BBS proposed another ban too: that Muslim women should stop wearing the *niqab* and *burkah*. This issue subsequently gained traction because of "security concerns" insofar as the wearing of the *niqab* was seen, even within the university context, as making it possible for potential male terrorists to impersonate women; or, for instance, to take examinations at the university under false pretenses.[16] Articulations of religio-cultural identity became targets for political projects aimed at harming, subordinating, and disenfranchising Muslims.

Meanwhile, in addition to the campaign mounted by the BBS, another extremist Buddhist group, the Ravana Balaya ("Ravana's force"),[17] launched a two week, 250 km pilgrimage procession from the sacred shrine at Kataragama in the country's southeast to the capital of Colombo, concluding with a high-profile ceremonial presentation of a petition to then President Mahinda Rajapaksa, formally demanding that the government address the problem of the certification of Halal food. Again, the implication for the importance of sacred places in political strategies, that is, as a syntactical feature for articulating political projects, was clearly invoked; for Kataragama is also a nationally known place of religious pilgrimage. Then, on the first night of Ramadan in August 2013, thugs allegedly associated with the Sinhala Ravaya broke into a mosque near Mahiyangana east of Kandy and smeared it with pig intestines. Subsequently, in the Grandpass neighborhood of Colombo on the night of Eid at the end of Ramadan in August, a mob of Buddhist outsiders attacked Muslims in prayer within a newly built mosque, in the process vandalizing this place of worship and injuring the incumbent imam. Time and place were carefully calculated in these instances so that the violence perpetrated gained maximum effect. Ritual time, ritual space, clothing apparel distinctively denoting religious identity, and ritually sacralized food became substantial issues for articulating ethnic alienation and anger.

While these acts of harassment and violence by militant Buddhists against the Muslim community became widespread, the intensity and severity of violence that broke out in Aluthgama in June 2014 raised tensions between Buddhists and Muslims to levels perhaps not seen in Sri Lanka since 1915. For some, it also evoked memories of 1983. The Aluthgama violence is described in much greater detail and is the subject of Farzana Haniffa's chapter in this volume, but I will briefly allude to some of its major moments because the anatomy of the purported incidents at Aluthgama is consistent with the "religious syntax of violence" that I have outlined thus far, except this time the catalyst was an alleged Muslim attack on a man in saffron robes, a Buddhist monk on a *poya* (full moon day). From a variety of media sources, what appears to have happened is that a "3 wheeler" taxi ferrying a Buddhist monk through the middle of the Muslim enclave of Dharga Town next to Aluthgama, 50 km south of Colombo, was unable to pass owing to a traffic block in front of a Muslim mosque in the middle of town. A scuffle broke out between the taxi driver and Muslims on the street. According to various accounts, the monk left the "3 wheeler" to either intervene or to assist his taxi driver and was pushed aside in the fracas. This incident was later interpreted as an physical act of violence perpetrated on a Buddhist monk by so-called Muslim extremists, although the police who arrived at the scene to investigate found no evidence for such a charge; and although the monk was brought to a local hospital, no evidence of a physical attack was determined by medical staff. In the following days, a rally was called by the BBS to take place in Aluthgama. More than 7,000 people, many of them outsiders, attended the rally during which Gnanasara Atthe Thero, general secretary of the BBS, delivered a fiery speech in which he threatened the Muslims with violence if they laid a hand on any Sinhala Buddhists and reminded the crowd that Sri Lanka was a Buddhist country and its police and army Sinhala people. How outrageous, he said, is it that the police and army would protect the

Marakkhalas (a derogatory term)? He said that he and his supporters are sometimes called "racists," and that he proudly and loudly affirmed the verity of the claim.[18] Following the rally, squads of Sinhalese armed with clubs, knives, and firearms stormed into Aluthgama and Dharga Town, torching Muslim-owned businesses and several mosques, sending some sixty people to the hospital with serious injuries, and killing three people outright. The riot continued after a curfew had been called, a curfew that was not enforced by the police and the Special Task Force that had been belatedly deployed, fulfilling Gnanasara's claims that the police and army are Sinhala-friendly indeed.[19] Just as the rioters acted with impunity, so the Sri Lankan government has given Buddhist extremists a free pass, leaving Muslim citizens to wonder about the chances of their future well-being.

Conclusion

From what I have presented, it is clear that the BBS has an ideological affinity with Myanmar's "969" movement led by the radical monk U Wirathu. Not only have the two groups referred to each other publicly, but Wirathu completed a high-profile public visit to Sri Lanka in September 2014 and announced with Gnanasara Thero that the "969" and the BBS would be coordinating international efforts to defend Buddhist interests in the future. A month before Wirathu's visits, leaflets had been distributed to announce a BBS rally in Mawanella, a town that saw Buddhist–Muslim violence in 2001, signed by the so-called 969 Mahasena ("969 great army"). There is also evidence that the BBS, like Arakanese Buddhists in Myanmar and like Wirathu in the July 2014 troubles in Mandalay, has attempted to use gender strategically in its attempts to create violence against Muslims. (In early June 2014, two young Sinhalese women in the upcountry town of Badulla concocted a story that Muslim clerks in a Muslim clothing store had attempted to spy on them while they tried on new garments, and within moments a large crowd of BBS supporters were amassed in front of store. Fortunately, in this instance, police aggressively dispersed them before mayhem could break out.)

From this consideration, it seems clear that elements of religious culture provide a syntactical element to the generation of emotions that spill over into violent actions undertaken by one community against another. Elements of religious culture become flashpoints kindling excitement conducive to the violent articulation of political projects. This is not to deny the reality of economic factors in the equation but only to highlight that these elements of religious culture (ritual, symbol, sacred time, and sacred space) are syntactical dynamics likely to resonate with those who can be mobilized in the interest of asserting dominance by means of ethnic violence. Buddhist religious culture is not above violence but in some instances is inextricably entwined with it.

NOTES

1. For detailed account of this specific incident, see S. J. Tambiah (2011: 641–647) in *The Sri Lanka Reader*.
2. See John Clifford Holt, *The Religious World of Kirti Sri: Buddhism, Art and Politics in Late Medieval Sri Lanka* (New York: Oxford University Press, 1996), 97–108; and John Clifford Holt, "Religion and Processes of Modernization in Contemporary Sri Lanka," in *History and Politics: Millennial Perspectives*, eds. Gerald Peiris and S. W. R. de A. Samarasinghe (Colombo, Sri Lanka: Law and Society Trust, 1999), 237–250.
3. "Toward a Theory of Ritual and Violence: The Recent Sinhala Experience," *The Sri Lanka Journal of the Humanities* 17–18 (University of Peradeniya Golden Jubilee Commemoration Double Issue, 1991–1992): 65–74. Here I was quite consciously arguing against the theories put forward by Rene Girard in his *Violence and the Sacred* (Baltimore: Johns Hopkins University Press, 1979).
4. Leonard Woolf, *Diaries in Ceylon, 1908–1911* (Dehiwala, Sri Lanka: Tisara Press, 1962), 241–242.
5. *Pancasila*, or the observance of not killing, stealing, lying, engaging in sex, or taking intoxicants.

6. See H. L. Seneviratne, *Rituals of the Kandyan State* (Cambridge: Cambridge University Press, 1978).
7. John Clifford Holt, *Theravada Traditions: Buddhism and Ritual Cultures of Sri Lanka and Southeast Asia* (Honolulu: University of Hawaii Press, 2017).
8. Synopses of various accounts of the 1915 riots are available at http://www.sangam.org/articles/view2/?uid=1060
9. For Fa Hien's account of the cultic life he observed in 5th-century Anuradhapura, see Fa Hien, "Anuradhapura: Fifth Century Observations by a Chinese Buddhist Monk," in *The Sri Lanka Reader: History, Culture, Politics*, ed. John Clifford Holt (Durham, NC: Duke University Press, 2011), 44–49.
10. For a stunning, alarming, and yet eloquent poem documenting and yet memorializing the dead of Nallur, see Jean Arasanayagam, "Nallur," in *The Sri Lanka Reader: History, Culture, Politics*, ed. John Clifford Holt (Durham, NC: Duke University Press, 2011), 557–558.
11. Luke Heslop, "On Sacred Ground: The Political Performance of Religious Responsibility," *Contemporary South Asia* 22 (2014): 23.
12. Gananath Obeyesekere, *The Cult of the Goddess Pattini* (Chicago: University of Chicago Press, 1983), 50–70.
13. See and hear the speech by a BBS monk available at http://www.youtube.com/watch?v=_mtealqPOjg
14. Heslop, "On Sacred Ground," 27–28; it should be noted that although skirmishes occurred at the Dambulla mosque and the prime minister also called for its removal, the local power of Muslim officials and the inaction taken by the president of Sri Lanka has resulted in the fact that the mosque remains in place today.
15. Available at http://www.youtube.com/watch?v=_mtealqPOjg; at one rally in Kandy, one BBS monk event went so far as to make a speech in which he asserted that Muslims ritually spit three times on food that they prepare for Sinhala–Buddhist consumption.
16. Personal communications with faculty at the University of Peradeniya, June 2014.
17. Ravana is a reference to the antihero of the Hindu classic epic *Ramayana* whose magnificent palace is in Lanka, the venue of Sita's captivity after her abduction by Ravana. The association here is with

the great brute force attributed to the character of Ravana as well as the seemingly proud claim that his home was Lanka.

18. For a video and rough English translation of relevant portions of this speech, see http://www.youtube.com/watch?v=-fPMWD8f9lE
19. Of the many news reports about the Aluthgama riot and its significance in the political context, the following article is one of the most balanced and accurate: http://www.cnn.com/2014/07/17/world/asia/sri-lanka-bodu-bala-sena-profile/

BIBLIOGRAPHY

Abeyasinghe, T. B. H. (1986). "Muslims in Sri Lanka in the Sixteenth and Seventeenth Centuries," in M. A. M. Shukri, ed., *Muslims of Sri Lanka: Avenues to Antiquity*. Beruwala, Sri Lanka: Jamiah Naleemia Institute. Pp. 129–145.

Abeysekara, Ananda (2002). *Colors of the Robe: Religion, Identity, and Difference*. Columbia: University of South Carolina Press.

Ali, Ameer A. C. L. (1981a). "The Genesis of the Muslim Community in Ceylon (Sri Lanka): A Historical Summary." *Asian Studies* 19: 65–82.

Ali, Ameer (1981b). "The 1915 Racial Riots in Ceylon (Sri Lanka): A Reappraisal of Its Causes." *South Asia* 4(2): 1–20.

Ali, Ameer (1986). "Politics of Survival: Past Strategies and Present Predicament of the Muslim Community in Sri Lanka." *Journal of the Institute of Muslim Minority Affairs* 7(1): 147–170.

Ali, Ameer (1989). "Muslim Participation in the Export Sector of Sri Lanka 1800–1915," in M. M. M. Shukry, ed., *Muslims of Sri Lanka: Avenues to Antiquity*. Beruwala: Jamiah Nalieemia Institute. Pp. 235–252.

Ali, Ameer (2001). *Plural Identities and Political Choices of the Muslim Community: The Survival Game*. Colombo, Sri Lanka: Marga Institute.

Ali, Ameer (2012). "Point of View: An Aggressive Brand of State Religion vs. Others." *Lakbima News*, May 12, 2012. http://www.slmuslims.com/index.php?option=com_content&view=article&id=181:point-of-view-an-agressive-brand-of-state-religion-vs-others&catid=67:opinion&Itemid=56

Ali, Daud (1999). "Introduction," in Daud Ali, ed., *Invoking the Past: The Uses of History in South Asia*. New Delhi: Oxford University Press. Pp. 1–12.

All-Ceylon Buddhist Congress (2006). *Bauddha Toraturu Parīkṣaka Sabhāvē Vārtāva*. Colombo, Sri Lanka: Visidunu Prakāśanayaki.

Allport, G., and L. Postman (1965). *The Psychology of Rumor*. New York: Russel and Russel.

Amarasuriya, Harini, Zainab Ibrahim, Iromi Perera, and Halik Azeez (2015). *Of Sacred Sites and Profane Politics: Tensions of Religious Sites and Ethnic Relations*. 2 vols. Colombo, Sri Lanka: Secretariat for Muslims.

Ameen, A. G. H. (2003). "Wakfs Law in Sri Lanka." *Neethi Murasu* 39: 38–44.

Amunugama, Sarath (1991). "Buddhaputra and Bhumiputra?" *Religion* 21: 115–139.

Anes, M. S. M., V. Ameerdeen, and A. J. L. Wazeel (2008). *Ilankayil Inakkalavarankalum Muslimkalum* [Muslims and Ethnic Violence in Sri Lanka], 2nd ed. Colombo, Sri Lanka: Islamic Book House.

Anwar, Kombai S. (2013). *Yadhum: A Tamil Muslim's Journey in Search of His Roots and Identity* (Documentary film [English and Tamil versions]). Chennai, India: Media Kombai.

Appadurai, Arjun (1981). "The Past as a Scarce Resource." *Man*, New Series, 16: 201–219.

Aqsha, Darul (2010). "Zheng He and Islam in Southeast Asia." *The Brunei Times*, July 13, B10.

Arasanayagam, Jean (2011). "Nallur," in John Clifford Holt, ed., *The Sri Lanka Reader*. Durham, NC: Duke University Press. Pp. 557–558.

Asad, M. N. M. Kamil (1993). *The Muslims of Sri Lanka under the British Rule*. New Delhi: Navrang.

Azeez, I. L. M. Abdul (1907). *A Criticism of Mr. Ramanathan's "Ethnology of the Moors of Ceylon."* Colombo, Sri Lanka: Moors' Union. Reprint, Colombo, Sri Lanka: Moors' Islamic Cultural Home, 1957.

Bartholomeusz, Tessa (2002). *In Defense of Dharma: Just War Ideology in Sri Lanka*. New York: Routledge.

Bauddha, Jatika Balavegaya (1963). *Catholic Action: A Menace to Peace and Goodwill*. Colombo, Sri Lanka: The Bauddha Pracharaka Press.

Bell, H. C. P. (1892). *Report on the Kegalle District of the Province of Sabaragamuwa*. Colombo, Sri Lanka: G. J. A. Skeen.

Berkwitz, Stephen (2008a). "Religious Conflict and the Politics of Conversion in Sri Lanka," in Rosalind I. J. Hackett, ed., *Proselytization*

Revisited: Rights Talk, Free Markets and Culture Wars. London: Equinox. Pp. 199–230.

Berkwitz, Stephen C. (2008b). "Resisting the Global in Buddhist Nationalism: Venerable Soma's Discourse of Decline and Reform." *Journal of Asian Studies* 67: 73–106.

Blackton, Charles S. (1967). "The 1915 Riots in Ceylon: A Survey of the Action Phase." *The Ceylon Journal of the Historical and Social Studies* 10: 27–69.

Bond, George (1988). *The Buddhist Revival in Sri Lanka*. Columbia: University of South Carolina.

Brass, Paul (1991). *Ethnicity and Nationalism: Theory and Comparison*. New Delhi: Sage Publications.

Buddhaghosa. (1960). *The Illustrator of Ultimate Meaning (Paramatthajotika); Commentary on the Minor Readings*. Translated by Bhikkhu Ñāṇamoli. London: Pali Text Society.

Casie Chitty, Simon (1834). *The Ceylon Gazetteer*. Ceylon: Cotta Church Mission Press. Reprint, New Delhi: Navrang, 1989.

Catholic Union of Ceylon (1963). *Catholic Action According to the Balavegaya*. Colombo, Sri Lanka: Senger Publications.

Centre for Policy Alternatives (2012). *Brief Note: Legal Frameworks Governing Places of Religious Worship in Sri Lanka*. Colombo, Sri Lanka: Centre for Policy Alternatives.

Centre for Policy Alternatives (2013). "Attacks on Places of Religious Worship in Post-war Sri Lanka." Colombo, Sri Lanka: Centre for Policy Alternatives.

Cheran, R. (1999). "Sri Lanka: Human Rights in the Context of Civil War." *Refuge* 18: 4–9.

Chua, Amy (2004). *World on Fire: How Exporting Free Market Democracy Breeds Ethnic Hatred and Global Instability*. London: Arrow Books.

Comaroff, Jean (2009). "The Politics of Conviction: Faith on the Neo-Liberal Frontier." *Social Analysis* 53: 17–38.

Daniel, E. Valentine (1996). *Charred Lullabies: Chapters in an Anthropography of Violence*. New Jersey: Princeton University Press.

Daṡ, Veena (2006). *Life and Words: Violence and the Descent in to the Ordinary*. Berkeley: University of California Press.

Davy, John (1821). *An Account of the Interior of Ceylon, and of Its Inhabitant: With Travels in That Island*. London: Longman, Hurst, Rees, Orme, and Brown.

De Bussche, Captain L. (1999). *Letters on Ceylon Particularly Relative to the Kingdom of Kandy*. New Delhi: Asian Educational Services.

Deegalle, M. (2004). "The Politics of the Jathika Hela Urumaya Monks: Buddhism and Ethnicity in Contemporary Sri Lanka." *Contemporary Buddhism* 5(2): 83–103.

Denham, E. B. (1912). *Ceylon at the Census of 1911*. Colombo, Sri Lanka: H. C. Cottle, Government Printer.

Department of Archaeology (1997). *Administrative Report of the Director-General of Archaeology for the Year 1997*. Colombo, Sri Lanka: Department of Archaeology.

Department of Archaeology, Divisional Office, Avisawella (2013). "*Devanagala Purāvidya Sthānayē Mäṇum Kaṭayutu Sambandavayi*" [Concerning the Surveying Activities at the Devanagala Archaeological Site]. December 12, 2013. Reproduced in Mawanella Peoples Friendship Forum, *Devanagala Samīkṣaṇa Vārtāva* [Devanagala Investigative Report]. Mawanella, 2014. Appendix 7.

de Silva, C. R. (1968). "Portuguese Policy Towards the Muslims in Ceylon, 1505–1626." *Proceedings of the First International Conference Seminar of Tamil Studies, Kuala Lumpur 1966*. Kuala Lumpur, Malaysia: International Association for Tamil Research.

De Silva, K. M. (1981). *A History of Sri Lanka*. Berkeley: University of California Press.

de Silva, Premakumara (2014). "Colonialism and Religion: Colonial Knowledge Productions on Sri Pada as 'Adam's Peak.'" *Sri Lanka Journal of Social Sciences* 37: 19–32.

DeVotta, Neil (2007). *Sinhalese Buddhist Nationalist Ideology: Implication for Politics and Conflict Resolution in Sri Lanka*. Washington, DC: East-West Center.

DeVotta, Neil and Jason Stone. (2008). "Jathika Hela Urumaya and Ethno-Religious Politics in Sri Lanka." *Pacific Affairs* 81: 31–51.

Dewaraja, Lorna. (1994). *The Muslims of Sri Lanka: One Thousand Years of Ethnic Harmony 900–1915*. Colombo, Sri Lanka: The Lanka Islamic Foundation.

Dewaraja, Lorna (1995). "The Indigenization of the Muslims of Sri Lanka," in G. P. S. H. de Silva and C. G. Uragoda, eds., *Sesquicentennial Commemorative Volume of the Royal Asiatic Society of Sri Lanka, 1945–1995*. Colombo, Sri Lanka: Royal Asiatic Society of Sri Lanka.

Dewasiri, Nirmal (2013). "'History' after the War: Historical Consciousness in the Collective Sinhala-Buddhist Psyche in Post-War Sri Lanka." International Centre for Ethnic Studies [ICES] Research Paper 9. Colombo, Sri Lanka: ICES.

Dharmadasa, K. N. O. (1989). "The People of the Lion: Ethnic Identity, Ideology, and Historical Revisionism in Contemporary Sri Lanka." *Sri Lanka Journal of the Humanities* 15: 1–35.

Dharmadasa, K. N. O. (1997). "Buddhism and Politics in Modern Sri Lanka," in Maduwave Sobhita, Kamburugoda Sorata, and Mendis Rohandeera, eds., *Bhikshauwa Saha Lankā Samājeya*. Colombo, Sri Lanka: Dharmaduthasrāma Pirivena.

Dirks, Nicholas B. 2001. *Castes of Mind: Colonialism and the Making of Modern India*. Princeton, NJ: Princeton University Press.

D'Souza, Victor S. (1973). "Status Groups Among the Moplahs on the South-west Coast of India," in Imtiaz Ahmad, ed., *Caste and Social Stratification Among the Muslims*. New Delhi: Manohar.

Effendi, Mohamed Sameer bin hajie Ismail (1965). "Archeological Evidence of Early Arabs in Ceylon," in *Moors Islamic Cultural Home, The First Twenty-One Years, Anniversary Souvenir*. Colombo, Sri Lanka: Moors Islamic Cultural Home. Pp. 31–38.

Fa Hien (2011). "Anuradhapura: Fifth Century Observations by a Chinese Buddhist Monk," in John Clifford Holt, ed., *The Sri Lanka Reader*. Durham, NC: Duke University Press. Pp. 44–49.

Fakhri, S. H. Abdul Khader (2008). *Dravidian Sahibs and Brahmin Maulanas: The Politics of the Muslims of Tamilnadu, 1930–1967*. New Delhi: Manohar.

Fanselow, Frank S. (1996). "The Disinvention of Caste among Tamil Muslims," in C. J. Fuller, ed., *Caste Today*. New Delhi: Oxford University Press. Pp. 202–226.

Fanselow, Frank S. (1989). "Muslim Society in Tamil Nadu (India): An Historical Perspective." *Journal Institute of Muslim Minority Affairs* 10(1): 264–289.

Farook, Latteef (2014a). *Mayhem During Curfew: Attacks on Aluthgama, Dharga Town and Beruwala Muslims*. Colombo, Sri Lanka: Author.

Farook, Latteef (2014b). *Muslims of Sri Lanka under Siege*. Colombo, Sri Lanka: Author.

Faslan, Mohamed and Nadine Vanniasinkam (2015). "Fracturing Community: Intra-group Relations among the Muslims of Sri Lanka."

International Centre for Ethnic Studies [ICES] Research Paper no. 16. Colombo, Sri Lanka: ICES.

Foucault, Michel (1991). "Governmentality," in Graham Burchell, Colin Gordon, and Peter Miller, eds., *The Foucault Effect: Studies in Governmentality*. Chicago: University of Chicago Press. Pp. 87–104.

Frydenlund, Iselin. (2005). *The Sangha and its Relation to the Peace Process in Sri Lanka: A Report for the Norwegian Ministry of Foreign Affairs*. Oslo, Norway: International Peace Research Institute.

Gamage, Ariyasena U. (2014). *Devanagala Survey Report 2014*. Mawanella, Sri Lanka: Mawanella Friendship Association (in Sinhala).

Girard, Rene (1979). *Violence and the Sacred*. Baltimore: Johns Hopkins University Press.

Gombrich, Richard and Gananath Obeyesekere (1988). *Buddhism Transformed: Religious Change in Sri Lanka*. Princeton, NJ: Princeton University Press.

Goonesekere, S. (2000). *Muslim Personal Law in Sri Lanka: Some Aspects of Law on Family Relation*. Colombo, Sri Lanka: Muslim Women's Research and Action Forum.

Gosh, Anjan. 2008. "The Role of Rumour in History Writing." *History Compass* 65: 1235–1243.

Government of Ceylon (1959). *Budha Śasana Komiṣan Vārtāva* [Buddha Sasana Commission Report]. Colombo, Sri Lanka: Government Press.

Guha, Ranjit (1983), *Elementary Aspects of Peasant Insurgency in Colonial India*. New Delhi: Oxford University Press.

Gunawardana, R. A. L. H. (1990). "The People of the Lion: The Sinhala Identity and Ideology in History and Historiography," in Jonathan Spencer, ed., *Sri Lanka: History and the Roots of Conflict*. London: Routledge. Pp. 45–86.

Gunawardana, R. A. L. H. (1995). *Historiography in a Time of Ethnic Conflict: Construction of the Past in Contemporary Sri Lanka*. Colombo, Sri Lanka: Social Scientists' Association.

Gupta, Charu (2009). "Hindu Women, Muslim Men: Love Jihad and Conversions." *Economic and Political Weekly* XLIV 51: 13–15. December 19, 2009.

Guruge, Ananda (1965). *Return to Righteousness: A Collection of Speeches, Essays and Letters of Anagarika Dharmapala*. Colombo, Sri Lanka: The Government Press.

Guruge, Ananda (1967). *Anagarika Dharmapala*. Colombo, Sri Lanka: Department of Cultural Affairs.

Haniffa, Farzana (2005). "Under Cover: Reflections on the Practice of 'Hijab' Among Urban Muslim Women in Sri Lanka," in *Gender and Social Change*. Colombo, Sri Lanka: Centre for Women's Research. Pp. 61–87.

Haniffa, Farzana (2008). "Believing Women: Piety as Politics amongst Muslim Women in Contemporary Sri Lanka." *Modern Asian Studies* 42(2–3): 347–375.

Haniffa, Farzana (2012). "Conflicted Solidarities? Muslims and the Constitution Making Process of 1970--1972," in Asanga Welikala, ed., *The Sri Lankan Republic at Forty: Reflections on Constitutional History Theory and Practice*. Colombo, Sri Lanka: Center for Policy Alternatives.

Haniffa, Farzana (2014). "Competing for Victimhood Status: Northern Muslims and the Ironies of Post-War Reconciliation, Justice and Development." International Centre for Ethnic Studies [ICES] Research Paper No 13. Colombo, Sri Lanka: ICES.

Haniffa, Farzana, et al. (2015). *Where Have all the Neighbors Gone? Aluthgama Riots and Its Aftermath: A Fact Finding Mission to Aluthgama, Dharga Town, Valipanna, and Beruwala*. Colombo, Sri Lanka: Law and Society Trust.

Haniffa, Farzana (2016). "Minorities in the Post-War Context: the Case of the Muslims of Sri Lanka," in Amarnath Amarasingham and Daniel Bass, eds., *Post War Sri Lanka: Problems and Prospects*. London: Hurst.

Harrison, Frances (2014). "The Agony of Sri Lanka's Muslims." *Newsweek* [Pakistan edition], June 30.

Harvey, D. (2007). *A Brief History of Neoliberalism*. Oxford: Oxford University Press.

Hasbullah, S. H. (2004). "Justice for the Dispossessed: The Case of a Forgotten Minority in Sri Lanka's Ethnic Conflict," in S. H. Hasbullah and Barrie M. Morrison, eds., *Sri Lankan Society in an Era of Globalization: Struggling to Create a New Social Order*. New Delhi: Sage. Pp. 221–240.

Hassan, Said Fares (2013). *Fiqh Al-Aqalliyyat: History, Development, and Progress*. New York: Palgrave MacMillan.

Herath, Dammika and Harshana Rambukwella (2015). "Self, Religion, Identity and Politics: Buddhist and Muslim Encounters in Contemporary Sri Lanka." International Centre for Ethnic Studies [ICES] Research Paper no. 15. Colombo, Srilanka: ICES.

Herr, Ranjoo Seodu (2006). "In Defense of Nonliberal Nationalism." *Political Theory* 34: 304–327.

Heslop, Luke (2014). "On Sacred Ground: The Political Performance of Religious Responsibility." *Contemporary South Asia* 22: 21–36.

Ho, Engseng (2006). *The Graves of Tarim: Genealogy and Mobility across the Indian Ocean*. Berkeley: University of California Press.

Holt, John Clifford (1991–1992). "Toward a Theory of Ritual and Violence: The Recent Sinhala Experience." *The Sri Lanka Journal of the Humanities* 17–18 (University of Peradeniya Golden Jubilee Commemoration Double Issue): 65–74.

Holt, John Clifford (1996). *The Religious World of Kirti Śrī: Buddhism, Art, and Politics in Late Medieval Sri Lanka*. New York: Oxford University Press.

Holt, John Clifford (1999). "Religion and Processes of Modernization in Contemporary Sri Lanka," in Gerald Peiris and S. W. R. de A. Samarasinghe, eds., *History and Politics: Millennial Perspectives*. Colombo, Sri Lanka: Law and Society Trust. Pp. 237–250.

Holt, John Clifford (2017). *Theravada Traditions: Buddhist Ritual Cultures of Sri Lanka and Southeast Asia.* Honolulu: University of Hawaii Press.

Horowitz, Donald L. (1980). *Coup Theories and Officers' Motives: Sri Lanka in Comparative Perspective.* Princeton, NJ: Princeton University Press.

Hussainmiya, B. A. (1986). "Princes and Soldiers: The Antecedents of the Sri Lankan Malays," in M. A. M. Shukri, ed., *Muslims of Sri Lanka: Avenues to Antiquity*. Beruwala, Sri Lanka: Jamiah Naleemia Institute. Pp. 279–309.

Imtiyaz, A. R. M. and Amjad Mohamed-Saleem (2015). "Muslims in Post-war Sri Lanka: Understanding Sinhala Buddhist Mobilization against Them." *Asian Ethnicity* 16: 186–202.

Inden, Ronald (1990). *Imagining India.* Bloomington: Indiana University Press.

Indrapala, K. (1986). "The Role of Peninsular Indian Muslim Trading Communities in the Indian Ocean Trade," in M. A. M. Shukri, ed.,

Muslims of Sri Lanka: Avenues to Antiquity. Beruwala, Sri Lanka: Jamiah Naleemia Institute. Pp. 113–127.

International Alert (2008). *Words that Kill: Rumours, Prejudices, Stereotypes and Myths amongst the People of the Great Lakes Region of Africa*. Nairobi: International Alert.

International Crisis Group (2007). *Sri Lanka Muslims: Caught in the Crossfire*, Asia Report No. 134, May 29, 2007.

Ismail, Qadri (1995). "Unmooring Identity: The Antinomies of Elite Muslim Self-Representation in Modern Sri Lanka," in Pradeep Jeganathan and Qadri Ismail, eds., *Unmaking the Nation: The Politics of Identity and History in Modern Sri Lanka*. Colombo, Sri Lanka: Social Scientists' Association. Pp. 55–105.

Izberk-Bilgin, E. (2012). "Infidel Brands: Unveiling of Alternative Meanings of Global Brands at the Nexus of Globalization, Consumer Culture and Islamism." *Journal of Consumer Research* 39: 663–687.

Jackson, Michael (2007) *The Politics of Storytelling: Violence, Transgression, Intersubjectivity.* Copenhagen, Denmark: Museum Tusculanum Press.

Jameel, S. H. M. (2013). *Ilankayp Paaraalumanraththil Muslimkal* [Muslims in Sri Lankan Parliament]. Colombo, Sri Lanka: Kumaran Books House.

Janardhanan, Arun 2015. "Hardline Lanka Buddhists to Launch Party, Say Inspired by BJP, RSS." *Indian Express*, January 21, 2015.

Jayawardena, K. (1983). "Aspects of Class and Ethnic Consciousness in Sri Lanka." *Development and Change* 14: 1–18.

Jayawardena, K. (1984). "Class Formation and Communalism." *Race and Class* 26(1) (Summer): 51–62.

Jayawardena, K. (1990). *Ethnic and Class Conflict in Sri Lanka*. Colombo, Sanjiva Books.

Jayawardena, K. (2000). *Nobodies to Somebodies: The Rise of Colonial Bourgeoisie in Sri Lanka*. Colombo, Sri Lanka: Social Scientists' Association.

Jeganathan, Pradeep (1995). "Authorizing History, Ordering Land: The Conquest of Anuradhapura," in Pradeep Jeganathan and Qadri Ismail, eds., *Unmaking the Nation: The Politics of Identity and History in Modern Sri Lanka*. Colombo, Sri Lanka: Social Scientists' Association. Pp. 106–136.

Jeganathan, Pradeep (1997). "All the Lord's Men: Recollecting a Riot in an Urban Sri Lankan Community," in Michael Roberts, ed., *Sri Lanka: Collective Identities Revisited*. Colombo, Sri Lanka: Marga Institute.

Johansson, Andreas 2016. *Pragmatic Muslim Politics: The Case of Sri Lanka Muslim Congress. Lund Studies in the History of Religions 37*. Lund University, Sweden.

Jones, Robin Noel Badone (2015). "Sinhala Buddhist Nationalism and Islamophobia in Contemporary Sri Lanka." BA honors Thesis in Anthropology. Bates College, Lewiston, ME. http://scarab.bates.edu/honorstheses/126

Kahaṭapiṭiya, Lakṣman (2008). *Siṃhala Urumayē Ran Ayipata Ellāvala Medhānanda Hāmuduruvō*. Colombo, Sri Lanka: Dayawansa Jayakody.

Kapferer, Bruce, Annelin Eriksen, and Kari Telle (2009). "Introduction: Religiosities toward a Future—in Pursuit of the New Millenium." *Social Analysis* 53: 1–16.

Kearney, Robert N. (1967). *Communalism and Language in the Politics of Ceylon*. Durham, NC: Duke University Press.

Kemper, Steven (1991). *The Presence of the Past: Chronicles, Politics, and Culture in Sinhala Life*. Ithaca, NY: Cornell University Press.

Kemper, Steven (2015). *Rescued From the Nation: Anagarika Dharmapala and the Buddhist World*. Chicago: University of Chicago Press.

Kiribamune, Sirima (1986). "Muslims and the Trade of the Arabian Sea with Special Reference to Sri Lanka from the Birth of Islam to the Fifteenth Century," in M. A. M. Shukri, ed., *Muslims of Sri Lanka: Avenues to Antiquity*. Beruwala, Sri Lanka: Jamiah Naleemia Institute. Pp. 89–112.

Knoerzer, Shari (1998). "Transformation of Muslim Political Identity," in Mithran Tiruchelvam and C. S. Dattathreya, eds., *Culture and Politics of Identity in Sri Lanka*. Colombo, Sri Lanka: International Centre for Ethnic Studies.

Kolor, Kimberly (2015). "Ornamenting Fingernails and Roads: Beautification and the Embodiment of Authenticity in Post-War Eastern Sri Lanka." BA Thesis in Religious Studies. University of Pennsylvania.

Lawrie, Archibald (1972). *A Gazetteer of the Central Province of Ceylon*. 2 vols. Colombo, Sri Lanka: Government Printer. First published in 1896–1898.

Liyanage, Amarakeerthi. (2013). "Islamic Culture and the Challenge of Buddhist Fundamentalism." *The Island*, April 13. http://www.island.lk/index.php?page_cat=article-details&page=article-details&code_title=77949. Accessed March 14, 2015.

Liyanage, Chamila (2014). *Approaching the Extinction of a Race: An Enquiry into the Population Trends in Sri Lanka*. Colombo, Sri Lanka: Bodu Bala Sena [in Sinhala].

Mahadev, Neena (2014). "Conversion and Anti-Conversion in Contemporary Sri Lanka: Pentecostal Christian Evangelism and Theravada Buddhist Views on the Ethics of Religious Attraction," in Juliana Finucane and R. Michael Feener, eds., *Proselytizing and the Limits of Religious Pluralism in Contemporary Asia*. Singapore: Springer. Pp. 211–235.

Mahroof, M. M. M. (1994). "Community of Sri Lankan Malays: Notes Toward a Socio-historical Analysis." *Journal Institute of Muslim Minority Affairs* 14: 143–155.

Maitri Sahana Padanama (2013a). "*Devanagala Api*" ["We are Devanagala"]. Public Notice.

Maitri Sahana Padanama (2013b). "*Devanagala Hatana*" ["Battle of Devanagala"]. Public Notice.

Malalgoda, Kitsiri (1976). *Buddhism in Sinhalese Society, 1750–1900: A Study of Religious Revival and Change*. Berkeley: University of California Press.

Marx, Karl (1972). *The Eighteenth Brumaire of Louis Bonaparte*. Trans. Moscow: Progress Publishers.

Mauroof, Mohamed (1972). "Aspects of Religion, Economy, and Society among the Muslims of Ceylon." *Contributions to Indian Sociology* 6: 66–83.

Mawanella People's Friendship Forum (MPFF) (2014). *Devanagala Samīkṣaṇa Vārtāva* [Devanagala Investigative Report]. Mawanella.

McGilvray, Dennis B. (1982a). "Dutch Burghers and Portuguese Mechanics: Eurasian Identity in Sri Lanka." *Comparative Studies in Society and History* 24: 235–263.

McGilvray, Dennis B. (1982b). "Mukkuvar vannimai: Tamil Caste and Matriclan Ideology in Batticaloa, Sri Lanka," in Dennis B. McGilvray, ed., *Caste Ideology and Interaction*. Cambridge: Cambridge University Press. Pp. 34–97.

McGilvray, Dennis B. (1989). "Household in Akkaraipattu: Dowry and Domestic Organization among the Matrilineal Tamils and Moors of

Sri Lanka," in John Gray and David J. Mearns, eds., *Society from the Inside Out: Anthropological Perspectives on the South Asian Household*. New Delhi: Sage. Pp. 192–235.

McGilvray, Dennis B. (1998). "Arabs, Moors, and Muslims: Sri Lankan Muslim Ethnicity in Regional Perspective." *Contributions to Indian Sociology* 32: 433–483.

McGilvray, Dennis (2004). "Jailani: A Sufi Shine in Sri Lanka," in Imtiaz Ahmad and Helmut Reifeld, eds., *Lived Islam in South Asia: Adaptation, Accommodation and Conflict*. New Delhi: Social Science Press. Pp. 273–289.

McGilvray, Dennis B. (2008). *Crucible of Conflict: Tamil and Muslim Society on the East Coast of Sri Lanka*. Durham, NC: Duke University Press.

McGilvray, Dennis B. (2011). "Sri Lankan Muslims: Between Ethno-nationalism and the Global Ummah." *Nations and Nationalism* 17: 45–64.

McGilvray, Dennis B. (2016). "Islamic and Buddhist Impacts on the Shrine at Daftar Jailani, Sri Lanka," in Deepra Dandekar and Torsten Tschacher, eds., *Islam, Sufism and Everyday Politics in South Asia*. London and New York: Routledge.

McGilvray, D. and M. Raheem. (2007). "Muslim Perspectives on the Sri Lankan Conflict." *Policy Studies* 41. Washington, DC: East-West Center.

Medhananda, Ellawala (2005). *The Sinhala Buddhist Heritage in the East and the North of Shri Lanka*. Colombo, Sri Lanka: Dayawansa Jayakody.

Metcalf, B. D. (2002) *Traditionalist Islamic Activism: Deoband Tablighis and Talibs*. Leiden, Netherlands: ISIM.

Minayeff, I. P. (1885). "The Sandesa-Kathā." *Journal of the Pāli Text Society*.

More, J. P. B. (1991). "The Marakkayar Muslims of Karikal, South India." *Journal of Islamic Studies* 2: 25–44.

More, J. P. B. (1993). "Tamil Muslims and Non-Brahmin Atheists, 1925–1940." *Contributions to Indian Sociology* 27: 83–104.

N.a. "'JHU will not help any party to form new govt.'" *Daily Mirror*, April 5, 2004.

N.a. "New Buddhist Union Formed." *World Buddhism*, April 1963, 16–18.

Najimudeen, A. M. (2002). *Muslimkalum Kalavarac Cuulalum* (1815–1915). Matale, Sri Lanka: Author.

Nissan, Elizabeth (1985). "The Sacred City of Anuradhapura: Aspects of Sinhalese Buddhism and Nationhood." PhD diss., London School of Economics.

Nissan, Elizabeth (1989). "History in the Making: Anuradhapura and the Sinhala Buddhist Nation." *Social Analysis* 25: 64–77.

Nuhman, M. A. (2007). *Sri Lankan Muslims: Ethnic Identity within Cultural Diversity*. Colombo, Sri Lanka: International Centre for Ethnic Studies.

Nuhman, M. A. (2009). "Gate Mudaliyar M. S. Kariapper: Kilakku Muslim Arasiyalin Vidivelli," in *Gate Mudaliyar M. S. Kariapper Ninayvu Malar*. Kalmunai, Sri Lanka: Gate Mudaliyar M. S. Kariapper Commemoration Committee.

Obeysekere, Gananath (1979). "The Vicissitudes of the Sinhala Buddhist Identity through Time and Change," in Michael Roberts, ed., *Collective Identities, Nationalism and Protest in Modern Sri Lanka*. Colombo, Sri Lanka: Marga Institute. Pp. 279–313.

Obeyesekere, Gananath (1983). *The Cult of the Goddess Pattini*. Chicago: University of Chicago Press.

Obeyesekere, Gananath (2010). "The Demoness Kali and the Lord Buddha: Sense and Reference in a Buddhist Text on Revenge and Violence." *International Journal of Ethnic and Social Studies* 1: 41–72.

Ong, A. (2006). *Neoliberalism as Exception: Mutations in Citizenship and Sovereignty*. Durham, NC: Duke University Press.

Osella, Filippo and Caroline Osella, eds. (2013). *Islamic Reform in South Asia*. Cambridge, England: Cambridge University Press.

O'Sullivan, Meghan (1997). "Conflict as Catalyst: The Changing Politics of the Sri Lankan Muslims." Special Issue, *South Asia: Journal of South Asian Studies* 20: 281–308.

Pieris, P. E. (1939). *Tri Sinhala: The Last Phase 1796–1815*. Colombo, Sri Lanka: The Colombo Apothecaries Co.

Raghavan, M. D. (1971). *Tamil Culture in Ceylon: A General Introduction*. Colombo, Sri Lanka: Kalai Nilayam.

Rahula, Walpola (1974). *Heritage of the Bhikkhu*. New York: Grove Press.

Raja Mohamad, J. (2004). *Maritime History of the Coromandel Muslims: A Socio-Historical Study of the Tamil Muslims, 1750–1900*. Chennai, India: Government Museum.

Ramanathan, Ponnambalam (1888). "The Ethnology of the 'Moors' of Ceylon." *Journal of the Royal Asiatic Society, Ceylon Branch* 10: 234–262.

Rampton, David and Asanga Welikala (2005). *The Politics of the South: Part of the Sri Lanka Strategic Conflict Assessment 2005*. Colombo, Sri Lanka: The Asia Foundation.

Ricci, Ronit (2014). "Asian and Islamic Crossings: Malay Writing in Nineteenth-century Sri Lanka." *South Asian History and Culture* 5(2): 179–194.

Roberts, Michael (1994). Mentalities: Ideologues, Assailants, Historians and the Pogrom Against the Moors in 1915. In Michael Roberts, *Exploring Confrontation: Sri Lanka—Politics, Culture and History*. Chur, Switzerland: Harwood Academic Publishers. Pp. 183–212.

Rogers, John (1990). "Historical Images in the British Period," in Jonathan Spencer, ed., *Sri Lanka: History and the Roots of Conflict*. London: Routledge.

Rogers, John D. (1994). "Post-Orientalism and the Interpretation of Premodern and Modern Political Identities: The Case of Sri Lanka," *Journal of Asian Studies* 53: 10–23.

Rogers, John D. (1995). "Racial Identities and Politics and Early Modern Sri Lanka," in Peter Robb, ed., *The Concept of Race in South Asia*. New Delhi: Oxford University Press. Pp. 146–164.

Samaraweera, Vijaya (1977). "Arabi Pasha in Ceylon, 1883–1901." *Islamic Culture* 50: 219–227.

Sanjiva, K. (2014) "*Devanagala Ginikandak Viya Häkiya*" ["Devanagala Could Become a Volcano"]. *Rāvaya*, January 26.

Sannasgala, P. B. (1964). *Sinhala Sahitya Vamsaya*. Colombo, Sri Lanka: Lake House.

Saunders, Doug, "Kingship-in-the-Making," in John Clifford Holt, ed., *The Sri Lanka Reader: History, Politics, Culture*. Durham, NC: Duke University Press, 2011. Pp. 731–733.

Schalk, P. (1988). "Unity and Sovereignty: Key Concepts of a Militant Buddhist Organization in Sri Lanka MSV, Movement for the Protection of the Motherland." *Temenos* 24: 55–87.

Schonthal, Benjamin (2012). "Buddhism and the Constitution: The Historiography and Postcolonial Politics of Section 6," in A. Welikada, ed., *The Sri Lankan Republic at 40: Reflections on Constitutional*

History, Theory, and Practice, vol. 1. Colombo, Sri Lanka: Centre for Policy Alternatives. Pp. 201–218.

Scott, David (1995). "Dehistoricising History," in Pradeep Jeganathan and Qadri Ismail, eds., *Unmaking the Nation: The Politics of Identity and History in Modern Sri Lanka*. Colombo, Sri Lanka: Social Scientists' Association. Pp. 10–24.

Scott, David (1999). *Refashioning Futures: Criticism after Postcoloniality*. Princeton, NJ: Princeton University Press. 1999.

Sebastian, Aleena (2013). "Matrilineal Practices among Koyas of Kozhikode." *Journal of South Asian Studies* 1: 66–82.

Secretariat for Muslims (2015). "Anti Muslim Sentiment in Sri Lanka: Hate Incidents of 2014." Digital report at http://secretariatformuslims.org. Colombo, Sri Lanka: Secretariat for Muslims.

Seneviratne, H. L. (1978). *Rituals of the Kandyan State*. Cambridge, England: Cambridge University Press.

Seneviratne, H. L. (1999). *The Work of Kings: The New Buddhism in Sri Lanka*. Chicago: The University of Chicago Press.

Shokoohy, Mehrdad (2003). *Muslim Architecture of South India: The Sultanate of Ma'bar and the Traditions of Maritime Settlers on the Malabar and Coromandel Coasts*. London: Routledge Curzon.

Shukri, M. M., ed. (1989). *Muslims of Sri Lanka: Avenues to Antiquity*. Beruwala, Sri Lanka: Jamiah Naleemia Institute.

Silva, K. T. (2013). "Rival Nationalisms, Collective Violence and Discourse of Entitlement in Urban Sri Lanka." Presented in a workshop on *Violence, Insurgencies, Deceptions: Conceptualizing Urban Life in South Asia*, May 6–7, 2013, organized by Asia Research Institute, National University of Singapore.

Smith, D. E. (1966). "Political Monks and Monastic Reform," in *South Asian Politics and Religion*. Princeton, NJ: Princeton University Press.

Social Scientists' Association (1984). "Introduction," in *Ethnicity and Social Change in Sri Lanka*. Colombo, Sri Lanka: Social Scientists' Association. Pp. i–ix.

Spencer, Jonathan, ed. (1990). *Sri Lanka: History and the Roots of Conflict*. London: Routledge.

Spencer, J., et al. (2015). *Checkpoint, Temple, Church and Mosque: A Collaborative Ethnography of War and Peace*. London: Pluto Press.

Sri Lanka Muslim Congress (2014). "Aftermath of Aluthgama: Fact-Finding Report of Aluthgama Anti-Muslim Pogrom," June 2014. Digital report at www.slmc.lk, Colombo, Sri Lanka: Sri Lanka Muslim Congress.

Stewart, James John (2014). "Muslim–Buddhist Conflict in Contemporary Sri Lanka." *South Asia Research* 34: 241–260.

Sumathipala, K. H. M. (1968). *History of Education in Ceylon, 1796–1965*. Colombo, Sri Lanka: Tissa Prakasakayo.

Tambiah, S. J. (1986). *Sri Lanka: Ethnic Fratricide and the Dismantling of Democracy*. Chicago: University of Chicago Press.

Tambiah, S. J. (1992). *Buddhism Betrayed? Religion, Politics and Violence in Sri Lanka*. Chicago: University of Chicago Press.

Tambiah, S. J. (2011). "The Colombo Riots of 1983," in John Clifford Holt, ed., *The Sri Lanka Reader*. Durham, NC: Duke University Press. Pp. 641–647.

Tamil Lexicon (1982). Chennai, India: University of Madras.

Tennekoon, N. S. (1988). "Rituals of Development: The Accelerated Mahaväli Development Program of Sri Lanka." *American Ethnologist* 15: 294–310.

Tennekoon, Serena (1990). "Newspaper Nationalism: Sinhala Identity as Historical Discourse," in Jonathan Spencer, ed., *Sri Lanka: History and the Roots of Conflict*. London: Routledge. Pp. 205–226.

Thawfeeq, M. M. (1972). "The Fight for the Fez," in M. M. Thawfeeq, *Muslim Mosaics*. Colombo, Sri Lanka: Al Eslam Publications and the Moors' Islamic Cultural Home. Pp. 128–131.

Thiranagama, Sharika (2011). *In My Mother's House: Civil War in Sri Lanka*. Philadelphia: University of Pennsylvania Press.

Tschacher, Torsten (2014). "The Challenges of Diversity: 'Casting' Muslim Communities in South India," in Robin Jeffrey and Ronojoy Sen, eds., *Being Muslim in South Asia: Diversity and Daily Life*. New Delhi: Oxford University Press. Pp. 64–86.

Turner, Alicia Marie (2014). *Saving Buddhism: The Impermanence of Religion in Colonial Burma*. Honolulu: University of Hawai'i Press.

Udagama, Sarath (2014). "The Devanagala Uproar." *Ceylon Today*, January 16.

Uwise, M. M. (1986). "The Language and Literature of the Muslims," in M. M. M. Mahroof et al., *An Ethnological Survey of the Muslims of Sri*

Lanka from Earliest Times to Independence. Colombo, Sri Lanka: Sir Razik Fareed Foundation. Pp. 150–165.

Uwise, M. M. (1990). *Muslim Contribution to Tamil Literature*. Kilakarai, Tamil nadu, India: Fifth International Islamic Tamil Literary Conference.

Vadlamudi, Sundar (2016). "Merchants in Transition: Maritime Trade and Society of Tamil Muslims in the Indian Ocean World, ca. 1780–1840." Ph.D. Thesis in History. University of Texas, Austin.

Vaijayavardhana, D. C. (1953) *The Revolt in the Temple: Composed to Commemorate 2500 Years of the Land, the Race and the Faith*. Colombo, Sri Lanka: Sinha Publishers.

Vatuk, Sylvia (2014). "Change and Continuity in Marital Alliance Patterns: Muslims in South India, 1800–2012," in Ravinder Kaur and Rajni Palriwala, eds., *Marrying in South Asia: Shifting Concepts, Changing Practices in a Globalising World*. Hyderabad, India: Orient Blackswan. Pp. 28–48.

Weber, Max (1965). *Politics as a Vocation*. Minneapolis, MN: Fortress Press.

Wickramasinghe, Nira (2012). "Producing the Present: History as Heritage in Post-War Patriotic Sri Lanka," International Centre for Ethnic Studies [ICES] Research Paper 2. Colombo, Sri Lanka: ICES.

Wijenayake, Vishaka (2014). "Bodu Bala Sena, Population Control and Reproductive Rights."

Wijethunge, Shan (2004). *Sangha Power! Discussion Led by Shan Wijethunge with the Venerables Who Registered for the Sri Lankan Polls on Feb 24, 2004*.

Wilson, A. J. (1988). *The Break-up of Sri Lanka: The Sinhalese—Tamil Conflict*. New Delhi: Orient Longman Limited.

Wilson, A. J. (2000). *Sri Lankan Tamil Nationalism: Its Origins and Development in the 19th and 20th Centuries*. New Delhi: Penguin Books.

Wimaladharma, Kapila (2003). *Sacerdotal Succession of Sri Lankan Buddhist Monks: Since 1753 Higher Ordination*. Kandy: Varuni Publishers.

Wimalaratna, K. D. J. (1989). "Muslim under British Rule in Ceylon 1796–1948," in M. A. M. Shukri, ed., *Muslims of Sri Lanka: Avenues to Antiquity*. Beruwala, Sri Lanka: Jamiah Nalieemia Institute. Pp. 415–452.

Wink, André (1990). *Al-Hind: The Making of the Indo-Islamic World*, Vol. 1: *Early Medieval India and the Expansion of Islam, 7th–11th Centuries*. Leiden, Netherlands: Brill.

Woolf, Leonard (1962). *Diaries in Ceylon, 1908–1911*. Dehiwala, Sri Lanka: Tisara Press.

Woolf, Leonard (2000). *The Village in the Jungle*. Chennai, India: Oxford University Press.

Yalman, Nur (1967). *Under the Bo Tree: Studies in Caste, Kinship, and Marriage in the Interior of Ceylon*. Berkeley: University of California Press.

Zuhair, Aysha (2014). "Is BBS the New Face of Buddhist Revivalism?" in *Farook, Latheef*, ed., *Mayhem During Curfew: Attacks on Aluthgama, Dharga Town and Beruwala Muslims*. Colombo, Sri Lanka: Author. Pp 265–269.

NOTES ABOUT CONTRIBUTORS

Philip Friedrich is a PhD candidate in the Department of South Asia Studies at the University of Pennsylvania. His research interests include the political and social history of medieval and early modern South India and Sri Lanka, historical interactions between Buddhism and other religious traditions, and relations between courtly and monastic domains of thought and practice. His dissertation examines the "minor" royal courts of 13th- and 14th-century Sri Lanka as sites of regional political and religious dynamism.

Farzana Haniffa is Senior Lecturer in Sociology at the University of Colombo. She obtained her PhD in Anthropology from Columbia University in 2007. Her research and activist interests since 1999 have concentrated on the social and political history of Muslim communities in Sri Lanka. She has published research articles about Islamic reform movements; the history of Muslims' involvement in electoral politics; the Muslim community's exclusion from the peace process in Sri Lanka; northern Muslims' place in discourses regarding return, resettlement, and reconciliation; and the mobilizing of hate rhetoric against Muslims. Haniffa serves on the Social Scientists' Association's management council and is Chair of the Board of Directors of the Secretariat for Muslims.

John Clifford Holt (PhD, Chicago) is William R. Kenan, Jr. Professor of Humanities in Religion and Asian Studies at Bowdoin College. He is the author or editor of many books, including *Buddha in the Crown: Avalokitesvara in the Buddhist Traditions of Sri Lanka* (1991), for which he was awarded an American Academy Book Award for Excellence; *The Religious World of Kīrti Śrī: Buddhism, Art, and Politics in Late Medieval Sri Lanka* (1996); *The Buddhist Visnu: Religious Transformation, Politics, and Culture* (2004); *Spirits of the Place: Buddhism and Lao*

Religious Culture (2009); and *The Sri Lanka Reader: History, Politics and Culture* (2011). *Theravada Traditions: Buddhism and Ritual Cultures in Sri Lanka and Southeast Asia* is coming in the very near future. He was awarded an honorary Doctor of Letters from the University of Peradeniya in 2002 and selected as University of Chicago Divinity School Alumnus of the Year in 2007. He has four times received senior fellowships from the National Endowment of the Humanities and a John Simon Guggenheim Foundation fellowship in 2014.

Dennis B. McGilvray is Professor Emeritus of Anthropology at the University of Colorado, Boulder, and President of the American Institute of Sri Lankan Studies. His ethnographic research is focused on the Tamil-speaking Hindus and Muslims of Sri Lanka's eastern region, supplemented with fieldwork in Tamilnadu and Kerala. His books include *Symbolic Heat: Gender, Health & Worship among the Tamils of South India and Sri Lanka* (1998); *Muslim Perspectives on the Sri Lankan Conflict* (with Mirak Raheem; 2007); *Crucible of Conflict: Tamil and Muslim Society on the East Coast of Sri Lanka* (2008, 2011); and *Tsunami Recovery in Sri Lanka: Ethnic and Regional Dimensions* (coedited with Michele Gamburd; 2010).

M. A. Nuhman, Retired Professor of Tamil, University of Peradeniya, Sri Lanka, is a well-known scholar, poet, literary critic, linguist, and a creative translator in Tamil. He taught linguistics, Tamil language, and literature at several universities in Sri Lanka and abroad. As an author, editor, and translator he has published 35 books in Tamil as well as in English—including three collections of his poems and four collections of poems in translation—apart from a large number of articles and poems published in various journals and magazines. His books include *A Contrastive Grammar of Tamil and Sinhala Noun Phrase* (2003), *Sri Lankan Muslims: Ethnic Identity within Cultural Diversity* (2007), and an enlarged 2nd edition of his Tamil book *Marxism and Literary Criticism* (2014).

Benjamin Schonthal is Lecturer in Buddhism/Asian Religions at the University of Otago in New Zealand. He received his PhD in the field of History of Religions at the University of Chicago. His research examines the intersections of law, politics, and religion in late-colonial and contemporary Southern Asia, with a particular focus on Sri Lanka. HIs dissertation, *Ruling Religion: Buddhism, Law and Politics in Contemporary Sri*

Lanka, won the 2013 Law and Society Association Dissertation Award. He is currently President of the New Zealand Association for the Study of Religions.

Kalinga Tudor Silva holds a BA from the University of Peradeniya and PhD from Monash University, Australia. He is professor emeritus in Sociology at the University of Peradeniya. Whereas this university has been his base for over 40 years, he also served as the Executive Director of the Centre for Poverty Analysis (2002–2003) and the Executive Director of the International Centre for Ethnic Studies (2009–2011). He assumed duties as the resident director of the ISLE (Intercollegiate Sri Lanka Education) Program in 2015. His latest book, *Decolonization, Development and Disease: A Social History of Malaria in Sri Lanka* (2014), deals with malaria as a development-induced disease.

Jonathan A. Young is Visiting Assistant Professor at the College of the Holy Cross in Worcester, Massachusetts. His work examines the history of Buddhist monks as political agents, particularly in Sri Lanka. He also conducts research on the growth of Buddhism in South and Southeast Asia including investigations of trans-regional networks of exchange, literary techniques used in the production of Buddhist subjectivities, and interreligious conflicts.

INDEX